Sunday Dinners, Moonshine, and Men

TATE BARKLEY

Micro Publishing Media
Stockbridge, Massachusetts, 01262

Printed in the United States of America

First Printing, 2023
ISBN 978-1-953321-22-0

Micro Publishing Media, Inc.
PO Box 1522
Stockbridge, MA 01262
www.micropublishingmedia.com

This book is dedicated to my mom, Linda Ann Tevepaugh Barkley, whose unconditional love, courage and fierce commitment to her children made each of us exceptional in our own way.

We love you, Mom!

"Another great dividend we may expect from confiding our defects to another human being is humility—a word often misunderstood. To those who have made progress in AA., it amounts to a clear recognition of what and who we really are, followed by a sincere attempt to become what we could be."

— *Twelve Steps and Twelve Traditions*, Page 58

CONTENTS

PART ONE

Sunday Dinners

CHAPTER 1

TATE G.

My Dad had done some hard living throughout his life, but it still came as a shock when he had his first heart attack in September 2003. The Dad I knew was tough as nails. He was robust in both physique and personality, with a full head of sandy brown hair and a beard and mustache that aligned with his gregarious and animated manner. For many years, Dad was my favorite drinking buddy.

When my sister Brandy called me the first time that day, she said Dad was having some chest pains. Then she called back and said he was having a heart attack and that I should head to the hospital. I was surprised but not overly concerned about the news. I felt like his habits had caught up with him, giving us all a chance at an "I told you so." He had cheated death so many times that I honestly didn't think this could be anything serious.

Dad had the gift of gab, so much so that he constantly talked the angels out of taking him, and he wore his close calls like badges of honor. He must have given Ma and Pa Barkley many sleepless nights. Aside from the countless car wrecks he had been in where he walked away without a scratch, there was one particular story he loved to tell. Each time it got bigger and bigger.

He loved to talk about his "white lightning" days back in his home state of North Carolina. We were all skeptical of his obvious embellishments, but his brother, my Uncle David, not a man prone to lying, more or less vouched for him. In the late '50s in North Carolina, there remained a rather sizable part of the community that preferred corn liquor from a still, otherwise known as "moonshine" or "white lightning." Dad and Uncle David both "ran moonshine" just after high school. Dad came by this career honestly and may have been inspired by his grandma, Mary Isabella Sharp Barkley, who was known to be one of the best moonshiners in North Carolina. She took great pride in her product, and no one messed with her.

As I passed a truck on the highway on my way to the hospital I felt a twinge of fear for my dad, but then dismissed it. I even laughed: "Nope, Dad will be okay. He is always okay." I thought about his moonshining days. The way the story went, he was given a 1954 Dodge Coronet stripped down for speed and storage of the liquor.

Dad would laugh and say, "Bub, (that was my nickname) there was a man who would pay me $75 for each delivery. That was big money in those days." He'd add, "Bub, I would pick up a load of liquor just outside Marion, North Carolina. My job was to deliver it to a spot in High Point, safe and sound, and return the car to Statesville without a scratch, no problem, right? But one time..." he dragged out the word "time" so I would know what was coming. Something would always go terribly wrong, leading him to narrowly survive. I used to laugh at his tall tales, but I couldn't help but listen intently every time.

"But one time, I picked up a load of moonshine at a small run-down farm about a half mile off State Highway 221, like usual. I remember it was a summer day in 1958 and it was hot as Hell. The same snaggle-toothed farmer helped load about 10 boxes of booze. The farmer never spoke much, so neither did I. Uncle David was supposed to come in and pick up a load about 20 minutes behind me. They liked to stagger the pickups. Less chance of getting nabbed.

"This day felt like all the others, so I headed south on the highway. I swear on a stack of Bibles I was cruising at the posted speed as I approached the little town of Gilkey. Bub, I rounded a steep curve just before town and there he was for sure: A highway patrolman pulled in behind me and hit his lights and sirens. The whole purpose of being given a supercharged car like the '54 Dodge Coronet I was driving was to ensure I never got caught by law enforcement. It was built for quick getaways.

"So it began. I hit the gas and took off. But I couldn't go pedal to the metal with all the intense curves. We were in the mountains where the roads are steep and a long ways down."

I likely heard this story a thousand times, but this part always made my stomach jump.

"At first the patrol car was almost on top of me. Son, he could reach out and touch me. He was so close. I had to move in and out of these curves and could never get to a place where I could open her up. This Dodge Coronet was built for speed, but I just needed to catch a break so I could get some distance from the patrolman. I knew my moment was coming because luckily, about three miles into the chase, there was an extended stretch of straight road. When we finally made it to that straight stretch, I floored it, and that Coronet roared! Within 30 seconds I was breaking away and leaving the cop in my rearview. I kept it floored. That guy wasn't going to give up and I knew I was in for it if he caught me.

"I was home free as I sped off down the road. I loved that car. It was smooth and as close to flying without really leaving the ground. But then I saw the patrolman. He wouldn't give up and was closing in on my rear. I pushed down on the gas as hard as possible, then swung my arm over the seat to take a good look behind me, and I didn't see him so I figured I was in the clear. When I swung back around, I was just in time to see a huge curve in the road right in front of me.

"And for the love of God! There was a farm tractor with a huge trailer full of hay only a few feet away. I had to slam on the brakes, and I was going fast. Never do that, Bub. I turned hard left to avoid the tractor-trailer and started to spin!"

Sometimes Dad would stand up and act out this part of the story for emphasis.

"The next thing I remember, the car was teetering on two wheels about to fall off this steep road. Not even a split-second prayer would'a helped because it was too late."

It didn't matter that I knew with all logic that he had survived the accident. Hearing him say "it was too late" always made me quiver. I was in that car with him imagining what I would have done in his shoes.

"The Coronet rolled over and over and over. I remember tumbling around inside the car. We didn't have seatbelts back then or nothing, and we wouldn't have worn them if we had. I bounced around like a ball inside that car. And I guess I passed out. The next thing I remember was waking up to the intense smell of moonshine and gas. I was lying on my back on the ceiling. The car had rested on its top. Thank goodness I could feel my body. But then I realized the car was about to blow and I had to get out. I crawled through the passenger side window. The car had tumbled about 300 feet down the side of the road. I looked up and there was the highway cop and your Uncle David both screaming at me to run. It took a second for me to understand what they were saying, but I had already figured out that a crash, booze, and gasoline was not a good combination.

"I began to crawl up this embankment. It was slow going. I was still disoriented, and my body was struggling to move. I kept hearing "hurry, hurry" and then I heard this *hiss*, a really intense hiss, and the next thing I knew I heard an explosion and this wave of scalding air passed over my body. When the heat subsided a bit, I scrambled up the side of the embankment as fast as I could. When I arrived at the top, your Uncle David lifted me to my feet. The car was burning like crazy below. The cop, David, and I just watched it burn without saying a word.

"Then the cop grabbed my arm and said, 'Boy, you should be dead! Do you get that or are you just plain ignorant?'

"I was in too much shock to mouth off at him and just said, 'Yes, sir, I get it, I get it.' It was true, Bub, I did get it. It happened so fast, and it was pure luck or the Good Lord that saved me. The patrolman never introduced himself and did not have a name tag. He grabbed my elbow and said, 'Boy I ought to haul you off to jail for a hundred reasons right now! But I do not have a radio and I have to hustle up to town to get the fire department out here before we have an out-of-control blaze on our hands.' He turned to David and said, 'I want you to load this boy up and go! I better never ever see either one of you in this county again.' The patrolman then squeezed my arm and said, 'Boy you damned near died. Now, you have to explain to whoever loaned you that car and whoever is expecting that moonshine what happened, so I guess that will have to be punishment enough for now. Yes sir, I knew what you were up to! Now both of you just get!'"

It was funny that, while I was driving to the hospital, this particular story had come to mind. Dad had danced with death before, but it occurred to me that it was while doing something he wasn't supposed to be doing. That was also like Dad. He always got away when he should have paid a heftier price.

Like this heart attack. He was still smoking despite everyone telling him to stop, and he still drank. In fact, that was one of the ways we related to one another. Together we walked into biker bars and redneck pool halls across the South, and no one ever messed with us. That is why I felt like this was yet another dance. My dad stood six feet even with broad shoulders and a solid frame, larger than life, formidable, and bulletproof. I never feared anything or anyone when I was out drinking with him. He was indestructible and made me feel the same way.

On one occasion during my junior year of college, Dad and I broke down between Austin and Houston, Texas. The only refuge in sight was a biker bar just outside the small town of Paige, Texas. We were driving the pride of Dad's fleet, a 1971 blue- and white-striped Chevy pick-up with three-speed on the steering column and a souped-up V-8 350 engine. Dad loved this truck, but on this day, the engine was overheating something fierce. Dad tried to baby it for a few miles but to no avail: the steam poured out from underneath the hood. We managed to make it into the gravel parking lot of this bar, which must have had two hundred Harley-Davidson motorcycles parked in it. Our Chevy was not cooling down and was not going anywhere anytime soon. As we got out of the truck, Dad looked at me and said, "Bubba, this could be tricky." My family nickname was "Bubba," but Dad always called me "Bub," so I knew this was as close to him using my full name as he got. He smelled trouble.

As we passed through the screen door and into the bar, the chatter we had heard from the outside stopped, and all two hundred angry bandido-looking men turned to glare at us in complete silence. I admit I felt a wave of fright go through me. But Dad stood tall, swept the room with his eyes, and said loudly, "So, can we get a beer in here or not?" If I could have, I would have grabbed his hand like a five-year-old and run out of there, but then Dad broke the silence again with a loud, "I'll take that as a 'yes.'" Dad walked straight to the wooden bar at the center of the place with me close behind, loudly tapped his knuckle on the bar, and said, "Two Miller Lites, please, and the beverage of choice for the owner." The bartender was about 5 feet 6 inches, an easy three hundred pounds with tatted-up arms and a scraggly gray beard. He waddled up to us from behind the bar. Scowling, he scoffed at our order. "Miller Lites, huh?"

Dad retorted, "Two bottles or cans, whatever you got, and I am buying a drink for the owner." The bartender mumbled and the place returned to a low roar. I thought to myself, *I guess we can stay without getting our asses kicked.* Within two minutes, an older, weathered warrior-looking man at least

60 years old, about 6 foot 3 inches and heavyset, in biker gear walked toward us from behind the bar. He had a full salt-and-pepper beard and at one time might have been considered good-looking. I could feel my anxiety creeping back.

The man looked at Dad and said, "So you want to buy me a drink? I drink Cuervo tequila, and never alone."

Dad elbowed me gently and said, "Bub, you up for a little tequila?"

I looked at Dad and the owner and said, "Always."

Dad turned to the ornery-looking bartender and said, "Three Cuervo shots."

We stood in silence as Dad passed the three shots to us, held up his glass, and said, "God Bless Texas."

Three shots and two beers later we learned the owner's name was "Testy." We did not ask why. By the time all was said and done, Testy had agreed to let Dad leave his truck at the bar until such time that he could afford to come back and get it. Testy gave Dad a tarp to cover up the truck and several of us pushed it out of the way behind the bar. Dad always said, "It helps when you can hold your liquor."

I called my college roommate Greg to come pick us up in Paige. By the time Greg arrived, Dad and I were three sheets to the wind drunk, but we managed to get in and out of the bar without loss of life or limb.

On my drive to the hospital, I chuckled to myself as I thought about that day. I loved drinking with Dad. We had the best time. But when I quit drinking, things changed between us, and they changed fast.

I was glad Dad called my sister Brandy first when he had chest pains. I would likely have downplayed them, as is my tendency. I might have told him he was alright, when clearly he wasn't.

Each of us kids held our roles in the family hierarchy. Brandy, the youngest of five, was the family healthcare provider since she had trained as an X-ray and CT Scan technician. In many ways she was the most like Dad, or at least it looked that way to me because, just like Dad, when she smiled, she could light up a room with twinkling blue eyes and natural blonde hair. People gravitated toward both of them. She is someone Dad took seriously, so when Brandy told Dad that she had called an ambulance, he did not object.

When I got to the hospital, I went straight to the emergency room. I could see my mom had been crying. For a minute I thought I was too late.

Mom stood up and grabbed my hand. "He's in the back. I'll take you to him."

I was relieved that he was still alive, but that feeling of worry was all too familiar.

Aside from accidents and some foolish choices of drinking partners, Dad had truly cheated death several times. These stories had no need for embellishment and made us all think he had a charmed life. Not a year earlier, Dad had been working a refinery "shut down" in Lake Charles, Louisiana. He had been a mere 50 yards away when a massive explosion and chemical leak ripped apart a section of the plant. Dad told me he could hear this "odd gurgling" in the air, and he yelled to his crew, "Get on the ground, now!" Dad was unhurt and unfazed. His crew was fortunate that they were far enough away from the explosion's direct path to not get burned, and only 100 yards away from where the refinery kept its ventilation suits. Dad and his crew quickly outfitted themselves with ventilators, and he helped organize the varied crews on site in putting out the fire and plugging the chemical leak.

Then, two years before his heart attack, Dad had contracted Legionnaires' disease while supervising the construction of a new natural gas power plant in Arizona. They called us twice during his first night in the hospital saying he would die any minute because his lungs were giving out. Before the flights could even be arranged, they called a third time to say he'd made a miraculous improvement overnight. None of us saw Dad as someone who could die. But I always had a deep fear he was someone I could lose.

I was taken aback when I saw him in the hospital bed. He looked pale, unkempt. He usually had a deep color and took good care of his hair. For many years he kept it almost hippy length and he always brushed, crafted, and even used hair spray to keep it just so. Now hair went every which way. His voice was weak and even more raspy than usual. He was a smoker, so he always had mild rasp, but like his personality, his voice was usually firm and smooth. In the hospital bed with an IV drip, he looked small. Feelings of anger were bubbling up, and I had no idea why.

◆ ◆ ◆

Dr. Patel, a well-dressed South Asian man with only a slight hint of an accent, began speaking as soon as we were all present at Dad's bedside.

"The test shows a significantly blocked artery that we need to clear with a stent." I noticed my dad's eyes widen. "I am told I am very good at my job." Dr. Patel smiled warmly, and I saw him relax slightly. "I will leave you to discuss," he added, nodding at me.

Dad called me to his bed. He looked at me and smiled as broadly as ever. I wondered if they had him on drugs. He seemed too happy.

But then he turned serious and said, "Bub, this is no big deal, but just in case something happens, you are to give the truck to Reggie and Leighann and gather my guns. The guns are worth a fortune, so do not rush it. Wait for the right buyers."

I was amused with how his brain worked. My Dad rarely hunted anymore, but he had built a great collection of rifles and shotguns. He even bought an old Tommy gun, a damn machine gun, for reasons that were beyond me. I just said, "Okay, Dad."

He snapped, "I mean it, Bub. This is important! Dad loves you, but you can get so impatient and scattered-brained. Handle it with care." His brow creased as he barked out his orders. I shook off the insults and nodded quietly.

Now there was the Dad I knew. I started to understand why anger was rising into my throat. So much of my life had been dictated by this man and his needs. As a child, there were times we didn't know where he was or if he would be coming back home. I was forced to be "man of the house" when out of the blue, he would waltz back into our lives expecting everything (and everyone) to fall back into place. The Kingdom of Tate G.

"Bub, are you hearing me," he rasped. He weakly banged his fist on the bed tray they had set in front of him. I didn't know why it was there in the first place because he couldn't have any food or water. Maybe Mom put it there to keep him from getting up. In that moment I saw something in him that touched my heart. That was always the way it was with him. One minute I could be as mad as hell at him for everything in our past. Then I would see a softness in his eyes that would remind me of the moments of kindness and connection that I longed for from him.

"I hear you, Dad," I said. "I will take care of everything. Everything will turn out okay."

I needed a cigarette. I had quit for the hundredth time without telling anybody. I figured this didn't count, and I had my emergency Marlboro in the glove compartment. "I will be back, Dad." He grabbed my hand as I turned away. I squeezed it back but kept walking.

CHAPTER 2

THAT POOR BOY AIN'T EVER GOING TO BE NORMAL

obriety is a tricky thing. You can feel accomplished and proud about not taking a drink, but still ignore some of the things that helped bring you to the rooms of AA. I had become a pro at ignoring things and a master of self-repression, particularly when it came to Dad.

Tate G. was not around when I was born on April 13, 1965, at Iredell County Hospital in Statesville, North Carolina. I didn't know he would have any kind of role in my life. My birthday was the same day that the Beatles recorded the famous song "Help." It was as if God was trying to give me a sign from the very start. Sitting in silence did not come naturally to me. Too many thoughts bubbled up and now I could no longer drown them out with booze. When I got back inside the hospital it was the typical waiting, observation, and tests. Sitting alone with my thoughts, I let my thoughts drift to our past. It wasn't all bad. It couldn't have been.

My earliest memory was eating oatmeal in a highchair in a trailer, sitting next to my older sister Vickie. It is only in hindsight and by comparing memories that I realized exactly how shitty that place was. The man who owned the trailer park also owned a dump truck business right next door. Our trailer had a dirty white exterior with a faded brown stripe down the middle of it and a small set of steps with chipped cement. The trashy furniture was rented, but it wasn't the inauspicious surroundings that stuck with me. It was the energy of the place that I remember most vividly. Something wasn't right. Children don't notice things like faded furniture or cracked paint as much as they notice feelings and interactions. There was an undeniable tension between my mother and my father, a man named Gene Kirkman. They acted more like strangers than a married couple. I think the uncomfortable chill in that trailer was only matched by my near-constant confinement to a croup tent.

Everyone says I was born with bad lungs, which is why I spent most of the time in a croup tent at one of the Iredell County hospitals being nebulized so I could breathe. I am sure I had some true respiratory affliction, but I also think children reflect the dysfunction they experience around them. My parents at the time were feeling suffocated.

My constant sickness served another purpose. No one had to focus on the stressful marriage because everyone was always worried about me. Both sets of grandmothers doted on me and worried so hard they had me believing I could die at any moment. I heard them whisper, "That poor boy ain't never going to be normal." I didn't know what that word meant, but I knew it was something I could never be. It turned out they were right. Just not in the way they predicted.

◆ ◆ ◆

In 1955, my mom was sixteen years old and working as a sales clerk at Efird's, a department store in Statesville. In those years, Statesville had a population of about 19,000. Although forty miles north of Charlotte, a city with over 200,000 people, Statesville was the center of our world.

Efird's was in a two-story brick building downtown. They had a little bit of everything. It was a bargain hunter's paradise because its concept was based on buyouts and bankruptcies. The owners had followed the approach created by the Belk brothers by pricing their items low and only accepting cash. This way of doing business was great for farming communities in North Carolina. Belk's eventually took over Efird's and became the largest chain in North Carolina.

My mom worked in the girls' department at Efird's when Gene Kirkman came in and started flirting with her. I can't picture him as suave or romantic, but I know he was nice to her, and that was something she liked. My mom cared for herself by curling her hair appropriately and ensuring she wore the right "conservative" clothing. I noticed in her school photograph that her lipstick was perfectly applied, and Mom highlighted her deep-set eyes and perfectly arched brows with just the slightest amount of makeup.

Mom's parents raised her to become a wife who would hopefully marry well. Grandpa Tevepaugh, my mom's dad, was a supervisor at a furniture plant, so they were considered middle class. As bright as my mom was, it wasn't expected for her to be a sales clerk as a career. She was taught to be a good Christian wife, and to raise children.

Gene had an added advantage over any of the boys who wanted to date my mom. Even though he was older than she was, she knew he was in college studying to be a preacher. When he asked her out, she said, "Yes." They dated off and on during the rest of high school, and I guess she figured he was a good bet. And her parents loved him. He was everything they wanted in a son-in-law, at least on paper. When they heard he planned to become a preacher that was all they needed to hear. They liked him so much they assumed he would be the one Mom would marry. My mom has no recollection of when and how Gene proposed to her, so I guess it was uneventful. They were engaged for about a year, and then on a beautiful December Sunday in 1958, Linda Ann Tevepaugh married Frank Eugene Kirkman in the United Methodist Church. There were bridesmaids, a ring bearer, and a nice article in the local newspaper. This was a pinnacle event in the Tevepaugh household, and I am sure the wedding was the talk of their small town. My older sister Vickie was born a few years later, in 1961.

Gene Kirkman came from a different type of family than my mom. His father, Frank, died when Gene was young. Grandma Kirkman was not the typical stay-at-home housewife because she was the sole breadwinner after Frank died. Frank had worked for the phone company and left her some AT&T stock that, along with working at what eventually became Belk's Department Store, kept her comfortable, but I am sure she saw Mom as a good catch for her son.

Another one of my first memories is Grandma Kirkman's home place. After Gene's father died, they moved in with her kin to have a roof over their heads. The house seemed enormous to me, and I loved exploring it. They lived downstairs primarily, as the upstairs, like most other houses at that time, did not have heat. Most of the second floor was used for storage. I remember going upstairs in the spring and summer and finding lots of old toys. I especially loved playing with the wooden puzzles I found in a wooden rack. The back of the pieces felt rough like burlap.

There was military equipment, including a helmet, a fake parade rifle, and a soldier's backpack. But my favorite things were the picture books. I sat next to the wall by the only window that opened. It had a fan blowing to keep the heat out of the downstairs. I poured over the yellowed pages with illustrations of faraway places. They may have been children's encyclopedias, but it was obvious no one had looked at them for a very long while. I always took great care of the things I found in my secret upstairs world.

I liked being alone, but if it was a Sunday, I listened for the call to dinner. In the downstairs was a dining room with a huge table. We rarely ate at that table and instead sat at a smaller table in the large kitchen. I remember something about Grandma Kirkman having an ice business. It is hard to imagine now that this could be a way to make money, but her family got electricity in the 1930s while most of the people in the area didn't have any, even in the '60s, when I was born. They had a machine that made ice blocks, and a very old Black man named Arthur used to come by and sell the ice for them. They wouldn't let me near it. I remember Arthur though. He was overly polite to my grandma, looking down when he came to get the ice, but Grandma was always respectful and kind. Arthur talked to me and smiled, and I loved that he noticed me.

I found out later that Grandma Kirkman didn't really make any money from the ice business. She kept it going because of Arthur and the Black folks who still didn't have refrigeration. Arthur got hurt in World War II and didn't have any other way of making a living. I think it probably cost more in electricity than it would ever have earned back. She didn't shut it down until all the Black folks in the holler had electricity and refrigeration.

Grandma Kirkman was a doting and definite matriarch. She liked to feed me sweets and she could bake. I was a very fat boy, but I didn't think anything of it until other people pointed it out. I just knew I liked food, and when it was given to me by Grandma Kirkman, I felt loved. I hated to leave her house and go back to the trailer. There in the Loray Trailer Park, Vickie and I knew to be quiet or play outside.

Things weren't working out for Mom and Gene as her parents had hoped they would. He was showing very little interest in being a preacher by that time and had not only dropped out of his studies, but he had also taken a job with the phone company. We still all went to church, even if it was just to please Grandma Kirkman. I loved going to Church because it was always followed by the greatest dinners. Grandma Kirkman's weekly Sunday dinners were the things of southern hospitality legend. Looking back, I think those Sunday dinners were what gave me the few moments of a happy childhood that I remember. There I could be a kid. At home, I felt off. The knots in my stomach didn't match my family's insistence that everything was, in fact, okay. I know Mom wished it were true. She was dedicated to us and made sure we were fed and clothed, but with each day, I could see the life oozing out of her.

One day we arrived at Grandma's house early and I got to bear witness to the cooking. "What are you doing with that?" I asked as Grandma pulled out a massive hammer-shaped mallet.

"I am going to pound the cube steaks," she explained. Grandma was in a well-matched skirt, blouse, sweater, and pearls. She used her discount at Belk's department store to make sure she was always well dressed. She also made sure I had new clothes even though we had to shop in the husky department where everything fit me better.

Grandma wore an apron with pockets so she wouldn't ruin her clothes and pounded away on the steaks until they were exactly the thickness she wanted.

She would add a bit of salt, a bit of pepper, and set the steaks in the refrigerator until we returned from church. She made it look so easy. Those steaks tasted like magic. Magic in those days involved frying the steaks in a great big dollop of Crisco. She would get the grease good and crackling-hot and then add the meat. The smell alone made my mouth water. After the steaks were about done, Grandma would add flour to the drippings and residue, forming a gravy. Watching Grandma cook was like watching a choreographed dance. Next came the russet potatoes boiled with bacon grease from a tin she left by the stove, followed by the chorus of green beans with a spoonful of the not-so-secret, magic ingredient. The potatoes were a featured performer at Sunday dinner. Grandma placed the cooled potatoes in a bowl and pulled out her hand mixer. She let me pour in the milk and a big old stick of real butter. Then, of course, the bacon grease for good measure.

All the while we were making lunch, Grandma was reheating the peach cobbler she had made earlier in the week, usually on Friday afternoons. Her neighbor had a huge peach tree with sweet fruit that just *needed* to be in the cobbler. No store-bought pie crusts for us. I'm not sure if they even had them in Stony Point, North Carolina, at that time. Grandma rolled out the crust and the extra dough would go on top in a crumble with cinnamon and lots of sugar. No wonder I was fat.

As I got older, there were times I had fun around Gene, the man I called "Dad." It always felt awkward though, like we didn't know what to say to each other. Even as a little kid I could see something wasn't quite right. Kids monitor their parents to learn how to feel. I was feeling like there was always some disconnect even if I did not have the words to express it at the time.

Gene drove a cool 1966 Ford Mustang with an eight-track player that distracted us from the expanding gulf between us. I would sit on the floorboard in the front passenger side with Vickie on the seat. We listened to Johnny Cash and Loretta Lynn and annoyed each other. Sometimes we would hear Gene humming along to the music, but he was just as much a background noise as the cassettes.

Gene Kirkman never tried to control or discipline me. Sometimes he would scold Vickie for some misdeed or another, but it wasn't just because she was the older sibling. With me, he was oddly hands-off.

I think I noticed Gene less because of Grandma Kirkman. Aside from her cooking, she was one of the kindest, sweetest and most Christian women I ever knew. I didn't understand religion beyond the stories I heard in Church, but I had a sense that many people talked about walking in the footsteps of Jesus. To me, Grandma Kirkman truly walked that walk. That may have been why Gene was planning to become a preacher. After he left his mother's house, his motivation to preach followed suit. He seemed to have lost his moral compass along the way. At first, I didn't know why Gene and Mom spoke less and yelled more, but eventually I found out.

Gene started staying out late during the week when, before, he used to be home about the same time as Mom, who had recently found a new job in the shipping office at the Langley Processing Plant, a good employer at the time and a lot of locals worked there. The plant made white and colored fiberglass for curtains, drapes, and other household goods. Every little thing must be made somewhere and that was one of the biggest contributions to the economy coming out of Statesville. It also happened to be the reason I was born. What I could make out of Gene and mom's fighting was the name "Kat Clore." I thought it was funny when Mom said, "Yeah, you went bowling." But under her breath, she whispered, "Kat Clore, the whore." I didn't know what it meant, but I knew it couldn't be good. One day she put Vickie and me in the car and we just left. A lot of the furniture and things in the trailer were rented so there wasn't much else to take.

Leaving Gene Kirkman was probably for the best. A loveless marriage running on fumes, a nauseatingly brown trailer with an interior mood to match—something had to change. Mom, Vickie, and I moved into the aptly named Center Street Apartments located on "Center Street" in Statesville. It was a two-story brick apartment building right across the street from Statesville Senior High, and it was certainly a hell of a lot better than the trailer park. Center Street had a sense of optimism, a fresh start. Gene's presence had been like a shadow in our trailer. I didn't feel like we lost much as we unpacked our clothing and the few pots and pans we brought along. Mom had to start over. She had no credit and no money yet and everything familiar was changing.

Grandma Tevepaugh never said anything against Gene because she knew she had really pushed Mom to marry him. "He seemed so promising," she said, but only once. She never questioned my mom about leaving Gene. In fact, she helped us get back on our feet by co-signing for the water, lights, and apartment lease. She also co-signed for my mom to purchase furniture on credit at Gordon's Furniture Store.

This new place meant freedom, but I didn't know Mom already had a new life in mind for all of us. Now that Mom was a single parent, she needed something else—childcare.

CHAPTER 3

MISS SAWYER'S NURSERY SCHOOL

I had never been around a lot of other kids, even at church, where I was usually with one of my grandmas or Mom and didn't venture beyond. I didn't bond right away with Miss Sawyer, the owner of the nursery school. She was a bleach bottle blonde about the same petite size as my mom. Miss Sawyer seemed friendly enough, but her assistant was a skinny old woman with yellowish-brown teeth stained by tobacco. She wore cat eye glasses and a permanent scowl. She oversaw lime green Kool-Aid and cheap store-bought cookies for snack time which she administered after our forced nap. I remember all of us laying on blankets pretending to sleep. If you moved or opened your eyes, old Miss Yellow Teeth would furrow her brow so we knew she meant business. I hated her and I hated being around kids all damn day. I wanted to go home or to Grandma Kirkman's house.

Still, one kid did become my friend. He was the weirdest kid in class, which immediately endeared him to me. Today we would probably call him autistic, but back then the old folks would just say "he ain't quite right." His name was Eric and he had odd features. His eyes seemed far apart, and his head seemed misshapen, like someone needed a plunger to pull him from the womb. But that is not what set him apart. He couldn't speak more than a few words and paired them with gibberish. He tried to communicate with hand gestures, but as he became more frustrated, he would flail his hands around like he was spastic. You could look into his face and see his frustration, but he seemed kinder than the other children and I just liked him.

As one would expect, you couldn't put a boy like Eric in a room full of children without a bully emerging from the group. That bully was a red-headed, snot-nosed boy named Timmy who took every opportunity to pick on Eric and call him "retard." Both Miss Sawyer and old Miss Yellow-Teeth saw what was happening but didn't do a thing.

One day, I had enough of Timmy pushing Eric around. I didn't do anything dramatic, I just said, "You shouldn't do that." I was not schooled in the way of bullies so I wasn't expecting him to turn on me too. I wasn't a "retard," and I was just sticking up for my friend.

Timmy immediately shouted, "Shut up, porker." The other kids started to laugh and called me "porker" in unison. I shouldn't have been shocked, but I hadn't realized that was how they saw me. I don't know if it was my embarrassment or if I was standing up for Eric, but something came over me that I never felt before. It was like a volcano of rage that ended with my fist on Timmy's nose. And suddenly he was bleeding.

I don't know why that incident always stuck in my mind. When I thought about it over the years, I think it surprised me that I didn't see myself as a porker then, any more than I saw myself as an alcoholic when I got older. I was clearly overweight because I ate too much. But until that moment in that nursery school classroom, I wasn't self-conscious about it. No wonder I liked being friends with Eric. I also remember the punishment. I got put in the naughty chair by the old Miss Yellow Teeth, and no one even asked why an otherwise shy and passive child would haul off and punch Timmy hard enough to draw blood. When my mom came to pick me up, she listened and nodded her head as Miss Sawyer told her about my crime.

Mom said, "Was that boy mean to you?"

"Yes," I mumbled, waiting for her to yell at me. I knew from church that I wasn't supposed to hit.

"Okay" was all she said back to me. At that moment I felt she understood me. And she would show me many times through the years how unconditional her love truly was.

◆ ◆ ◆

Seeing my dad at the hospital brought up a lot of memories. He looked so fragile in his hospital bed. I couldn't help but remember the very first time I laid eyes on him. I was still attending Miss Sawyer's nursery school, but most of my memories of that time are a blur. I remember keeping to myself a lot. I guess the other kids didn't want to mess with me, but that also meant I played alone. Even Eric seemed scared of me.

One day Miss Sawyer took me by the hand and led me from the playground to the chain-link fence behind the school. Miss Sawyer had a big smile on her face as we approached a tall, strikingly handsome man leaning against the fence.

He said, "Hi there, are you ready to go?" It took me a minute to realize he was talking to me.

I had never seen a man so well dressed. He reminded me of the men I saw on the pages of the Sears catalog, dressed in tailored slacks and a pullover polo that fit him perfectly. He had beautifully shined brown shoes matching his belt. And he was so tall.

"Michael, this is Mr. Tate Barkley. He is going to take you home today."

In those days it would never have occurred to anyone not to send a kid home with a strange man. But evidently, my mother and Tate had it all arranged. Looking back, I could see Tate's charm right from the start. Miss Sawyer's typically stoic personality was now more like a giggling teenager. She was flirting with him, and he was flirting back like it was just the way he talked to everyone. It came naturally.

This elegant giant picked me up and seat-belted me in the front seat of his 1969 Plymouth Fury. It was the biggest and newest car I had ever seen, a beautiful shiny brown filled with all kinds of knobs and dials. I remember how much I wanted to touch them but didn't dare. There was something about this man that made me feel special. I instantly liked him, but at the same time, I was unsettled.

It felt strange when he brought me to Grandma Tevepaugh's house. It was immediately obvious that she didn't like the man. He had been introduced to me as Tate, and Grandma Tevepaugh seemed to call him "Ted" purposely. Grandma gave him a smirk of clear disapproval, but it seemed to roll by him. That would continue to be their relationship for the rest of her life.

My Grandma Tevepaugh would always remain a fan of Gene Kirkman. I think it was because of who she thought he would be. When they met, he told her he would be a Presbyterian Minister. My grandma always wanted her family to stay close to the good Lord, and she seemed to forget that not only was Gene Kirkman not a minister, but he also had no intention of becoming one.

Grandma Tevepaugh knew something I didn't know and would have no clue about until I was eleven years old. This big tree of a handsome man was my birth father. There was a type of connection I didn't feel from Gene, but I had no idea that there was blood between us. I was too young to understand these things anyway. But this was another case of my gut telling me something I couldn't figure out.

Grandma Tevepaugh didn't like Tate Barkley because she knew he had been intimate with my mother while she was still married to Gene. For all I know, she may have figured he was just a no-good man, and because of him her daughter would be going to hell for her sins. On top of everything, he had made her pregnant while also married to someone else. The one thing I know for sure is that my mother and real father must have loved each other very much to put up with all the chaos they caused to be together as a family.

It wasn't until I was a grown man that my mother told me what was happening back then. When Vickie was born in 1961, my mom went to work in the shipping office at the Langley Processing plant. My dad, Tate, who was married to a woman named Martha at the time, also worked at the plant. Martha and my dad had a daughter, Jane, born one year before Vickie.

My mom worked at the plant and took care of Vickie while Gene went bowling at night. Only he wasn't bowling. This is when he met the divorcee Kat Clore who lived only a few houses down from my mom's best friend. Statesville is a small town. It wasn't long before Mom's best friend spotted Gene's car late into the night parked in front of Kat Clore's house. Mom decided she was not going to share Gene with Kat Clore, the whore, so she stopped sleeping with him altogether.

Mom and Tate had been flirting at work and they got involved in a passionate affair. I was their love child, but the law at the time was that if a child was born during a marriage, it was presumed to belong to the husband. My mom said she and Gene lived together platonically until 1968 when she finally had enough and left.

I know more incidents tipped the scale to her leaving the marriage. Any woman raised in the way Mom was knew there would be a small-town scandal. Mom was in love with the charming Tate, but a disappointing home life gave her the fuel to make the break. Mom wanted to be a good wife and mother and worked hard at it. If Gene had been truthful and said he just made a mistake, she might have forgiven him. But everything about him and their life together was a lie. My mom's parents may have taught her to be a lady, but she had and still has pride and good sense. I also know my mom needed a dreamer, and Tate Barkley was certainly that.

The next time he picked me up from Miss Sawyer's, he took me on an adventure I would never forget. After buckling me into the shiny Plymouth, he drove me to the Statesville Municipal Airport. Tate was a private pilot at the time and co-owned an Arrow airplane with some doctors, at least I think he owned part. I learned later that I could never be fully sure what to believe when Tate was spinning a yarn. He always went for the most impressive version of the facts. I wouldn't have cared if it was his plane or not because the next thing I knew, he took me up in the air. He may as well have been Superman himself. He flew us over the town and pointed out our apartment when we got to Center Street.

"That's where you live," he said over the noise of the engines.

I pressed my nose against the window and looked for landmarks. I had never been on a plane or met anyone like Tate. I was hooked. It was the first time I felt connected to a man. I didn't understand the concept of a father, but I knew I was safe with him even though I was up in an airplane.

When I got home, I was still floating on air and couldn't wait to see him again. Then, out of nowhere, he was gone. I hardly knew him, and I never missed Gene when we left him, but with Tate I immediately felt sad, like I was grieving.

I don't think I even felt like eating. Even though Mom and Gene were separated on the way to divorce, we still went to Grandma Kirkman's for Sunday Dinner every so often. Even her cobbler didn't cheer me up. She never said anything, but I am sure she understood how confusing my life had become.

All these years later, with my father now in the hospital, it occurred to me that the feelings coming up were not new. From the moment I met him, I constantly feared losing him, just as I had that first time. So many times, he would go just away without us knowing where he was, but this first time was the worst. After that, it would take a long time for me to trust that he would stay, and I don't think I ever got over the feeling that someone I love could just up and leave.

I don't know how long it was before we saw Tate again. I had settled back into a life without him as if he were nothing but a fantasy. With Miss Sawyer's School, green Kool-Aid, cheap cookies, and occasional posturing with Timmy, life went on. Mom worked, we visited Grandma Tevepaugh, and we went to Church on Sundays with Grandma Kirkman. It felt settled and okay.

Then Mom came home with some news. No warning, just an announcement. "We're moving to Florida with Tate," Mom said. There was to be no response from Vickie and me and no discussion about how we felt about leaving. I vaguely remember feeling queasy after the news, and my breathing became difficult. I worried that I would wind up back in the hospital with Croup again, so I hid it from everyone as much as I could.

CHAPTER 4

I JUST WANT TO HOLD THE BABY

The news at the time was full of stories about Cape Canaveral, astronauts, and the Kennedy Space Center. After flying in an airplane, space travel interested me. These were the years of men going to the moon. I should have been excited about Florida, but I wasn't.

We saw Tate four or five times before we made the move. He seemed standoffish, or maybe it was me. I didn't want to get close to him like before because I couldn't figure him out. I also didn't know how to behave around him. It always seemed there was some unspoken expectation that I should say something, but I never knew what to say. My time with Tate before the move felt even more awkward than when I spent time with Gene.

I didn't want to leave North Carolina. It all just seemed so weird. I was unsettled and nervous from the moment Mom made the pronouncement. I was only five, but even five-year-olds feel things they may not be able to express. But my mom was the center of my world, and she seemed happy with Tate. That was all that mattered, I guess.

The actual move was abrupt. When you are that young, you don't realize everything around you. All I remember is, "We are leaving tomorrow." That was it—no long goodbyes. I don't even remember saying goodbye to my two grandmothers or Gene. Some things stand out so clearly for me, but that scene in my mind is like a quick cut to a commercial.

The next thing I remember is living in an honest-to-goodness Florida house. It was in a subdivision called Sunland in Sanford, Florida. The air smelled different, like it had water in it, and we had a garden with a big piece of coral rock in front. I remember periwinkles, little flowering plants that do well in Florida's sandy soil. There were windows in every room of the house, and they rolled out. Unlike the old wooden house in North Carolina, this one was made from pink cement blocks. We only had window air conditioners in two of the rooms, so I think the cement structure was to keep the house cool.

Another difference with the Florida house was a lot of sliding doors. All the doors were sliding, even the doors between the bedrooms. My bedroom and Vickie's were connected by a sliding door. We both loved the backyard because not only was it big, but it also had an orange tree and a grapefruit tree. To us, the house was a major step up. Looking back, it wasn't the palace I thought it was. It was an old house by Florida standards and always in disrepair. The furniture brought from North Carolina didn't fit right, but it was what tied us to home. Although it was unspoken, Vickie and I were resigned to making the best of our new life.

I had hardly gotten used to our move when Mom hit us with more news. We were only in Sunland for a few days when she announced, "You are going to have a baby sister very soon." I must have been young if I hadn't noticed she was pregnant.

Then she told me Tate was the dad. I didn't know what to make of this as I didn't know he was my real dad. I think I was a bit jealous but also excited. Vickie didn't take it well;she stayed in her room most of the time. I was filled with a million questions, but there was tension in the house, so I tried to stay out of everyone's way.

I had no sense of time back then. Having a baby sister "soon" could have meant tomorrow or next year. But, as children do, I blended into my new environment with more ease than I would have expected. I met a boy named Andy about my age next door. He and I rode bikes, ran around, examined bugs under magnifying glasses, and chased lizards. The weather was warm, and I liked the smell of orange blossoms. It was just like blending in with a local accent.

Living with Tate Barkley was not like living with Gene. Gene hardly noticed me and never asked me to do anything. Tate gave me chores to do and reminded me that I was part of a family living under his roof. I wasn't sure I liked his control, but on the other hand, I did anything I was told. I was young, but apparently not too young to clean trash cans and the bathrooms. I may not have liked it at first, but the truth was after doing chores and running around with Andy, I went from a sickly, super chubby white kid who could barely breathe to a lean, tan, blonde-haired, blue-eyed picture of health within only a couple of months. I was never sick a single day in Sunland.

Throughout my life with Tate, it aggravated the hell out of me when he was right. Even now, as a grown man with a career, success under my belt, and sobriety, I could still feel like that little six-year-old waiting for my orders whenever I was around him. I wanted to please him so he wouldn't go away. If he said to do something, I did it without question and did it the best I could. I think that's why there were times he could hurt me more than anyone else on the planet.

I felt good when I finished something for Tate, and even if he didn't compliment me, if he didn't say anything, I knew I had done something right. That was good enough for me. We were all settling into a routine when my baby sister, Leighann, came along. There was so much excitement in the house when Mom went to the hospital that Vickie and I scrubbed everything from top to bottom. It was as if we were awaiting the arrival of a princess. We couldn't wait. Then Mom came home with the most beautiful little thing I had ever seen. I was fascinated that something so small could have everything a big person has. She had little fingers and toes complete with little nails. She had big blue eyes and a tiny nose that made me melt. I loved her from the minute I saw her.

The best part was seeing Tate so excited. We had never seen him so filled with joy. He could joke, laugh, or be stern, but this was complete abandon. I only wish I could have captured that moment forever.

I loved Leighann deeply from the first minute I saw her. I remember looking up at Tate and saying, "What do I do?"

"You love her like you've never loved anyone," Tate said, laughing. So, I did, and to this day I've never stopped.

Mom had been home from the hospital for less than a week when Tate returned to work. He was on the road a lot as a fabric salesman in those days. Vickie and I cleaned the house daily. We knew how to wash clothes and complete every chore inside the house. Vickie would stand on my back so she could reach the clothesline in the backyard since we didn't have a dryer. We vacuumed, dusted, and I cleaned the bathrooms. I took great pride in the sparkling bathrooms.

With Leighann home, my days took on a different dimension. I watched

Mom clean Leighann and change diapers. Leighann would drink formula, which had to be warmed. I wanted to know everything, and Mom and Tate let me be involved. One afternoon, Tate called me to the stove. He asked me to hold out my arm. He had Leighann's baby bottle in his hand, and he shook the bottle up and down so the milk would fall to the inside of my forearm. The first few drops were cold.

"You want her milk to be warm, nice and warm, but not hot," Tate explained. "She needs to drink it without getting burned."

The thought of burning her scared me so I asked him to show me the exact right temperature. I wanted nothing more than to feed her and take care of her. I don't know why I was so obsessed with her. It never occurred to me that I would never have any babies of my own. I was just a natural nurturer.

I watched as Tate placed the bottle in the pot with the water and turned on the stove. We watched and waited. Twice, he pulled out the bottle and sprinkled it over our arms. Finally, he said, "Feel this." He sprinkled it on my arm. "This is the temperature, feel it, remember it."

Now, I knew the temperature the milk had to be. He asked that I take the bottle back to my mom. From that day on, I knew by sense when the milk was ready, but I always tested it before I gave it to Leighann.

Tate's trust in me with Leighann's baby formula was surprising, since Tate called me "scatterbrained." This is another way that I hadn't seen myself until Tate made a thing about it. We internalize the messages our parents give us. That is why it was so amusing to me that now he was putting me in charge of his precious guns and other items while thinking he could be on his deathbed. I was six years old at that time, and I was taking care of a baby. And even though he worried, I never came close to burning the house down. It never occurred to me until I got sober that he may have been projecting onto me. Either way, he would scare me by saying, "How would you feel if you burned the house down with all of us in it?"

The thought terrified me. To this day, I identify as someone who rushes and is scatterbrained. I am sure I was at my worst when I was a drunk. Of course, scatterbrained would not have described the fog and the danger I created for myself and others when I was drinking. But then I could dismiss it because of the alcohol. But inside me, I always carried the burden that I was flawed and not really capable of caring or loving like other people.

Despite Tate's concerns, I was always careful with Leighann. But I was never allowed to hold her on my own. I even learned to change her diapers, which were the cloth kind. We didn't have the money for Pampers. The more responsibility I took, the more I kept asking Mom if I could hold Leighann. She always said, "Not yet," and that Leighann was too young and fragile.

I remember being frustrated as I did my chores. I wouldn't hurt the baby. I just wanted to hold her. As Leighann grew, she would recognize me and smile and react to me. If she was awake, I was usually with her. It was a full day every day.

Tate and Mom were still protective of Leighann, but through her, I became closer to Tate. Tate would often feed Leighann while watching the news. We were a Walter Cronkite family. It seemed that everything was about "Vietnam." I began to recognize the faces of Richard Nixon and Henry Kissinger and the endless footage of the fighting taking place there. While Tate and I watched the news he began sharing his commentary with me. It was different from being with Gene.

These moments may have been what eventually sparked my interest in politics. Tate would get all fired up about "Tricky Dick." It was 1971, and he clearly didn't trust the man. Tate always talked about the news when I was there with him and Leighann. He would pontificate and educate all at the same time. I was too young to appreciate it fully at the time, but looking back, I realize that even though he thought I was scatterbrained, he never talked down to me when he analyzed the news for me, but just shared it like I was another adult.

Leighann had a magical way of making me feel closer and less apart from Tate. I liked that Tate would frequently direct conversation toward me. He would lay out his expectations which gave me structure. When he left for work every day, he always gave me a chore list. Raking the entire yard and bagging it was the biggest chore on my schedule. This was also the only chore for which I received any money. I would get 25 cents for raking and bagging the yard, and then walk up to the 7-Eleven store to get a comic book.

Tate was personable, animated, and without fear when it came to people. Within weeks of moving to Sunland, we knew all our neighbors on our street and the adjacent one. Often, I would walk with him in the evening so we would meet many people on these walks. The best part about meeting these people was he would put his hand on my shoulder and proudly say, "This is my son." Frankly, it confused me, but I liked it.

One of Tate's early lessons stuck with me later in life as I tried to understand the man and what made him do the things he did.

Tate said, "When you look at someone, you'll know what's needed. Some people like you to be sweet; some people want you to be a nervous wreck, and others just want you to respect them. You'll know what each person needs from you when the time comes." He was talking to a young child, knowing I wouldn't understand, but his words stuck with me, and later they helped me understand him. He was a character, but I grew very attached to him and the life he gave us in Florida.

While the summer of 1971 was filled with joy, a new baby sister, and a budding relationship inside a family, like most things in my young life, it all came crashing down.

Andy and I were playing near the orange tree when a tall, thin older man pulled up to the house in a Black Plymouth Fury. This man was wearing a white Resistol cowboy hat and a brown suit like President Lyndon B. Johnson used to wear. He walked part of the way up the driveway when Tate, sitting in the carport reading the paper, sprang up to meet him.

Tate was close enough to where I could hear, and I remember the man asked if they could talk inside. And Tate said, "No." He looked around toward me and said, "Michael, go inside. Andy, go home. Both of you, now."

I went inside but ran to the window to see what was happening. The man handed Tate some papers, and I watched Tate become angry. I could hear him yelling at the man but couldn't understand what he was saying. When Tate stormed into the house, I ran into my room to hide so he wouldn't know I had been listening. All I knew was something bad had happened, and I was not about to get in Tate's way. He went straight to the bedroom, and I heard muffled voices. Then I heard my mother shriek and start crying. I was afraid someone had died. I had never heard her so upset. At that point, I had to see what was going so I ran to the bedroom door and yelled for my mom.

Tate yelled back, "It's fine. Go outside now."

I knew nothing was fine, and my mother's tears worsened it. No one would tell me anything. I felt sick to my stomach. Tate was on edge and even stopped commenting to me about the news. I was worried about everything. Mom and Tate went to Orlando and left Vickie and me with Andy's family. When they returned, they called us into the living room. Tate said, "Your Mom and I went to Orlando to see a lawyer."

I knew what a lawyer was, and I knew it had to mean something serious. Mom started crying and couldn't even look at us. Finally, Tate put his hand on her shoulder and said, "You're leaving to go back to North Carolina." I felt wide-eyed when he said it. And I remember saying, "When are we leaving?"

Tate said, "Two days."

"Where are we going to live?"

Tate looked at me, he knew that I was not getting the import of what he was telling me. He pulled me on his lap and said, "Just you and Vickie are going. You are going to live with Gene. The Court, the Judge, ordered it. I am going to fight like hell to change it, but you have to go for now."

I felt utterly confused. I asked, "Is Leighann not coming, or Mom?"

He said, "No, we will stay here." Tate's eyes began to well up with tears. It was the first time I ever saw him shed a tear.

I looked at him and said, "But who will watch the baby?"

My mom totally lost it at that moment. Tate paused and said, "I promise, we will watch the baby until you get back." Two days later, I had a grocery bag of things to take to North Carolina. Mom had packed a small suitcase for me, but Tate said, "No! If he wants to do this, he can buy them all new clothes, fuck him!" It was the first time I'd ever heard Tate say "fuck." The morning we left, we were in the living room and Tate said, "Are you ready? You okay?"

I responded, "I just want to hold the baby."

He said, "Sit back on the couch." He took Leighann from Mom and sat next to me. Tate gently showed me how to hold Leighann and then put her in my arms. I moved my arm until I had her cradled in both. Leighann and I looked at each other for what seemed like forever. Tate said, "Good job, but we have to go now." I gave Leighann back and walked out to the carport in tears. If a six-year-old can feel broken, I did.

CHAPTER 5

STONY POINT

The hospital made me think about all the times I had no idea what would happen. Ever since that first time we were sent back to Gene in North Carolina, I had always felt uneasy when things were out of my control. It amuses me when I also think about how often I was completely out of control when I was drinking, but it didn't seem to matter. Now, in the hospital, all the waiting was getting under my skin. No one could give us a clear answer about what to expect.

I felt my body tighten and my throat go dry. The first time I felt this way was when Vickie and I were in the back seat on our way to Stony Point, North Carolina. It seemed like we were always in the backseat of a car, wondering what was going to happen next. I don't understand why adults don't tell children anything. I was young, but I wasn't stupid. The hardest part was trying not to think about Leighann. We were on our way to Gene who was now living with Grandma Kirkman. I remember being confused. I loved Grandma Kirkman but felt torn. If I felt glad about seeing her, I felt like I was being untrue to my mom and Leighann.

In hindsight, I know we weren't the only children to be in a divorce tug of war between parents. But it made me feel nervous all the time. At least if someone explained things to me, I might have been able to anchor my worry. Instead, it was the not knowing that was always the worst. I could never settle anywhere, no matter how much I wanted to. I do not remember how we got to North Carolina exactly or with whom; Vickie and I stuck together and did what we were told. Gene was now dating an animated redhead named Nora. She smoked more than she ate. This lady was something and I was not sure how I felt about her. She was taller than Mom, wore heavy eye shadow, and had a single-minded determination seeping from every pore. At first glance, you knew who was calling the shots in this relationship.

The best part of Stony Point was Grandma Kirkman. She belonged to that part of the country and the red earth around us. Gene and Nora made a big fuss about how much they wanted Vickie and me with them, but once they got us they were barely around. They would go out at night and even during the day. But Grandma Kirkman was always around with us except when she had to work. So she was mostly home when we were home, and I was now going to a new school.

I don't know why at my age now this year was so important to me. I guess it was because it was a time when my memories were sharp, and the first time I really understood what it was like to live in the North Carolina backcountry. My world was now beyond Tate, my mom, and Leighann.

Stony Point was not far from where I was born in Statesville. But, aside from Associated Reformed Presbyterian (ARP) churches everywhere, a small grocery store, and a post office, there wasn't much else. At the top of the street where you turned to go to my Grandma Kirkman's house, there was a bankrupt tire shop. But I remember most the great big holler at the end of Grandma Kirkman's road where Arthur the ice delivery man lived.. A holler or hollow is the ground space between the hills. It's so hilly that often it can't be seen from the road. The folks who lived in this holler were a small community of Black people who had stayed close to the land their ancestors worked back when they were slaves. I am unsure if the people I knew back then would prefer I describe them as descended from slaves or formerly enslaved people. Still, all I know is they had a huge impact on me. All these families had been around the holler for generations, and no one ever seemed to move. I remember clearly that the old tire shop held the ghosts of a terrible past. It may have been abandoned, but it still displayed the signs of the old Jim Crow South in the back. The segregation signs were there for everyone to see, showing the way to the "Colored entrance," and to the front "for Whites only." I noticed these when I was a child and asked Grandma Kirkman about them. In hindsight, I wonder if the small community wanted the signs to remind their children what it had been like or if no one bothered to take them down. I know that as recently as 2021, anonymous members of the KKK sent veiled threats to over sixty residents who had voted to remove

Confederate monuments.

My Grandma Kirkman was not like most other old folks in North Carolina. When I asked her about the signs, she said, "Those were from ignorant people and an unfortunate time." Then she told me how God loves everyone, and so should I. I remember her words, but it was more how she behaved that stuck with me. Grandma Kirkman did seem to love, touch, and hug everybody she met. Color never appeared to be an issue for her, as she always helped and gave regardless of race.

People in Stony Point needed the help. They were proud people, but some were "dirt poor." I learned early what that expression meant. The soil in Stony Point was red clay, and I will never forget seeing children go to school without shoes, with their feet red and calloused. I only went to school with white kids and these white children were the poorest. Not only were they barefoot, but they also had torn clothes two sizes too big and dirty faces to match their feet. They looked like no one cared about them or watched over what they did. I missed my mother and sister, but even at that age, I saw that my life was better than most.

Thinking back, I can retrace every part of that little town and recall every inch of Stony Point Elementary. I remember the concrete walls and the faint smell of mildew emanating from the bathroom. We ate our lunches at our desks, and even though many kids had no lunch, we all got little paper milk containers. I always had a good lunch. My grandma always put something good in my little sack. I will never forget how my teacher, Ms. Sprinkle, who always wore shoes to match her dresses, always brought food to the class for the poor children to eat. I now know she must have been paying for the food out of her own pocket.

I watched as she gave easier questions to the poor children during spelling contests so she would have an excuse to give them a treat. At first, I felt cheated, but when I caught onto what she was doing it no longer bothered me.

Many things opened my eyes when we lived with Gene and Grandma Kirkman. As it was, Vickie shared a room with Grandma, and I had to share the front bedroom with Gene. Grandma Kirkman came into the room every night to say prayers with me, and she always made sure we blessed Mom, Tate, and Leighann. That prayer meant everything to me, and I was proud when I could say by myself without prompting: "Now I lay me down to sleep; I pray the Lord my soul to keep. If I should die before I wake, I pray the Lord my soul to take."

Grandma Kirkman never denied me anything or tried to manipulate my prayers, she just wanted me to pray, and she especially wanted me to know that God loved me.

When I was in the throes of alcoholism, I tried not to think about Grandma Kirkman and everything she taught me by example. Alcoholics don't take time to think about other people while drinking. All we want to do is get higher and higher while separating from real life. Grandma Kirkman was the kindest, most generous, and most merciful person I have ever known. To think about her while I was drinking would have added to my shame. It might have pierced through my denial, something I wouldn't have been able to stand. Only through sobriety can I reflect on everything she gave me and how she represented what it meant to be a faithful Christian.

Grandma Kirkman was not without her quirks. She could be frugal about certain things. But she was never frugal when helping others.

One day Grandma Kirkman took me with her to a store run by the church where they would gather and recycle shoes and clothes for the poor. I remember the place smelled old and the clothing was in large piles on picnic tables set up for sorting. I was in charge of matching shoes and putting them in a row. Grandma Kirkman reminded me about the children without shoes.

"But these shoes are too big for them," I said. "Some of these shoes will go for the parents," she replied. "They need good shoes too. It will help them come to church if they can cover their feet. So many people are too shy to come into church barefoot."

I realized she didn't mean shy; she meant embarrassed. She also bundled up grown-up pants, nice shirts like the ones Tate wore to work, and women's dresses. "The poor are God's special people. Always remember that."

When school had started, Ms. Sprinkle helped me get settled in class and I made some new friends. Grandma Kirkman was quick to help the poor, but she never wanted me to sleep over at anyone else's house, even when their parents invited me, even when they were members of the church. When I asked her why I couldn't go, she said, "Those mamas have enough on their plate right now."

Looking back, I realize my classmates were rock bottom poor. Many of the parents still worked in the fields around Stony Point. The lucky ones had parents who worked in the furniture plants or the textile mills up in the nearby town of Hickory. School buses would roam the county picking up kids, including the ones who lived up in the Brushies. The Brushy kids were hardcore Appalachian. The Brushy mountains are a deeply eroded spur of the Blue Ridge mountains that routed their way very close to Stony Point. Stony Point itself had some hills but mostly pasture and farmland. The affluent folks had pastures and farmland. The Brushies had the rocky land of the mountains.

When Grandma Kirkman saw one of my classmates wearing tattered clothes, she would bring a paper bag of clothes and give it to them after school. She always said, "Here, take this to your mama, tell your mama I don't know what to do with them." Grandma made sure to add, "Tell your mom I don't have any room in the store for these clothes. Would your mama kindly take them off my hands?"

Grandma Kirkman knew the Appalachian folks were too proud to accept outright charity from do-gooders. But she was clever enough to allow them their pride while giving them what they needed. She would always think of ways to try to help them. One particular day, my classmate Jimmy Fox was walking down the street. It was cold outside, and Jimmy was barefoot. He also didn't have a jacket. We didn't know where he was headed, but it seemed a long way away. My grandmother pulled over and asked me to get him.

"What are you doing walking all this way, Jimmy?" she asked.

"I missed the bus and have to walk home," he said, shivering.

"Did you call your mama to come pick you up?"

"We don't have no phone," he said, tucking his head down to his neck. "And we don't have no car, neither."

"Do you know the way home?" she asked.

"Sure, I do!" he answered.

"Well, hop in!" she said, opening the door before he could say no. Jimmy Fox hopped in the back seat of Grandma Kirkman's 1969 Plymouth, and off we went. We bounced down what seemed like every winding road in the county until we wound up on a rutted road.

"Turn here, please, ma'am," Jimmy said, pointing to a dirt road. At the end of the dirt road was a settlement with several small houses, two outhouses, a chicken coop, and a barn. None of the buildings looked nice and painted like Grandma Kirkman's house; some had doors off their hinges. I noticed both outhouses had half-moons carved in the doors and looked like they had been there for a long time.

I got out of the car with Jimmy out of curiosity. We played a bit at school, but until now I hadn't heard him say much. I also had no idea where he lived.

"Thank you, ma'am," Jimmy shouted as he ran to his front door. Before he got there, his mom came out of the house.

She eyed Grandma Kirkman and turned to Jimmy, "I was wondering where you were at, boy. Go inside."

Before Jimmy's mom could say anything, Grandma Kirkman said, "We saw him on the side of the road, and since he was a friend of my grandson," she said, pointing to me. "We just wanted to drop him off."

The two women stood in silence for what seemed like a few minutes.

"Hmn," Jimmy's mom nodded and said, "Thank ya." The woman motioned for Grandma Kirkman to wait a minute and I got back in the car.

When Jimmy's mom returned, she had two jars with her. "I put up these peaches last summer. I hope you like preserves," she said, handing them through the open car window.

"Thank you ever so much," Grandma Kirkman replied, taking the gift. Then she showed me how to help someone without making them feel less.

"You could do me one itty bitty favor," she said sweetly. "I am sure you know I work at the ARP Presbyterian church store in Stony Point. Why, I have these boxes of clothes in my trunk, and we don't have room for them anywhere. Could you take them off my hands?"

"Oh, we don't need any clothes," the woman protested while curling her lip.

"Well, alright," Grandma Kirkman replied. "I just don't know what I will do with them."

"Well, alright," Jimmy's mom said, walking toward the back of the car. "We will take them and figure out what to do with them if it will help you out."

Then Grandma Kirkman smiled at me, and the two of us took the six boxes of shoes and clothes to the front door.

"Oh, by the way," Grandma Kirkman continued, "we have some canned vegetables too that we were going to bring to our kin. But we won't see them until later in the month, and they have just been riding around in my trunk. I am afraid the jars will break. Will you take them too?"

I saw Grandma Kirkman put the jars in the trunk that very day. Mrs. Fox graciously accepted them along with the clothing.

As we drove away, I saw Jimmy and his mom standing at the front door waving at us. In that moment, I knew the delicate dance of charity.

CHAPTER 6

I WISH I WAS TAKING YOU ALL WITH ME

I got over my hatred of Nora for one reason: her kids. When I first met her, I had no idea she had three children of her own. We stayed at Grandma Kirkman's during the school week, but some weekends we would go with Gene to visit Nora in Hickory. Nora rented a huge white house overlooking a municipal swimming pool. Nora's kids, who were older than us, were Tony, Donna, and Ann. It was here I experienced my first crush. Tony was a high school swimmer, fun-loving, and generous with his time. He would take me to the pool and play in the water with me. I didn't know how to swim yet, so Tony would drag me around on his back like a baby whale or dolphin. Some people might say I was love starved for attention, and I am sure that was part of it. But no one will ever convince me that this wasn't my first crush.

I was happy when Tony was around. He was patient and kind and always made me feel like I was the center of attention. He probably saw me as a cute little brother, and I am sure I was adorable, pudginess and all. But when Tony went to the other side of the pool to hang out with girls his age, I felt real jealousy. I would have a secret emotional breakdown. He was sixteen or seventeen at the time, doing exactly the things he should, but inside my mind I was bewildered.

It is probably better that I was too young to understand anything about attraction because when we were not with Nora, Gene, and the other children at the pool, we were dedicated to the ARP church. A small town like Stony Point doesn't have a whole lot going for it, so church life is always important to the community. How I loved going to church on Sunday. The ARP Presbyterians sang the old hymns like "The Old Rugged Cross," "Bringing in the Sheaves," "How Great Thou Art," and others. If the pastor felt particularly progressive one Sunday, he might sing the Carter family's "May the Circle Be Unbroken." There was singing and preaching for the service, nothing fancy, not solemn rituals, just good church.

The church basement was plain but functional. It had a worn-out green carpet and beige walls adorned with drawings from our Sunday school classes. The church also used the classrooms for meetings and social gatherings. They probably also held AA meetings, but I wouldn't know about those rooms until much later in life. Church gatherings were the highlight for me. Women brought covered dishes and casseroles so we could hear the word of God with full stomachs. Wednesday night was Bible study, which also meant more treats and food. Grandma Kirkman brought me to everything she could, and I came willingly and happily. I know this made Grandma Kirkman happy. I sometimes watched her talking to the other women, and they looked over at me and smiled. I was her pride and joy, a good little boy who loved Jesus.

I was such a young innocent. I wouldn't realize how conservative these folks were until I began to think about my life during my early days of sobriety. They didn't even serve wine during the sacraments. Our blood of Christ was pure grape juice. And I have no idea what they would have thought of my being gay. Grandma desperately wanted those she loved to go to Heaven, so on some level I am glad she never knew about my later life. I held enough shame without feeling like she might have seen me as an abomination. Instead, I held her values in my heart throughout my recovery. But it was her real dedication to God that would help me during times of desperation. She was not a hypocrite. While other people talked about walking in Jesus' footsteps, I do not doubt that Grandma Kirkman walked by His side.

❖ ❖ ❖

I had adjusted to the rhythm of living with Grandma Kirkman, school during the week, some weekends at Nora's, and others being part of the church. I had almost stopped feeling the emptiness of missing my mom and Leighann. Then, without warning, Mom showed up for a visit. Mom wasn't alone when she arrived; she was with my Aunt Helen Tevepaugh. Aunt Helen was a pleasant woman with a generous soul and fiercely protected those she loved. She was married to my mom's older brother, Uncle Garland. He was a fine man with a heart to match, even though it was clear the ticker "wasn't working so good," as he would say. He always told us stories about how he served in the Third Army in Europe with George S. Patton, his eyes brimming with tears as if it was yesterday. I hadn't seen either of them since we left for Florida. Uncle Garland was the head of the Tevepaugh clan, and Aunt Helen was his second in command. I knew she was there for Mom, but I didn't know what to say.

I am sure Grandma Kirkman knew Mom was coming because she set out a tray of home-baked cookies and a pitcher of tea in the front "visiting room." Nora and two of her children were there, too. I don't know why anyone thought it would be a good idea to surprise me.

I remember that when Mom arrived, Aunt Helen broke the ice. She walked into the awkward scene and scooped me up in her arms. However, Aunt Helen did not cotton to fools. I caught her shooting daggers at Nora while she turned me around, put me on the floor, and said, "Look, look who I brought with me." I know everyone expected me to be happy, but I immediately started crying when I hugged my mom. These were not tiny tears of joy. They were a floodgate of pent-up sorrow that I could no longer push back. Being taken from Mom had left me deeply wounded.

I remember my mom holding me intently and Vickie joining in. Mom, Vickie, and I held each other until we were exhausted. Then Gene, who must have been hiding in the shadows, said, "Good, let's go sit. Now we can enjoy our visit." So, we all went to the front room at that point. I held on to my mother's legs until she set me down on an ottoman next to her while she sat on the loveseat. Vickie snuggled next to her, and Mom tried to make small talk.

"How are you doing, Son?" she sniffed, holding back tears. "I hear you like the water at the pool."

I wanted to tell her about how much fun I had with Tony and attending church, but I couldn't speak. My throat was closed and dry.

Thank goodness Grandma Kirkman redirected the attention from us by asking Mom all about Florida and Leighann. Hearing about my baby sister cheered me up. Although I missed her, it was less painful than being with Mom knowing we would be apart again. I could hardly focus; I knew Mom would have to leave. The Leighann stories were adorable; I could imagine what she must be like as she grows into a little girl. The conversation remained polite as Grandma Kirkman asked about all of Mom's family until it became tense and awkward. I had almost forgotten that we had school the next day. Gene was the one to remind us as a way to end the visit.

"The kids have school tomorrow, so we must say goodbye soon," he said as Nora nodded. My old resentment toward her bubbled up; I might have lashed out with internalized expletives if I was older. But at that age, and after being around Grandma Kirkman, I didn't. I could see Nora directing Gene.

Mom pulled me close and whispered, "I wish I was taking you all with me."

Gene overheard this and surprisingly lied, saying, "Well, Linda, I've talked with both kids, and they are happy here and want to stay!" I felt my knees buckle and wanted to throw up, but again I stayed silent. Seeing my mom opened the wounds of separation. I didn't care more about Gene, Nora, or even Tony than Mom and Leighann. I felt safe with Grandma Kirkman and loved her, but I wanted more than anything to be with my mom and my baby sister. What he said was not true.

Whenever I think about my childhood, this day haunts me. I was only a little boy, six or seven, and I was emotionally confused. Who should I love? Where is my loyalty, and how can I say something where no one will be hurt? How can I stay safe in the middle of this conflict? Later in my life, alcohol numbed the awful feelings, but what do you do when you are a child? Although I felt myself dying inside, I complied with what I thought Gene wanted me to say. Even though those were not my true feelings, I sensed that I would be stuck with Gene anyway and didn't want to make him angry with me. Looking back, I guess this was when I learned avoidance and pleasing people as a coping mechanism. Children will do what they can to survive.

I vaguely remember my mom asking me if I was ready to come home with her. I felt awful shaking my head "no." And I never forgot the look of hurt on Mom's face that day. When she reached the door, I couldn't handle it. I ran to her, grabbed onto her for dear life, and began sobbing again.

"Why didn't you bring Leighann to see me!" I asked. As Mom cried, she said, "Son, she is still too small to make the trip."

I know Grandma Kirkman hated what was happening. Mom and I were clinging to each other so hard that Grandma Kirkman had to unravel me, and Aunt Helen had to pull Mom away.

I don't think that I ever cried in my life more than I did that night. It's an experience that gives me an ache deep down five decades later. I remember following my mom down the steps of Grandma Kirkman's house. I ran out to her again, and my Aunt Helen eventually had to take me from my mom's arms and carry me back to the house.

When Aunt Helen brought me into the house, Nora's daughter, Donna, who was probably no older than 13 or 14, took me from Aunt Helen and closed the door. Instead of leaving me alone, she put her arms around me on the couch and we cried together. Maybe she felt a similar pain as a child from a broken home, but she helped me feel loved, safe, and seen the entire time. Perhaps only children can fully understand each other and what it is like when adults pull us into their conflicts. All children want is to know they are loved and what will happen to them next. I might never have stopped crying if it weren't for Grandma Kirkman and Donna.

◆ ◆ ◆

At the end of the school year, Vickie and I were allowed to go to Florida to visit Mom. Gene still had full custody of us, but Mom was allowed to have us for the summer. Gene, Nora, and Grandma Kirkman dropped us off at Grandma Tevepaugh's house, where we spent the night. Grandma Kirkman and Grandma Tevepaugh had always gotten along since the time they both cared for me when I was a sickly toddler. It was only out of separate loyalties that the two avoided unnecessary visits. Seeing them together made sense.

When Tate picked us up the following day, he had Uncle David and his kids with him, Pam and Bobby. We drove in separate cars and made frequent stops along the way that gave us a chance to hang out with Pam and Bobby. I could feel Tate's edginess, and all during the drive he would comment about Gene and how we weren't going back. I didn't want to hear any of this because, no matter what, everything felt wrong. I just wanted to feel safe and to see Mom and Leighann.

David and his kids had come down "to do Florida," so we got to do all the things we ever dreamed of doing. I have no idea if Tate would have taken the time alone with us, but we went to Disney World, Busch Gardens, New Smyrna Beach, and Cape Canaveral with Uncle David. That is another memory that sticks out in my mind. We had fun, and the sky was the limit. I am unsure where he got the cash, but Tate paid for anything we wanted. We rode rides and got snacks, balloons, and souvenir cups. We even stayed for fireworks at the very end of the night.

Eventually, we said goodbye to Uncle David and the kids and began to settle into life with Mom and Leighann. We had been gone so long; Leighann was walking and talking by this time. The day we got home, my mom took Leighann to a picture of me they had on top of the television.

"Who is that, Leighann?" Mom pointed.

"It… Bubba!" Leighann shouted and giggled.

My heart melted.

"I showed her your picture every day, Michael, and told her, 'That is your brother,'" Mom said, with the first laugh I had heard since before I went to Gene's. "Then Leighann started going to it herself, pointing and saying, 'That's Bubba.'"

Of course, that nickname stuck. Everyone in the family picked it up, but mostly Dad. Even when everyone started calling me by my middle name, "Tate," I was still Bubba to Tate G. It was hard for me to see him so weak in the emergency room. When he called me "Bubba," instead of a hearty "Bub," it worried me.

CHAPTER 7

APPLE JELLY AND CHEAP WHITE BREAD

I don't know how long I had been sitting outside the hospital. Finally, I broke down, bought myself a pack of Marlboro Lights, and grabbed a bench in the smoking area to process the situation. I closed my eyes feeling the warm sun on my face. Then, for a few moments, I stopped thinking. I had tamed my inner chatter, something I typically could not do without drinking. But now, five years sober, I consciously tried to maintain moments of complete calm as part of my program.

I was so deep in nothingness to be almost asleep. Then I heard, "Bubba, Bubba," the voice of my younger sister, Brandy. As I heard her voice, I smiled on the inside. Brandy-K, my youngest sister, born in 1975, was the only child born in wedlock to Dad and Mom.

"We need you," she said.

As I walked into the ER conference room, my mom turned to me and said, "Are you ready to talk to Dad?"

Despite our collective image of Dad as being indestructible, the whole family knew deep down that serious health problems were simply a matter of time given the way he lived. He was stubborn and not about to change. We had to involve him in the decision, especially if things could go wrong, so he would at least know what was happening. It was a matter of his pride.

Yet again, I felt pressure to make a decision for the family, something I had been doing since I was 10. I was feeling some sobriety fatigue bubbling up and wanted to call my sponsor but there was no time. I took a deep breath and said a silent prayer. Then the nurse came in asking us to get her when we were ready and decided to proceed. We all knew there was no other choice, so a stent it would be.

Dad looked at Mom and me and said, "Ok! I am as ready as I will ever be." Then he touched my arm and said, "Bub, did you hear me earlier or not?"

I looked at him and said, "Dad, I heard you! Take care of your guns and stuff." That made him smile. Then I got serious. "Dad, when you get out of here, you and Mom need wills, Powers of Attorney, and all that stuff."

Dad hesitated for a minute and answered with a grin, dripping sarcasm, "I know, Bubba, if only I had a son who was a lawyer." What could I say to that? Dad and I both busted out laughing. That was the marvel of Tate G. Barkley. Even during a cardiac event, he was still smiling and ribbing me.

◆ ◆ ◆

Laughing with my dad reminded me of that first summer back in Florida. We were blending as a family. I still believed at that time that Gene was my father, but I didn't miss him. I do not say that to be mean. I just always knew my place was with Mom and my sisters. My mom was pregnant again, and Vickie and I shared the chores to help her out. The best part of that summer was the time I spent with Tate. He saw that I was not such a good reader and worked with me to improve so I wouldn't be behind when I went back to school.

"Stony Point did you no good," he'd complain as he watched me struggle with words. Tate had an interest in World War II history and World War II aircraft. Once every couple of weeks, Tate would take me to the bookstore and buy me a book about the subject and we would read together. The first book we bought together was *Zero,* about the Mitsubishi aircraft that played a prominent role in the Pacific theater. Tate wasn't wasting my time with typical early reader books of the day about *Dick and Jane.* Instead, he gave me books like *Hellcats,* about the 12th Armored Division, a unit trained in West Texas that helped liberate the Nazi death camps.

Not only did we read these books together, but Tate also began building World War II model airplanes. He mostly let me watch. That summer he filled our house with the F4U Corsair, the F4F Hellcat, and every kind of World War II aircraft.

Tate was also true to his words. He refused to send us back to Gene when the summer was over. He told Gene, "You'll have to fight for them, and I've got possession." I guess Gene decided that he didn't want to fight because no one forced us to go back. Things felt right, and we were a family.

I got to see my friend Andy again, which meant we would start the school year together. Then in September, my second baby sister Kairy-Tate was born. Leighann was over a year old, walking and talking like you wouldn't believe. She would say "Bub" or "Bubba" a hundred times a day. We were stuck together like glue when I was not in school. I would pull her in her little red wagon or push her on her Big Wheel. I would carry her everywhere that she wanted to go. We walked together all over the neighborhood, even when I played with Andy. I wasn't about to let her out of my sight after missing her so much.

When Kairy-Tate came into our lives, Leighann wasn't the least bit jealous. And I relished the role of taking care of the baby again. I knew how to change diapers, heat up milk, check it on my skin, and burp the baby.

We hummed like a family by the fall of 1972. Mom had gotten better after being sick just after Kairy-Tate was born. I had two baby sisters and my older sister with me. Tate was involved in our lives, and I no longer felt so nervous all the time. I even loved my school, Idyllwilde Elementary, and I was thriving. After he had a second child with my mom, Martha finally gave Tate the divorce he wanted, so he and my mom were quietly married, which made us all official.

But then we had to return to North Carolina when Tate's dad, Pa Barkley, got sick. I couldn't help but think about this incident while waiting for my dad to go in for his procedure. In those days, Tate came from a long line of close-knit kin. Before the highway went in, the Barkley Family owned a good part of Iredell County and had a road in their name. The Barkley land included a long bisecting creek where my great-grandmother made her moonshine. The Barkleys were important to that land, and the land was important to them.

Tate got a call from a relative telling him Pa Barkley was sick and in a nursing home where the conditions were bad. Tate didn't need any details; he packed us into the car and drove straight through the night to Ma Barkley's place. His dad was in a rundown nursing home, lying in his excrement, filthy, unhealthy, and crying. I can't imagine seeing my father like that. It would break my heart.

This was a shining moment, no matter what Tate had done in his life. He immediately found a buddy, an ambulance, and brought his handgun. He was on a rescue mission.

When Tate got to the nursing home, he marched in and told the staff to get his father.

"I give you five minutes to get my father and bring him to me," Tate bellowed.

"But sir, the doctor says he needs to be here," the nurse protested.

"I don't care about any doctor," Tate said, flashing the handgun he had hidden in his jacket. The nurse got some other staff and immediately brought Pa Barkley to the ambulance. They didn't even wait to get him dressed.

I imagine Tate reassuring his Pa that he would never return to a nursing home. And he never did go back. Tate arranged a hospital bed and Pa went home to live with Ma Barkley.

That summer, we stayed in North Carolina for a while and visited with the Barkleys and Tevepaughs. I don't think Gene knew we were there, and we never made the time to see him. Instead, we drove back to Florida to start the new school year. But we didn't return to Sunland and the house we loved. The owner, who also became Tate's boss when he decided to try his hand in real estate, had sold it. Tate went to school and secured his real estate license and started working with Rosa Peyton, who owned Peyton Realty. Tate already had a connection to the family. During his junior year of high school, he lived in Sanford with his brother Pitt, a pilot stationed at the naval facility. While there he became friends with Larry Peyton, Rosa's oldest son. Returning to Sanford, Tate started his rise to riches.

Rosa Peyton was the first female real estate broker in the entire state of Florida. She was very savvy and owned extensive properties throughout central Florida along with a successful business. It seemed everything changed when Tate started working in real estate. The world just turned upside down.

Tate may have been pursuing his bliss in real estate, but he moved us into a cheaper house on a street called Rosalia Drive. It was an even older Florida house than the one in Sunland and was next to a railroad track. I am not sure if we were on the right or wrong side of it, but with the roll-out windows and screened-in porch, it was difficult to ignore the pounding of the trains. That sound became the background music of all my memories of the time. Sometimes even today, when I hear trains, my nerves get jangled.

I have never seen the kind of light pea-green color of the house on Rosalia Drive anywhere else. I can't imagine anyone purposely painting their house the color of vomit, so I figure it must have faded from something a little less disgusting. Or maybe my memories of that time are distinctively colored that way. Memories have a way of blurring into their most distinctive qualities.

At first, when Tate moved us into the Rosalia house, he made everything seem okay. Maybe it was cheaper and more affordable, but I still went to Idyllwilde Elementary School like I did when we lived in Sunland, so I was happy.

I thought it was great when Tate took it upon himself to take me to school every morning. He also picked me up in the afternoon, but he made it clear that if anyone asked me where I lived, I was supposed to tell them I still lived in Sunland. I didn't get it at first, but it was a ruse. The zoning for Sunland was for Idyllwilde, but the zoning for our Rosalia house was for Hopper Elementary School, a predominantly Black school. Hopper was not far from our house on Rosalia, but there were very few white kids. Tate insisted that I stay at a school where I had done so well the year before. He said it wasn't because Hopper was a black school; he just wanted me to stay where I was. Tate had absolutely no reservations about lying whenever he felt it was necessary and he was a world-class bullshitter. I probably witnessed millions of lies throughout the years over things he didn't need to lie about. Maybe that is why I eventually became an ethics professor.

To his credit, Tate kept his commitment to take me to school and pick me up daily—until he didn't. It was the picking up part that became an issue. Those early days at Idyllwilde with Tate picking me up formed one of my earliest resentments toward him.

At some point, Tate started picking me up in a soft red Monte Carlo accompanied by a woman named Marie Clark. I realize now, as an adult, the balls on that man. Tate was very nonchalant about Marie because he thought I was too young at the time to realize she was his girlfriend. Children can sense when things don't seem right, and being with Marie in the car was not right. But Tate knew I would be a good keeper of his secrets, so he didn't seem to care.

When I think about it, Tate was acting true to his nature. He always struggled with being settled into a non-chaotic lifestyle. I know he loved us, but at that time I don't think he particularly enjoyed having a family, and he didn't like to be bored at work. It was just too dull and uneventful to be a family man with a regular job. His pattern was to want some sense of adventure. For now, it was Marie Clark and fooling the school district.

One day, Tate forgot to pick me up from school. It wasn't unusual that he would run late to get me, but this was the first time he didn't show at all. I watched as each kid got on the bus or saw a parent drive up. I tried not to get scared and figured he was just late again. Eventually, I was standing outside all alone. I leaned into the wall of the building and tried to make myself invisible. The minutes seemed like an eternity, and I couldn't decide if I should go inside to make a call. I had been warned not to draw attention to myself, so I sat down and buried my head in my hands. I had no one to call anyway; we didn't have a phone.

Then the principal walked out of the front door as he did every afternoon and spotted me.

"What are you still doing here?" he asked, more confused than concerned.

"I'm waiting on my dad to pick me up," I said under my breath.

"We're closing the school and I can't wait any longer, so I'm going to take you home," he said. He didn't leave any room for protests. It was decided, and that was all there was to it.

I told him my address and the principal drove me to the other side of town. He didn't say a word the entire trip, but I could see he was taking note of where we were headed.

Finally, when we were almost to the house, he said, "I don't think you're supposed to be going to my school. You live too far away."

When we got home, the principal walked me to the door. Mom thanked him for the ride and let me inside. After that, my mom and the principal had a private discussion on the front steps. Of course, I couldn't hear what they said, but I knew it couldn't be good.

Tate finally made it home late that night. I overheard a muffled argument, and then Tate burst into my room.

"I thought I told you not to tell anyone where you lived. Now, see what you've done! You could have had them call me, or they could have taken you to the real estate office."

I felt so awful that night. It was all my fault, even though I would have had no idea how to call his office or where it was. I had disappointed Tate. I thought there would be no coming back from that. That was one of the first times I remember hating myself.

Now I would have to go to Hopper Elementary, a "Blacks only" school from its very beginning, but it was now integrating. I'll never forget the first day of class. I looked around, and almost all the other students were Black. Those early years were the beginning of actual integration. Hopper Elementary School had just started integrating in the early '70s. Unfortunately, like other southern states, Florida was way behind in implementing the landmark case of Brown v. Board of Education of Topeka.

Integration didn't come easy in this part of the country, and there were still known lynchings as late as 1968 in some southern states. In addition, the Jim Crow laws that legalized racial segregation were still on the books even though ordered otherwise by the U.S. Supreme Court.

I had never gone to a school so overwhelmingly Black, and I felt a little intimidated by it. Some of the other white students told me that the Black kids would beat up the white kids whenever they walked home from school. I was already anxious, and now I would be walking home from school every day.

Tate had worried that Hopper would be a backward school compared to the "white" Idyllwilde. That wasn't the case at all. Hopper Elementary was ahead of where I was. They were already learning cursive writing and mastering multiplication tables. I hadn't done any of that.

I started behind as usual, but I managed to catch up. Although Tate said he wasn't concerned that it was a Black school, I think he made assumptions about it. In my early days at Hopper, Tate often went to the school, claiming how smart I was. He tried to press the school into putting me ahead into the fourth grade. I know he didn't know the quality of my education, because back then, especially, southern whites were condescending when it came to Black people. Thankfully, the educators saw better and didn't think I was ready for the fourth grade. Even though I had been reading books about war and fighter planes and loved history, I was behind in everything else.

My teacher at Hopper noticed the types of books I checked out and suggested I read about something other than war. Ms. Arnold was a young, white, progressive, "I'm going to change the world" kind of teacher. Not only had she chosen to work at a primarily Black school, but she also didn't want kids reading about violence all the time. The first book she made me check out was about Jim Thorpe, the athlete.

I was worried about getting beaten up on the way home from school, but otherwise, I never much-noticed the color of my classmates. I loved reading and will never forget our school librarian. She did more for me than anyone to broaden my worldview. The librarian was a lean, older Black woman, at least 70 years old at the time. Her clothing looked right out of the 1920s, and she commanded respect from all the unruly children in her charge.

The librarian knew Ms. Arnold was monitoring my reading. One day she pulled me aside and said, "Listen, son, if you want to read, you check out any book you want, and it'll be just between us." This arrangement was sealed, and so was my friendship with the librarian. I would check out one book for Ms. Arnold's approval, and then I would check out a second book without Ms. Arnold knowing about it. You were only supposed to check out one book at a time in those days. The librarian thought that regulating my reading habits was total nonsense. She said, "as long as you are reading, you should be able to read whatever you want to." I am pretty sure the librarian sensed that I was a troubled kid. Reading became an escape and the library a haven.

We didn't live at Rosalia Drive very long, and I was never beaten up by any black kids on the way home from school. Maybe the other kids were warned by their ignorant parents of the dangers of integration. Who knows? One of my best friends was a boy named Lace. If there could have been a third-grade version of the character, Shaft, that was Lace. I spent a lot of time with his family and even spent the night. Meeting them, I could see why Lace was super cool. His parents were educated and interesting, and Lace was athletic, smart, and dressed as well as anyone our age could.

The biggest thing I noticed when I spent time with Lace and his family was, they all ate dinner together. And his parents were around all the time. They were professionals, not as common back then, and set a great example for their children and me. To be honest, they were the first successful Black folks I had met, but I had also never met any successful white folks.

I made other friends at Hopper. I gravitated to a chubby boy named Stevie, also Black, but whose life was more like mine. He was always laughing, cutting up, and getting in trouble. He just couldn't stay still, and he couldn't stay quiet. Stevie had trouble at home with his mom's boyfriend, who was a drinker. Stevie said the boyfriend didn't really care about him and his three brothers and sisters, so I am not sure if Stevie was acting out for attention or if he had some undiagnosed problem like ADHD or was on the Autism Spectrum. I just knew I liked him and related to him. He was funny and kind.

Stevie and I also made our first Asian friend, Chris, from the Philippines. Chris had five brothers and sisters. His mom was Filipino, and his dad was

White. His dad had been in the Navy in the Philippines and later decided to become a social worker back in the States. They lived in a Black neighborhood, which I found very odd. But they seemed to be happy. Chris's family had a volleyball net in their big backyard, so we spent most of our time there. Some familiar feelings surfaced during my afternoons with the neighborhood kids. I developed a crush on Mark, Chris's 14-year-old brother.

I would always go out of my way to be around Mark. I loved it when Mark would have to touch me or would have to communicate with me one on one. Mark was athletic and handsome. I am sure he looked at me as Chris's little friend. I didn't understand my feelings, but I always tried to be on Mark's team whenever we would play football or volleyball. I always wanted to be close to him.

One of the things that made me popular at Hopper was having what the other kids thought was a cool dad. Tate was selling real estate, so he often wore a suit and had a Cadillac, which was huge in those days. His 1974 silver two-tone Cadillac Sedan Deville was impressive. Whenever he would drop me off at school, everyone would "ooh" and "ahh" at the car. Tate Barkley was a cool cat cruising in a Cadillac dressed to the nines. Sadly, it was an illusion. We had no money, but to Tate, appearances were what mattered.

The times when Tate drove me to school became fewer and fewer. We didn't see him often while we lived at the Rosalia house. We had very little money, but Tate was too proud to ever allow us to get help from anyone. Everything in those days seemed to be a struggle and I remember my mom always seemed anxious. Another problem was with Vickie. She had not adjusted to Rosalia and now, in seventh grade, was miserable and not making friends. I hated to see her like that.

We had been broke before, but I never noticed it as much as I did during that time. Tate always had nice things and made promises of a better life, but now there was never any money for anything. I wasn't unhappy because I had my baby sisters and friends at school. But Tate was gone all the time, and we were getting regular visits from the "Cadillac Man."

The "Cadillac Man" looked like someone from a 1970s gay porn movie, something I would not see until many years later. But in hindsight, that is what he looked like, with a bushy mustache, short zip-up boots, a freshly ironed shirt, sharp sports coat, and gold chains around his open-collared neck.

This repo man drove a white Oldsmobile Cutlass Supreme and would beat on our door almost every day at random times, day or night. My mom would talk and talk and talk at the door, explaining that Tate would be back any time to handle it. I finally put together why Tate never allowed us to have a telephone. In fact, I think it wasn't until the ninth grade that I remember having a phone. So, I guess the repo man had no choice but to come to the house. Unfortunately for him, the Cadillac would not be there each time he showed up so he could not repossess it.

I now see it was another one of Tate's schemes. It makes me chuckle because he always thought he could and should get away with things. I later learned that he never paid a dime for that beautiful 1974 silver Cadillac he drove around. Tate somehow managed to drive away from the Cadillac dealership on a whole word-of-mouth credit deal. The poor "Cadillac Man" spent three months banging on our door to repossess the '74 Cadillac so the dealership could save face.

One day the "Cadillac Man" was beating on the door, so I told my mom I would handle it. When I opened the door, the "Cadillac Man" explained his purpose for the visit. I imagine Mr. '70s Porn Star Wannabe probably felt funny talking to a third grader and laughed when I told him we had no money, but I sure loved the Cadillac. He tried to be nice to me, but I know he lost patience when no adult would answer the door. In the days ahead, I kept being the one to reply to the knocking. I don't recall him ever doing anything illegal or threatening me in any way. He exercised patience that I am not sure I would have been able to muster under the circumstances.

While I was always glad when Tate came home at night, he would often be gone for days and days with no word, no call, or notice. It was tough on Mom. She didn't work and would stay home with us kids without a phone, little money, and no knowledge of her man's whereabouts

One day Mom walked all of us kids up to the phone at the corner store so that she could call Tate's work. The office said they assumed he had gone home. We made that trek to the payphone countless times, and the response was always the same. One particular night was especially bleak for us during his absence. My mom, my sisters, and I were down to nothing to eat, literally nothing to eat.

❖ ❖ ❖

It is painful to remember what it was like when there was no food in the house, and we had no idea where Tate was. Here I was in the hospital emergency room, waiting for my dad to be wheeled in for a heart procedure, and I couldn't help but have all my mixed feelings bubbling up to the surface. I thought I had processed much of this through AA, but anger can fester well below the surface. This is why they tell us to HALT! Do not allow yourself to get hungry, angry, lonely, or tired. We are always only one drink away from a relapse. I was all of the above, but Rosalia would not leave my mind.

◆ ◆ ◆

On that day, I remember Tate had been gone a while and I guess whatever money he used to leave for Mom to take care of us had run out. I remember thinking during those days about Stony Point and how well we would always eat at Sunday dinners at Grandma Kirkman's house. Mom had tolerated the move to Florida, but it was always Tate's place where he believed he would make his fortune. Now Mom was left alone, with few acquaintances, no friends, and nothing to feed her hungry children. I suppose nothing could feel more helpless for her. Mom would sometimes wait by the window crying, hoping that Tate would come home, hoping that he would come back and come back soon.

Now, there was nothing. We had water, but there was no juice. There was no bread. There were no Vienna sausages, there was no potted meat, and there was no baloney. There was nothing! Most of those things were staples that we ate around the house. But now, there was not even that stuff.

I remember an entire day that I did not eat at all. Tate was too proud to put me on a free lunch program at Hopper, so I didn't eat at school. He would have hit the roof if Mom had gone over to the neighbors and shared that we had nothing to eat. And, for whatever reason, my mom still believed in him.

That night I was lying in my bed and heard Tate finally come in the door. We had gone almost two days without eating, but as my mom promised, he was back. I am sure Mom had her hopes that somehow he would rescue us, but he wasn't much help. I was already in bed. I tried to sleep, but it wasn't easy on an empty stomach. I could hear Mom's voice uncharacteristically loud and aggressive as she opened the refrigerator and cupboards to show Tate they were empty. He was surprisingly silent. Then he stumbled to my room.

"Bub, do you have any change?" he asked. I got out of bed and reached under a blanket I had strategically placed to cover a small box of keepsakes. I dug out some change from the box. My mom emptied her purse, and we all searched between chair cushions and under things to see what we could scrape together.

Tate cleaned out the Cadillac, looking on the floorboard in the dark for coins as I held up the flashlight. We went through Vickie's room to see if she had any change and found a few more dimes.

By the time we finished the search, we had gathered a total of ninety-seven cents to our name.

Tate said, "Bub, let's go to the store." He and I walked four blocks to a corner store still open. I was angry at him, but at the same time I felt better that he was with me. That was always the familiar feeling. We had no stability, but having Tate home convinced all of us that now things would be okay.

I understand now that Tate painted pictures with his words. He wanted us to believe in him. As I walked by his side with ninety-seven cents jingling in his pocket, he told me about a big deal he had been planning in Orlando.

"Son, look at these houses," he said, pointing to the homes that lined the sidewalk. "I am going to be listing a lot of these houses." He touched a sign in front of one house that had a realtor's name on it. "You are gonna see my name on every sign up and down these blocks. Things will be very different for us."

I got caught up in his excitement, almost forgetting why we were walking to the store at a time when I should have been in bed. "Oh, Bub, I almost forgot to tell you about this big deal I got going in Orlando. It's near Disney."

Had I been older, I would have realized he was filling my head with bravado to deflect from the embarrassment of finding us all almost starving. At that age, I believed everything he said without question. Even if he was misguided, my memory of that time was of his irrepressible optimism with a fundamental belief in himself that was difficult to resist. I imagine he sincerely believed he was going to pull a rabbit out of the hat.

We walked in the pitch black to the convenience store. That night, he was my hero with the ninety-seven cents in his pocket and the "free" Cadillac parked in the driveway.

When we made it to the convenience store, we scoured the shelves. We bought a small jar of apple jelly and some cheap white bread. It was all we could afford with ninety-seven cents. We took it home, toasted the bread, because cheap white bread is better toasted, and we had jelly sandwiches.

That is what we had for breakfast and lunch the next day, and we finished it off at dinner. Honestly, I don't remember what happened when it was all gone. I guess Tate found some grocery money after that night. I do remember it was not the last time I would go hungry. The good thing I remember about that night was just being with him. After that, the rest took care of itself. I know now Dad had no idea about the basics of being an adult then. His world was himself, and we were all reflections in his mirror. There were times when he could shine a glow that would make you feel you were the only person in the world and the most important to him. I loved the man, then, and despite his barking orders at me now as if I were a six-year-old, I still love him.

Eventually, the Cadillac Man repossessed the '74 Sedan Deville. I would later learn he found Tate and the Cadillac outside a nightclub in Winter Park, Florida. Lucky for us, Tate's boss, Rosa Peyton, let him drive her 1972 white Sedan DeVille with a blue top. So we were back in style by the time we retreated from Rosalia.

◆ ◆ ◆

There was a lot going on at Hopper at the time too. As the end of the school year approached, there was a rumor that the Black kids would beat up the white kids on the last day of school.

Mr. Hanes, the school principal, was African American and as big as an NFL linebacker. At least, that is how he looked to me. He carried a paddle with him as he walked the hallways and, for effect, would sometimes hit it against his meat hook-sized hand. He kept the students in line with little more than his demeanor and expression, as I never saw him use the paddle even though he could. Back then, and especially in the South, corporal punishment was not only allowed but encouraged.

For some reason, I trusted the principal to watch over us. He proved himself on the last day of school by avoiding trouble in case the rumors were true. At first, I was scared shitless when he burst into the classroom, pointed to me and the few other white students, and said, "You need to come with me." His sternness startled me. Then Stevie piped up without raising his hand and asked, "Why is he leaving?"

"None of your business," the principal responded. "He's going early."

My Black friends had heard the rumors, so Stevie asked more urgently, "Is it because he's white?"

The principal said, "Yes."

At this point Lace signaled to Stevie, who got up from his chair, and stood by me. Lace said, "Well, we'll walk him home."

The principal looked them up and down and shook his head. "Boy, sit down."

Lace said, "He's our friend, so this is our business."

Stevie said, "Yes, sir. I am going too."

I think I was more scared than my friends watching the principal for his reaction. The three of us, all third graders, stood our ground in front of the entire class like a small posse.

The principal scanned us one more time and I might have seen a slight grin. "Y'all go. Hurry now." And the three of us left school early without incident.

But of course, nothing happened as the three of us walked to my house on the last day of school. It was also the last time I ever saw Lace or Stevie. A couple of days later, Tate blew in after several days' absence and said, "Pa Barkley's sick again. We're going to North Carolina."

CHAPTER 8

BUTCHER KNIFE IN THE BASEMENT

We left Florida without any goodbyes. It might have been because Pa Barkley was sick again, but I think it was because all of Tate's big dreams were not panning out. Tate was broke and needed the help of his family. This time we went to live with Tate's sister, my Aunt Helen Warren who lived in a house on Barkley Road.

I wasn't comfortable with Tate's family because it always felt like they didn't know how to treat me. I felt like an outsider with them, and I am not sure if they knew I was a true Barkley or not. Blood mattered above all for the folks in rural North Carolina. So, according to the law, I was Gene's son, an outsider, even though the resemblance to Tate was indisputable.

I spent that summer tending to my sisters and doing every chore around Barkley Road. My cousin Annie Jane and her husband Gary had a beautiful baby named Angela, but Gary tended to be on the lazy side. He mostly worked on his old Corvette and paid me a little bit here and there to do his chores. For example, Gary would pay me to take out his trash and remove Angela's dirty diapers from their house. I didn't mind. I did that kind of stuff at home and never got paid for my labor. Their little house was next door to Aunt Warren's place as Annie Jane was her daughter, so it wasn't far from us. Before they built their big brick home, Aunt Helen and Uncle Aaron Warren lived in the little house where they started their sandwich business, Warren Sandwiches. In Iredell County, you were considered rich if you had a brick home. After Gary and Annie Jane married, Aunt Warren gave them the little house so they could live nearby.

The Warrens were hard workers and earned that brick house. But unfortunately, Uncle Aaron died years ago, and now Aunt Warren had the big brick house all to herself. She allowed us into her home.

I had a plan that summer. I became very industrious and wanted to earn enough money to give a party for my sisters. So I went to the little house every morning to do whatever chores they had and then walked up and down Barkley Road looking for other small jobs. The people were all our kin in one way or another, and they always found something for me to do. I got paid in nickels and dimes; sometimes, they would hand me all the pennies they could find. Each day I put my money haul into a dish on my dresser and watched it grow.

I did everything asked of me. I just wanted money! I could see the party. We would have all the good stuff we never got to have. We would have Coke, Cheetos, and Little Debbie's oatmeal pies. I loved junk food and couldn't wait.

I can remember the smell of the "burn barrels" people used outside the back of their homes. There was no trash service on Barkley Road, so this became another way for me to earn money. I would pick up the trash in a red wagon and put it in the burn barrel. We burned everything in those barrels except for food scraps.

Many of our kin on Barkley Road raised hogs. Food scraps like apple peelings, potato peelings, or any other type of food waste went in a slop bucket, and almost every house had one. People paid me to collect the slop buckets to deliver to the hungry hogs. That was my summer until August. I was so proud of myself. After all the work, I had earned and saved forty-seven dollars. That was the most money I had ever had.

In early August, I spent a few days with my Uncle Garland and my Aunt Helen Tevepaugh. I hadn't seen Aunt Tevepaugh since the day she brought Mom to visit me at Grandma Kirkman's house and this felt like a vacation from the Barkley side of the family. I loved going to their house because they were warm and loving and had two of my favorite cousins, Renee and Robin. Vickie and I loved to hang out with them. We had fun and felt like real family. Aunt Tevepaugh gave me ten dollars as a belated birthday present.

When I returned to Aunt Warren's house, the first thing I did was run up to my room to put my ten dollars with my money. I looked on top of my dresser and found the little dish, but the money wasn't there. At first, it didn't register that the money was gone. I thought maybe I put it somewhere else, but I knew that was where I kept it. I looked everywhere I might have put it and realized I hadn't misplaced it.

"Mom!" I shrieked, a wave of anxiety and anger escaping onto my cheeks. "Something happened to my money; where's my money!?"

When my mom got to my room, I could see her eyes welled up with tears. I knew immediately it was worse than I imagined. She put her arms around me and said, "I'm sorry, no one stole your money. Tate had to borrow it, but I know he will pay you back. We needed it."

I pulled away from Mom and started crying. It would have been better if some stranger had stolen it. It felt worse that it had been Tate.

"He will pay you back," she insisted. But I didn't believe her.

"I had plans for that money," I cried. "I saved it up to have a party for my sisters! Why is he this way?"

Several weeks later, I was still sad and disappointed and too young to hide my feelings very well. I barely spoke and stopped doing any chores. I didn't even want to play with my sisters.

Looking back, I was walking around like a broken toy. I felt betrayed by Tate, again. I was so resentful that I didn't notice how sad my mother had become. Mom must have been sick of making excuses for Tate when he did something she knew would hurt me.

After several weeks of moping, Tate grabbed me by the shoulders and said, "What is up with you, Bub!"

This made me furious. How could he not know why I was angry? He didn't acknowledge that I could be mad at him for taking my money. He never spoke of it or offered to pay me back.

Instead, he shifted the conversation by saying, "Your mom is worried sick about you."

He kept pumping me for answers, and I was seething so much I could barely speak. Finally, I lied and told him I was worried about the girls. It didn't seem to bother him that what I said made no sense.

"Nothing is going to happen to the girls," he reassured me. "I won't allow it."

Instead of telling him the truth, I faked that I felt better after his gesture of concern. This was one of the first times, but would certainly not be the last, that I would fake my feelings and hold my tongue so my mom would not get sad, or just to keep the peace with Tate.

I knew Tate was never going to give the money back. Even by then, I knew him. I loved Tate, but I knew better than to trust him. I never really trusted him at any time, but he certainly couldn't be trusted with money. It was just who he was. I was trying so hard to love Tate the way I loved the girls and Mom, but I just couldn't. All I knew was that I was ten years old, and I felt helpless.

I never put it together, but stuffing my feelings over Tate taking my money led to another self-soothing habit. I spent a lot of time in Aunt Warren's basement, where they made all the sandwiches for their sandwich business. Each day she would bring home everything that did not sell. It was a stark contrast to the hunger I experienced living on potted meat, cheap white bread, and apple jelly. Aunt Warren was happy for the food to not go to waste. She told me, "If you don't eat it, I'll put it in the hogs' slop bucket." As a result, I got really fat. Not only did I become the de facto slop bucket, I felt like a little hog.

My Aunt Warren's house was immense. The downstairs basement alone was over 5,000 square feet. It had an industrial-sized kitchen and food preparation area. There was a massive walk-in freezer and an enormous pantry with a swinging door the size of a mobile home. There were three separate pantry places, and that was only half the downstairs basement. The other half of the basement was a catch-all for discarded clutter. There was a mess of old furniture, antiques, and things everyone on Barkley Road had outgrown or did not want anymore. I learned every inch of that basement and loved exploring.

Once again, I was settling into a life that felt comfortable. Tate was in and out, and I was almost over being upset with him. Then one weekend I was in one of the back rooms reading a book I found in the basement. My mom and Vickie were the only people I remember being home that day. There was no sandwich-making in the basement, and if I had been paying attention, I would have figured something was up.

Aunt Warren walked through the door, followed by my cousin Lewis, an Iredell County deputy sheriff. This visit was no social call. He pulled up in a Robin's egg blue Iredell County sheriff's car instead of his usual truck. Given his position in the Sheriff's department, Lewis looked like you would expect, with a cheesy grin, a great big old belly, and a mustache that needed constant attention. Tate had never spoken particularly well of Lewis, but he said he loved him because he was Uncle Pitt's son. My dad looked up to all his older brothers, but he worshiped the ground Uncle Pitt walked on when he was a kid, because Pitt flew F2F Wildcats and had engaged the Japanese early in World War II.

I heard my mom screaming, "You can't take them."

I heard Lewis's muffled voice saying something about an enforcement order, and I put together what was happening. My mom went outside, screaming angrily, "Tate is not here. You must wait. Tate is not here. Tate has to get here!"

I knew whatever was happening wasn't good. My heart started racing, so I ran downstairs to the only place where I felt safe. With all the nooks and crannies in the basement, I figured no one could find me until I could figure something out. So, I found a hiding place behind a pile of furniture in the corner. As I was bolting down the stairs, I overheard that Lewis had not only come to take me to Gene's, but he was also going to take my sister, Vickie. My first instinct was to fight. I ran out of my hiding place long enough to grab a butcher knife that was sticking out of a cutting board.

I don't know what I was thinking. I pulled my knees up to my chest, silent tears falling down my cheeks. My head felt like I was underwater; the only sound was my heart pulsating in my ears.

There was a commotion upstairs, and I could make out unfamiliar male voices calling my name. I began to shake and clutch the butcher knife so tightly that my hands began to cramp.

"Michael!... Michael!... Michael!" the men shouted. I heard a siren so there must have been other cops showing up.

Then I heard my mom hollering and pleading with them to leave. She sounded desperate. Mom had gone from mad to fiercely upset. Her tears only made me move further behind the furniture while covering myself with some old blankets and newspapers.

I heard Lewis come down into the basement. He looked all around, calling my name. I held my breath whenever he came near the back where I was hiding.

Had he looked harder, there is no way he wouldn't have found me. But he didn't seem to be working that hard. At one point, I heard Lewis talking to another man, probably also a cop.

"They told me he was here. I don't know. Nobody can find him now," Lewis said, sounding exasperated.

By this time, my cousin Jerry Tate and his parents, my Aunt Sis and Uncle

Charles had arrived. My Aunt Sis had been the only Barkley to embrace me and love me unconditionally.

"Where is Michael?" I heard my cousin Jerry Tate say, sounding concerned.

That got to me. I liked my cousin Jerry Tate. Then he said, "Maybe we should check the woods."

I remember thinking that checking the woods was a smart idea. I often walked through the woods to hang out on the big rock by Third Creek when I wanted to be alone. It was my cousin, Jerry Tate, that had shown me the way. Had I had more time to plan an escape, that is exactly where I would have gone. Jerry Tate told me all the stories of our great grandma, who kept her stills on the banks of Third Creek. The water was good, and her moonshine was the best. But she was most proud of her liquor.

I have no idea how long I hid in the basement, but it seemed to be a while. I was getting hungry and tired, but I didn't dare go to the pantry or put down the knife.

I calmed down, and now I could hear my Aunt Tevepaugh. As usual, she supported my mom, telling her everything would be okay. I also heard her telling Lewis and the other officers to come back another time when Tate would be home so they could straighten things out.

Lewis and several other deputies finally lost their patience. I heard Lewis raise his voice almost to a scream. "Now come on, everybody, someone must know where this kid is. We have a job to do."

I could feel the energy change upstairs. Lewis was frustrated. What began as an execution of a child possession order to return custody had now turned into a missing kid case. He went from yelling to pleading, which gave me some satisfaction.

If my mom hadn't started crying as more deputies arrived, I would have stayed in the basement until I died. In my mind, that was the plan. I did not want to go to Gene's and be away from my sisters again. I was sick of people deciding what was best for me, and now I was old enough to get very angry at the situation. It was plain unfair. I also wanted to be on Tate's side. I wanted him to be proud of me for standing up to the cops even though the law was likely in Gene's favor.

What I remember most is hearing my mom crying intensely. It was driving me crazy. I know my mom is a worrier; at this point, she was probably more concerned with whether I was safe than about sending me back to Gene's. I started resenting her tears because it made me feel guilty for hiding. I had little concept of time, but I am sure hours passed. I know we had family scouring Barkley Road looking for me. I wanted to be strong. Tate would be proud of me if I could hold out and be strong. But I broke down as I kept listening to her cry. Finally, I just couldn't take it anymore.

I crawled out from my hiding place and left the butcher knife downstairs. Then I tore up the stairs yelling for my mom. Meeting me at the doorway upstairs was my Aunt Tevepaugh. She immediately grabbed me and held me. For one brief moment, I had three of the women who loved me unconditionally, my mom, Aunt Sis, and Aunt Tevepaugh around me at the top of the stairs. I felt a little bit better.

Eventually, Lewis took me. But first, Lewis picked me up and took me to the back room. He told me, "I have to take you to your dad." I said, "Who?" He said, "Gene Kirkman, your dad."

"I want my mom and my sisters," I protested.

"This does not mean you cannot see your mom and sisters. I promise," he reassured me. He scooped me off the bed in the back room and took me out to the patrol car and put me in the back seat. I remember the bars between the seats.

At that point, my Uncle Charles lost it. Uncle Charles ran up to Lewis and looked like he was going to punch him.

"How dare you treat this kid like a criminal? Give him to me! I will drive him wherever he needs to go. He will not be in the back of a goddamn police car!"

After all his bravado in his uniform, Lewis looked frightened. The other deputies standing by their cars knew better than to get in between family.

Lewis relented. He opened the car door, and I ran to my Uncle Charles. "Sorry, Michael, I didn't mean anything by it. I was doing my job."

My Uncle Charles hugged me and took Vickie's hand and we both got in the back of Uncle Charles and Aunt Sis's 1968 blue Buick Electra. With two patrol cars following us, Uncle Charles drove us to the Iredell County Courthouse at his extraordinarily slow convenience. A six-mile trip took 40 minutes with my Uncle Charles grinning the whole time. As we parked at the courthouse, Vickie and I waited in the back seat. Finally, my legal dad, Gene Kirkman, walked up to the car. I'll never forget Uncle Charles's scowl when he told Gene Kirkman, "Get away from my car. Your time will come when you can have these kids. That's not now."

It wasn't long until the transfer of custody had taken place and we went back with Gene to his apartment. After everything, he was oddly ill-prepared for us. He had no clothes, beds, or food, so it wasn't long before we wound up back with Grandma Kirkman. That was fine with me. Frankly, I think Gene had moved on from me by this time. I remember no interaction with him really during this possession. But I was at Grandma Kirkman's which meant Sunday dinners and awesome love from her.

Even staying with Grandma Kirkman didn't last long. I am unsure how Tate pulled it off, but Vickie and I returned to them in pretty short order. Thinking back, I should have held a grudge that I was forced to hide like an animal in a basement, but I was just happy to be back home with my sisters.

CHAPTER 9

WHITE HOUSE, WHITE FLAG

It seemed like no time passed when a pleasant nurse named Deb came to us and said, "We are ready." I felt a touch on my elbow, and it was Dad. He looked at me and said, "I'm ready, Bub." My dad was visibly relieved by the confidence and bravado of Dr. Patel. People like that always made me suspicious, but my feelings didn't matter in this case. Dad liked him from the beginning, and that is all that mattered.

I told the nurse we were ready, and they put Dad into a wheelchair. When the orderly wheeled him away, the nurse said, "This usually doesn't take long, but stay close as there is risk, and we may need you. He will see you soon."

I knew there was a risk. There were rare cases when patients did not make it through this procedure, anything could happen. Once again, we gathered as a family in the waiting room. Mom looked anxious, and rightfully so. They had been through so much together but were still hanging tough. It was hard enough to be his son; I couldn't imagine what it must have been like for my mother to be Tate's wife.

Life for her was always fraught with disappointment and was certainly not the life her salt-of-the-earth family wanted for her.

Mom broke my train of thought by asking, "I wonder if this will get him to stop smoking?" We all laughed nervously, knowing Dad did nothing to make Mom feel better. Ultimately, Dad ruled the roost and Mom suffered and endured accordingly. I know she must have loved him, and I know I did, but when the siblings were alone, we often wondered how Mom could have stayed married to Dad all those years.

Just like Dad, Mom was the seventh child of seven, but otherwise they couldn't have been more different. They may have been from the same part of North Carolina, but Mom's people were townsfolk, which in those days was like being from high society.. Mom had four brothers and two sisters. The four boys each went to fight in World War II, and when they returned to Statesville, they surrounded their six-year-old baby sister with love and protection.

Grandma and Grandpa Tevepaugh were well-respected members of the Boulevard Methodist Church. Grandpa worked as a superintendent at the Sherill Furniture Plant in Statesville, a decidedly middle-class job. Even when Grandpa Tevepaugh became stricken with muscular dystrophy at age 60 and could no longer work, his employer continued to pay him a full salary until he died in 1960. As a result, the Tevepaughs were "comfortable" and raised their youngest girl to be a good Christian who would become a wife and mother someday.

It is no wonder they thought Gene was a better choice for Mom until he wasn't. Grandma Tevepaugh was suspicious of Tate from day one. I am sure it broke her heart when she was proven right time and again with his selfishness and unreliability. She wanted more for her daughter and her grandchildren.

Soon after being taken by Lewis and returned, I started fourth grade at Wayside Elementary School in Statesville with a teacher I hated, Ms. Krupp. She probably didn't stand a chance because, after everything that happened, I was in no mood for anything. Maybe I projected all my anger on her, but I swear she looked like a skinny witch with pale skin, a beak of a nose, and huge ugly glasses. Nothing made me happy, so I was surprisingly relieved when Tate announced we would be leaving Aunt Warren's for his new job in Wilmington, North Carolina. Tate seemed delighted, and at least a position with Dixie Air Compressors sounded normal. Tate always said he wanted to escape small minds and the simple people of Statesville. This job was his chance, and he didn't hesitate to make a move. Once again, there were no long goodbyes, just quick hugs, and off we went. Tate had Vickie call Gene from the road to tell him we were moving. Even then, I thought this was a chicken-shit move.

Mom must have noticed me scowling because she tried to cheer me up.

"Son, we will be in our own house again, finally. Then, things will be better," she insisted. But I had finally learned not to get my hopes up. As long as I was with my sisters, I could be happy, so I didn't much care about the rest.

As Mom had promised, we moved into a relatively nice, sparsely furnished house in Wilmington. It felt spacious, and I made friends right away with the next-door neighbor, a kid my age named John. We were barely in Wilmington long enough for it to make any real impression, but I remember the rain and that Mom was sick all the time. Tate was gone working or doing whatever when Mom developed an awful infection on her leg. Of course, we didn't have any money or health insurance, so Mom didn't go to the doctor right away. We tried every home remedy we could think of as I picked up the slack taking care of my sisters. Nothing worked, and Mom got so bad she finally had to go to the emergency room. They admitted her, and she got better. The ER doctor said Mom had come dangerously close to the point of no return with the infection. Once again, being broke haunted us when we were most at risk. Mom suffered for weeks on end because there was no money. There was never any money.

In spite of it all, we had a surprisingly good Christmas. The holiday fell during one of Tate's "I'll make it up to you all" moods. The best part was I got a present I really wanted, a *Planet of the Apes* lunchbox. The even better part of that Christmas was when Mom told us she was expecting again. I loved the joy of a new baby in the house. It brought us together, and even Tate was happy.

Tate left his job at Dixie Compressors in less than six months. However, Florida always seemed like his "promised land," and he wanted us to go back there so he could work again for Peyton Realty. I never figured out why Florida held such allure for Tate, but it seemed like his destiny to him.

I was excited about the new baby and didn't think much about the disruption of another move. Mom wasn't nearly as excited and was having morning sickness. I could see she was getting tired. This new baby would be her fifth, and the move was more than we could count. Mom was turning thirty-six, and I could feel how anxious she was about the new baby and all the instability.

I was so angry at Tate during this time, and I prayed for the guts to ask him why our life had to be the way it was. It wasn't fair. I realized that our lives had been nothing but chaos ever since I met the man. I'd seen examples of families working well together, who didn't move all the time and had regular food on the table. Tate seemed incapable of settling down. We were always living hand to mouth and wouldn't have had a television had Gene not given one to Vickie for Christmas the year before. It was a dinky 13-inch black and white TV for the whole family to watch. And we only had three pieces of furniture and some beds.

When we returned to Florida, we moved into an old white house given to us rent-free by Rosa Peyton. Rosa was a dignified and warm woman, but in my mind, she wasn't doing us any favors with this monstrosity of a house. Even in 1975, nobody wanted to live in a two-story pier and beam house with no central air and heat. We didn't even have a window unit for the heat of summer. There was no dishwasher, no clothes dryer or showers, only a bathtub. The only thing it had going for it was a huge front porch. The house was the largest we ever had, so we did have more space.

Tate had always fancied himself a gardener and landscaper, so he proclaimed "we" would make this the nicest house with the most beautiful yard in the neighborhood. By "we," he mainly meant me, but I couldn't help but get a little excited by the possibility of working by his side. Unfortunately, the way the white house was built, you could see underneath it, and that bothered Tate.

"Bub, we're gonna build a garden all around this house. A big mulch bed with native plants will hide all this," he said, gesturing to the space below the porch. I didn't see the problem with the space. I thought it looked like a great place to hide.

On two separate occasions, trucks dumped big mulch piles in our yard. It was my job to spread it around. It smelled rank, and I resented the sight of it. With each pile, I saw the air conditioner we didn't have. There were other things I didn't like about "our project." He didn't give me a wheelbarrow or wagon to move the mulch. I had to rely on an old cardboard box, which made the job twice as difficult. The task seemed endless and pointless. When Tate brought in the third and final load of mulch, it just broke my spirit. I had spent hours and hours spreading this Godforsaken mulch in the Florida heat.

That morning, I announced to my mom after Tate had left for the day that I was not going to spread any more mulch. My mom warned me not to defy Tate or it would make him angry, but I didn't care. He claimed to be the man of the house, and his word was law. But I didn't forget the times he let us down; my rage had been building over time, and I felt like if I had to scoop one more load of mulch, I would explode.

I guess I went on strike and refused to do the work. Mom was extraordinarily upset. I remember her almost begging me to do the work. I refused!

I waited for Tate to get home, my determination to see this through accompanied by a deep sense of foreboding.

At first, he was calm. Then he said, "What is this I hear from your mother that you stopped spreading the mulch?"

I looked straight at him and said, "I am sick of it. I have spread mulch day in and day out for what seems like an eternity."

Tate's face turned a dark shade of red, he took a deep breath and seemed to compose himself.

"You know, Bub," he said a little too calmly, "if you had just done the work like I told you, you would be done by now. But instead, you have refused and upset your mom."

I looked at Mom, standing just behind Tate. She looked like she could cry. She wasn't upset because I didn't spread the damn mulch, Mom knew Tate would be upset and he would create chaos and anger throughout the house. I saw it clearly as ever. Her job was to keep Tate happy. I can understand it in hindsight. She had to mollify Tate because she was in no position to lose a husband. Many women were in that position in those days and probably still are today. Mom had all of these kids and no money of her own and was far away from her family. She was stuck in this situation, whether she liked it or not. I felt terrible for her, but I was so sick of Tate.

As Tate lectured me, my body stiffened with resolve as I glared at him. He had not earned the right to tell me what to do and I wasn't going to do it. As I stood there the reasons I hated him raced through my mind. He did not exist to me for my first five years of life. He was never around when we needed him. We had no money, ever. Everything was a constant struggle. We never stayed still as a family. He had allowed me to be ripped away from my baby sisters TWICE because he couldn't do anything the right way.

There was only one thing that mattered to me, and that was my sisters. I stayed in a constant state of anxiety about them because of his antics. I was sick of it, and I was sick of him, and I hated mulch. The whole task was ridiculous. He figured laws and rules didn't apply to him.

As I seethed, for the first time, I wasn't afraid. In spite of Tate's known volatility, I had no fear of his reaction. My mom was worried for me, but that didn't upset me. I was just done with mulch and Tate. I was done with Florida. He could do whatever he wanted with me.

"I hate to do this, Bub," Tate said, "but you have to learn."

Dammit! He couldn't let me win even this one rebellion. Taking me by the arm, he led me into the bathroom, belt in hand. He quietly said, "Bub, lean over the tub," and his hand gently touched my back. I sensed he would whip me something fierce. But each blow of the belt stung equally. He never varied the intensity. He wasn't angry or out of control. As I leaned over that old bathtub, squeezing my eyes, refusing to shed even one tear, I resolved to hate the man forever.

Finally, after he finished, Tate said, "Go outside and do the job."

I did what I was told and was so angry that I finished moving the mulch in just forty minutes.

"See how little that took to do the job," Tate said when I came in to wash off the day. He acted proudly and thought he was right. He thought it was about the mulch. He had no clue what feelings were bubbling inside of me. Even now, when waiting for him to come out of surgery, these feelings are as strong as they were back then. Maybe it was typical pre-adolescent angst, but the mixed feelings about him never resolved. Even while smoking my cigarette outside the hospital, I could feel the anger I felt that day.

❖ ❖ ❖

Even though I took a stand that day, I returned to being his dutiful son. I let him win to keep the peace for my mother. I spread the damn mulch whenever asked, cut the grass, raked the leaves, and pulled weeds like a perfect little worker. When I wasn't doing yard work, I cleaned the bathrooms, took out the trash, and played with the girls. Although most boys had chores in those days, that wasn't where the resentment came in. Tate was never home. There were maybe four weeks when he was with us at that God-forsaken house, and we didn't know where he was the rest of the time. I felt more relaxed when he was gone, but it was difficult for my mom. Tate took the only car we had and left us with less money to live on each time.

I knew what we had to live on because I frequently bought groceries with what little money we had. My mom would stay home with the girls, and I would walk to the store. Mom and I had to do everything on foot during the day, and I didn't have a bicycle. Tate was gone even at night, so, if necessary, we had to walk to the grocery store in the dark. The grocery list was usually pretty simple. I bought off-brand mustard, no French's yellow mustard for us. We would buy the cheapest loaf of white bread, off-brand baloney, milk, and clear cereal bags on the bottom shelf in the cereal grocery aisle. Occasionally we would have enough for jelly, and potted meat as a special treat if it was on sale. Otherwise, we lived on these things with some beans and rice from time to time.

I felt important when I did the grocery runs by myself. I knew where everything affordable was in the store and would always go to one register where this older, heavy-set Black woman was on the checkout. My math was good, but sometimes the money didn't match the purchase. My favorite checkout lady would wink at me and sometimes take a dime or quarter out of her pocket to make the difference.

We weren't fooling anybody. The woman started asking me questions, and I told her I lived with my mom and sisters several blocks away. I even said to her that Mom was pregnant. Tate would have hated me for eliciting sympathy from a stranger, but it was something I learned early, and I know it served me well during my drinking days. The cashier lady eventually began to put pieces of gum and candy in my bag to take home with me without charge. She kindly said how lucky my mom was that I could do the grocery shopping for her. I knew she felt sorry for me, but I'd reached the point, even at ten, where I didn't care if people felt sorry for me as long as they could help.

Mom rarely walked to the grocery store especially when she was far along in her pregnancy. It was too hot, and time and again, we didn't have money to buy much of anything. Tate would occasionally come home with cash, and he and Mom would go to the grocery store to get some real things. But our supplies were still more of the same.

My sister Leighann was four by this time, and my sister Kairy-Tate was three. So the three of us were constantly together. The heat was so bad that summer that we stayed in the dining room where we had a floor fan. We didn't have a table, so we used it as a playroom and set up the small black and white TV. We had a small table in the kitchen where we ate, but sometimes Mom let us eat on small TV trays.

As kids will do, we made the best of the time together by acting out the TV shows and playing games we made up. We didn't have too much energy because of the heat, which made it easier for Mom to keep the place tidy. Vickie spent a lot of time in her room, though it was hot, and seemed very unhappy. After a few weeks, she went to see Gene and didn't return. It was the first time we had been separated from each other, and it felt unnatural to me.

My mom had tears in her eyes when she told me, "Son, Vickie will not be coming back. She will stay with her dad."

But I didn't understand at all. I immediately felt numb after hearing the news. I had been sad before but never without any feelings. It was as if I retreated into myself. I didn't say a word but walked out the front door and kept walking. Only in hindsight did I realize Vickie needed more stability. Being with Gene was better for her.

Tate had planted a large milk plant on the edge of the house that blocked off part of the exposed area beneath the porch. Without thinking, I slid behind it and hid. It felt cooler under there, and no one called for me. I felt a deep void and laid on my back under the house on the cool dirt where no one could see me. I prayed just like Grandma Kirkman showed me, and then I started to cry. I'm not sure how long I laid there. I needed to be alone.

After my tears were spent, I walked around the block a few times. I did not want to see anybody, but I knew it was time to go inside.

I was mostly sad that she would not be there for the new baby. My youngest sister Brandy-K was born on July 15, 1975. Brandy-K was born on the hottest day that summer. We used to joke that Brandy-K would come out looking like a fried baloney sandwich because we had eaten so many, and it was just so damn hot.

Tate was there for Brandy-K's birth, but unlike with the other babies, none of our family made the trip to help out. I don't think they could have handled Florida in the summer without a window AC unit, so Mom just had to do it herself. She had Brandy-K one day, and she came home very the next. Tate and I scrubbed the white house as best we could. It was just so old, and that house always seemed dirty. Tate was there constantly for about a week after Brandy-K was born. But he soon returned to his habit of disappearing for days.

When the afterglow of the first couple weeks of Brandy's birth passed, keeping her in baby formula and Pampers was a constant challenge. The money for Pampers soon ran out, and we switched back to using cloth diapers. Cleaning cloth diapers was a chore I hated, truly hated! We had to hand wash most of the time because we didn't have a washer and dryer at the house. I learned to go outside and do the initial cleaning with a tarp, a hose, and a bucket.

I got some reprieve from doing most things for my sisters when Mom got back on her feet. In my free time, I made friends with three boys around my age who lived nearby. Mike and his little brother Johnny lived in a single-parent home as we did. We couldn't count on Tate, so our lives were similar to theirs. Their mom was friendly but straightforward. Unlike Mom, their mom worked as a waitress at a breakfast place during the week and as a cocktail waitress on the weekends. Their mom looked even more stressed than mine. Mike and Johnny's mom let them stay home alone, so I spent a lot of time at their house. They had a color TV and we all liked the same shows. The best part was their mom bought all the good snacks every few weeks. Their cupboard was filled with real Kellogg's Pop-Tarts, Little Debbie's oatmeal cream pies, and Dr. Pepper.

We also had a whiny neighbor our age named Matthew, but we let him play with us because he had an above-ground pool. Matthew's house was old like ours, but his mom was not near as good of a housekeeper as my mom. As a result, it was always dirty, especially in the kitchen. As hungry as I was that summer, I always hesitated to eat anything from Matthew's kitchen. We may not have had much, but Tate and Mom taught me to keep things clean; to this day, I am uncomfortable around filth and clutter.

No one seemed to care that we had little money because everyone on that street was struggling to survive. Matthew's dad was a truck driver, and his mom worked part-time as a maid at a local motel.

I felt peaceful with my friends, especially Mike. He was the same age, skinny, blonde, and blue-eyed as me, except taller. These were pleasant, wholesome people, the kind you want in your life. I spent a lot of time with Mike, which made it confusing. Sometimes I would look at him without him knowing and imagine kissing him. I dismissed the feelings as quickly as they happened, but the image stuck in my mind all these years later.

As the summer closed, Mike would frequently go with me to swing my little sisters at the elementary school. He never joked or complained about my attachment to them. He would push them on the swing right along with me. Once in the late summer, when Mike and I were swinging with the girls, he asked me, "What do you want more than anything else?"

I thought for a moment and said, "I want to be able to buy whatever I want in the grocery store." Mike laughed and said, "You don't want much." It was my wish. I wasn't fooling.

Although I walked to school with my neighborhood friends, we were not in the same classes. There were two fifth grade classes and Mike was in the other one. I felt alone and embarrassed with myself almost all the time. I fully believed if all the kids knew about my situation, they would know I was less than them. They would see I was less brave, less smart, and certainly less rich. Yet, I felt something I would not identify until much later after hitting rock bottom with my drinking. What hung over me at that time was a deep sense of shame.

I am sure I telegraphed my emotions, and kids can smell low self-esteem a mile away. They would poke fun at me for random reasons, but mostly what I brought for lunch. Unfortunately, we lost my cool *Planet of the Apes* lunch box in the move. But even the lunchbox wouldn't have hidden what I brought with me in soggy brown paper bags. While other kids would get fruit cups, potato chips, and sandwiches, maybe even chocolate pudding cups, I was still eating baloney or a potted meat sandwich and some dry cereal. That was it. To make it worse, I had to take the brown bag home after each lunch so that we could reuse it. My mom made a point of reminding me every day to bring the bag home.

While I was at school, I missed my sisters and worried about them. It was difficult to concentrate, and I was miserable.

Tate was gone for extended periods, and it seemed as if he left less and less food each time he disappeared. We had nothing. We had nothing but total, complete, and unadulterated dependence on Tate.

He may have bad-mouthed the closed minds of Statesville, but he followed their code. He made it clear you don't air dirty laundry and don't tell the neighbors our problems. So we didn't. We just sat in that hot fucking house, hungry, and waiting for Tate.

Eventually, he stayed gone for two weeks without a word from him or anybody. During that time, we were almost entirely out of food and couldn't even scrape together enough change for cheap white bread or apple jelly. We were scared to death to tell our neighbors because we were so programmed not to make Tate look bad or he would be pissed. Mom and I would look at each other and ask ourselves what we were supposed to do. Finally, one evening I decided to do something. That night my mom and I had split our final two pieces of bread and one slice of baloney and ate a leftover cup of black-eyed peas. Fortunately, there had been enough food for the girls and Brandy-K still had a bit of milk. But there was no milk for breakfast the next day, except what little we saved for her.

I was afraid to piss off Tate. But I felt compelled to do something. I went to Mom's purse, looked up Rosa Peyton's home number in the little address book, and wrote it down. There was a payphone a few blocks away. I dialed the number and she answered.

"This is Michael, Tate, and Linda's boy," I said, trying to sound more grown-up than I was. She and I had met several times before.

"Well, how can I help you, young man?" she answered, sounding pleasant but confused.

"Do you know where Tate is?" I asked firmly.

"No, is he not at home?" she replied.

"He's not home and has not been home for many days." I insisted. "We do not have much food. Could you tell him to bring some food and come home? Brandy-K is also out of milk. There was not much left there. Could you please tell him that as well?" I blurted out, almost like a whine. I didn't want to sound like a baby. I just wanted Tate to come home.

There was silence on the other end of the phone for a long time. I remember saying, "Ma'am," and then she responded: "Are you okay?"

I said, "Yes. We just need Tate to come home."

Rosa softly said, "I'll let him know when I see him."

The day after I made the phone call to Rosa Peyton, she came by the white house. You could always tell when Rosa Peyton was coming. She drove a big, new, beautiful blue Fleetwood Cadillac. Rosa was a big lady who was always well dressed and perfectly manicured. She wore just the right amount of jewelry; on this day, she wore a subtle white pearl necklace and a navy-blue dress. I loved her dresses. Her hair was always perfectly swept back neatly, never out of place, with just the right amount of makeup. She was my idea of a sophisticated and successful woman, with a voice persuasive and kind yet intelligent and firm.

I shouldn't have been surprised when Rosa dropped by the house and said, "I just thought I'd come and check on y'all." I hadn't told Mom about the call, so I hoped she wouldn't be upset with me.

Mom asked me to watch the girls while she and Rosa sat together. I kept looking at them to gauge Mom's reaction. Rosa soon waved me over, hugged me, and then hugged the girls. She had told Mom that even though Tate was supposed to work for her, she also hadn't seen him in weeks.

Mom was pissed, not about the call to Rosa, but that I took the dime without asking her. She told me that taking things out of her purse was like stealing. She said she was saving that change to buy more milk in the morning and that that dime was necessary.

"Mom, I had to take the dime. We need to find Tate. We can't live like this," I insisted. I hadn't talked to my mom that way, and I think she was surprised.

Later that day, Rosa came back by the house. She brought two big jugs of milk, peanut butter, a lot of bread, lunch meats, and some other things, especially things the girls would enjoy, like canned fruit. Mom thanked Rosa profusely for helping. Finally, it seemed that we had gotten a reprieve.

I told Mom later that day that we needed to try to find Tate. Several more days passed, and he still wasn't there. About a week after Rosa Peyton had dropped off the food, I heard a knock at the door. An elderly couple was standing on the porch holding groceries. When I answered the door, they introduced themselves and the gentleman said, "Is this the Barkley house?" I said, "Yes." Pointing at the brown grocery bags, he said, "This is for you and your family." I remember the couple so distinctly. The man was wearing a cap and large black frame glasses. His wife had white hair and wore gray polyester pants and a brown windbreaker.

By then, my mom had come to the door holding Brandy-K. They were so very gracious in every way. They asked if they could bring the groceries in and set the bags on the table. There was no presumption. It seemed the bags just kept coming and coming and coming. I was mesmerized.

At one point, my mom said, "Maybe, Son, you should ask them if you can help."

I realized I had been standing there doing nothing, so I said, "Can I help carry some groceries?"

And he said, "No, that's fine. You just need to relax." No one had ever said that to me before. This was like a dream come true. The people were so generous, and all I had to do was sit back and watch a parade of food as it danced into the house.

They brought us a feast: Real chicken and real hamburger meat, brand-name Kraft macaroni and cheese, not the knock-off version we were used to, two big jugs of milk, and canned fruit and fruit cups. There were snacks of every kind, even potato chips, things we never got to eat! They even brought bags of nuts, including the exotic Spanish nuts I still love. One of the best things was the brand-name cereals all the other kids got to eat. They brought Frosted Flakes and Cap'n Crunch and actual Rice Krispies. We never got to have chocolate milk, but they brought us that too!

I remember this so clearly, as if it was yesterday, because their kindness was overwhelming. I saw the relief wash over my mom's heart when she saw the parade of supplies she would have for her children. I don't think people realize how it feels to be food insecure. We were on a high. When they finished, there were over 14 bags of groceries, not including a sack of potatoes and a big box of canned goods. The people smiled at us and said, "There you go." The gentleman said, "Thanks for letting us in. It was good to meet all of you." They acted like we were doing them a favor, which was initially perplexing to me. Then I remembered how gracious Grandma Kirkman was when helping the poor. For the first time, I realized now we were the poor. They wanted to preserve our pride. We thanked them profusely as they left.

Unfortunately, the food ran out, and about three weeks after the kind couple brought us the groceries, the electric company cut off the power to the white house due to nonpayment. After two weeks without electricity, the city also shut off the water. Tate had been gone for almost two months. It was a total disappearing act. There was no money, not even a penny at this point. And now we had almost totally exhausted the food those fine people had brought us.

One of our neighbors, Ms. Wilson, came over one afternoon to ask if she could pick something up for us. My mom, being the proud person she was, with Tate's misguided voice echoing in the back of her mind, said, "No, we are fine." I thought, "We are not fine, and evidently we aren't fooling anyone."

On that same day, Ms. Wilson came back and said, "I've made a mistake." She handed us two big milk jugs and said, "I bought too much milk this time, so here you go. Why don't y'all take this? I don't feel comfortable taking milk back to the store."

My mom said, "Sure, but we do not have a refrigerator working at the moment."

Ms. Wilson said, "Why, that's okay. I'll keep a jug at my house and a jug here. My husband is fixing up an ice chest now." What Ms. Wilson had said was the truth. Twenty minutes later, Mr. Wilson brought over a big ice chest. It had lots of ice, orange drinks, and a cold jug of water. He placed the jug of milk in the ice chest then looked at me and said, "Son, before you go to school, come to my house and get ice. It's okay. I'll be up."

Life without electricity was quite the adjustment. It was not like we missed the air conditioning since we never had it, but the girls and I sure missed the 13-inch black and white TV. So I arranged to take the girls to Mike and Johnny's after school to watch TV. Mike and Johnny were so accustomed to having my sisters around, they didn't care if I brought them.

We were resourceful with the electricity situation, but I worried that because I couldn't water the lawn, when Tate returned, he'd be angry the grass had dried out. He had me so trained that it bothered me not to water the plants, but we also had no way to flush a toilet, boil water, or wash things.

For whatever reason, Tate had several enormous bags of charcoal on the back porch and a Weber grill with tons of lighter fluid. I learned that if you get a thin bottom pot and strike up a fire on a Weber barbecue grill with some charcoal, you can heat the water up for a bottle sooner than you think. So Mom and I became pros at blowing on the fire and the charcoal until it got really hot, and I could warm up Brandy's milk bottle.

We were surviving without Tate. It didn't take too much hot water mixed with cold water to get a warm bath, wash your hands, or wash your face. We could keep ourselves clean. I kept an almost continuous fire on the Weber grill. I would heat several pots of water and it wasn't long before we figured out just how much warm water we needed to clean everything and everybody. The bigger challenge was getting the water. I knew that for us to have water, we needed the kindness of our neighbors. We would have to break down and tell the neighbors our situation. Mom and I realized we were making a decision that would piss Tate off, but Mom agreed there was no choice. I still get so angry at myself thinking about how we let things go that long without reaching out for help. But that was how it was. Finally, I walked across the street with a big green yard bucket. I knocked on the door, and Mr. Wilson answered and said, "Mike, what's going on?"

"Could I borrow some water?" I asked sheepishly. "We are having water problems."

Mr. Wilson belted out a belly laugh and just said, "Yes, sir." He directed me to an outside faucet and proceeded to fill up my green water bucket. We stood there and just watched the water. We didn't say anything.

Mr. Wilson was retired Navy, and his wife was a little bit of a busybody, but a good busybody. They were no fools. Thankfully, the Wilsons were good neighbors. We were already getting ice daily, so needing water wasn't a surprise. Once the bucket was filled, I grabbed the handle and turned to thank him. "You know, you can have as much water as you want. It'll be okay. Just in case that one bucket is not enough," he said.

For a moment, I felt confused. I'd not thought much past the first bucket. I just looked up again and said, "Thank you. I'll likely be back over."

When I got home, I decided to see how far one bucket of water would get us. I started with the bathroom. If you filled the back of the tank up, you could flush the toilet without running water. It took almost one full bucket to fill up the toilet tank.

So, I returned to Mr. Wilson's for more, and he was still standing outside smiling. "Help yourself. I'm going back in. You don't need to ask anymore. Just come get your water. Okay?"

"Yes, sir," I said. As time went on, we established a routine. The Wilsons would allow me to bring my big green bucket over to their outside faucet, and I would fill it up and bring it back to my house, first thing every morning before school. Then, as soon as I got home from school, I would get my big green bucket, and fill it up again to replenish everything Mom and the girls had used during the day.

Every now and then, Mr. Wilson would carry over an extra bucket of water or two. The Wilsons were such nice people but compared to Tate they seemed dull. It's odd, but that's how I remember them. They were ordinary people whose lives were functional. They didn't seem to have big dreams, nor were they chasing windmills. I learned something valuable from them, but it would take many years before I stopped craving the excitement one gets used to when every day is a roller coaster ride.

I learned another lesson that summer about assumptions. Our next-door neighbor was scary looking. He was what my people might have called "white trash," but only if no one was listening. Obviously, he and his family were struggling like we were. It also didn't take long for them to figure out that we had run out of water. One day the man was sitting on his front porch as he watched me haul my green water buckets from the Wilsons. He walked over and looked at me. I didn't know what he was going to do. Even though we were poor, Tate always dressed like he was rich. This man wore dirty jean shorts, flip flops, had a big beer belly, and was shirtless. His torso was covered in tattoos, and he looked sweaty.

He said, "Boy, are y'all out of water?"

I said, "Yes, sir, we don't have any water."

"All right, then," he said and walked away. I knew we had permission to take water from Mr. Wilson, so I couldn't imagine what this man wanted.

Thirty minutes later, he walked to our house and banged on the door. When I answered, he said, "Boy, you got a hose?"

"Yes, sir," I replied.

"Well, get it for me." He said, "Get me the hose."

So I went outside and got it for him. He hooked up the water hose to his faucet and we ran it across the yard. We took down a window screen and opened the window in the main bedroom where we had our bathroom. Then the man ran the hose to the bathtub. He then proceeded to duct tape around the hose and window screen to "keep the mosquitoes out."

"You can use the water anytime you need it," he said, ruffling my hair. At this point, my mom came in to see what the commotion was.

He turned to her and said, "This will do for y'all until they shut my water off too." Then he chuckled and went back home.

One night when I was with Mike, I decided to tell him the truth.

"We don't have any water or lights at our house," I said. I felt tears well, but I didn't want to look like a sissy. So I bit my bottom lip to make them stop.

"No water?" he asked innocently. "What happened?"

"Tate's been gone," I told him. Of course, he knew what that meant, or he figured it out real quick.

"Well, I'll just ask my mom if you can move in with us, and that'll solve that problem," he said. He believed it, and I wished it could've been that simple.

"Please don't ask your ma about it," I pleaded. "My dad would kill me if anybody else knew."

"Okay, I won't, but at least let me help," he said. Mike disappeared for a minute and returned with his hands stuffed with five packages of Little Debbie's oatmeal cream pies. He pushed them toward me and said, "I'll tell my ma I was hungry."

I will never forget that gesture. But I didn't know I wouldn't see Mike again after that day.

I saw my mom watching from the window when I got to the house. She seemed dazed. I had noticed that each day her spirits were worse and worse. I was excited about the treat I had to share with my family, but I sensed something was about to change.

After we got the girls to bed that night, Mom sat with me on the front porch. I was grateful for a cool breeze but felt anxious. I knew Mom had been crying again about Tate being gone, and even though we had been figuring things out, it was only a matter of time before we could no longer sustain our life. We both knew that Mom had a huge decision to make, and she turned to me to help decide.

"Son, what should we do?" she asked me. I was ten years old and felt the world's weight on my shoulders.

I was tired too. I was tired of seeing my mom cry, and my baby sisters have so little. I remember that I had no doubt: I said, "Mom, we have to go. We have to go now." Mom looked at me and said, "I know, Son. It's time to leave." It was probably the best and firmest decision we ever made.

Mom walked to the Wilsons' to borrow their phone. Her first call was to Tate's mom, Ma Barkley, to whom she spilled everything. Finally, we got over the concern about making Tate look bad.

Before she hung up, Ma Barkley told her, "Someone will be there to get you very soon." Mr. Wilson gave Ma the address and surprisingly told her we would be staying with them until our kin arrived. After the call, Ma Barkley told Aunt Biddy to gather up the kin and get us. It took a few days for Aunt Biddy and Aunt Duree, Uncle Roy's wife, to reach us at the Wilsons'. We packed what little we had in their station wagon and left Florida for good.

I never told Mike, Johnny, or anybody I was leaving. Mom said it was probably for the best. We just needed to leave as fast and quietly as possible. She didn't want Tate to know we were leaving. She knew he would be angry as a snake.

Mom worked out that we would stay with Ma Barkley once we arrived. I was proud of her because she defiantly told the Barkley's that we were their responsibility, and they would have to help us since it was Tate who abandoned us. They should have all been on her side, but when we arrived at Ma Barkley's, there was a houseful of kin and Tate had already called with his side of the story. Yes, Tate had finally returned to the white house the day after we left.

Everyone made a big "to do" over the girls when we arrived. They rushed past me to pick up the girls and welcome them "home." When I got out of the car, I stood by an old magnolia tree in Ma Barkley's front yard. This tree would become my oasis, my quiet place in the months to come. Then, finally, some of my aunts led my sisters away from the chaos that was about to ensue.

I could hear arguing, but Mom held her ground. It makes me furious thinking about it, but Tate had told Ma Barkley that it was Mom who abandoned him and denied leaving us high and literally dry for over three months. He even blathered something about only wanting Leighann and Kairy-Tate back with him, which stuck me like a knife. But Mom continued to assert, "This family, Tate's family, will care for me and these kids!"

CHAPTER 10

RETURN AND GOOD RIDDANCE
TO BARKLEY ROAD

Sitting with my mom and sisters in the waiting area while Dad was getting his heart stent was complicated. This was my fifth year of sobriety, and I had gotten my life back together, but Dad could still get under my skin. I thought I had gotten over the anger I had toward him, but it kept bubbling to the surface. He wanted all his loved ones around him here so he could rely on us, and for the first time aside from a few near slips, it made me think about having a drink. I never wanted to return to those days of blackouts and hopelessness. I thought about calling my sponsor, but he knew I was at the hospital and figured I could handle things. But it felt phony. My program was about rigorous honesty, and there was so much Dad didn't know about me, but it was par for the course. In my early years, everything I knew about him was a lie.

◆ ◆ ◆

My Ma and Pa Barkley's house on Barkley Road was called "The Home Place." It was where the Barkley kin would go whenever they were down and out. By this time, Ma Barkley was 78 years old, and Pa Barkley had recently passed away. Ma was in no mood to pick up the pieces of her youngest son's mess, especially since she hated that he had broken up with his first family. Ma loved Martha and her granddaughters, Jane and Lisa, Dad's daughters. She also saw divorce as a sin. That part was too bad because, from what I heard while there, she always spoke ill of Pa Barkley. I could never figure that out.

We were dependent on others again with no real place to go. After Tate told his ridiculous lie about how he wanted "his" kids, Tate disappeared again. We bounced between people's houses for almost 7 months, and my resentment toward him grew. Even though Tate would have hated it, Uncle Charles took us to get government assistance, which helped out a lot. At least we wouldn't starve, and we got health care at a government clinic. After a while, Tate returned, claiming he wanted to be a family again. We didn't know where he had been all that time, so I did not want to see him, let alone live with him. I was doing good in school and was used to life without him. We bounced around from house to house, but the school stayed the same. Tate's siblings saw that I wanted nothing to do with him when he returned, so one night, my Aunt Sis, with whom we were now living, sat me down with Mom in her kitchen. She set a small glass of beer in front of me. They had never done this before, so I imagined it had to be bad.

"Go ahead and take a drink," Aunt Sis said, motioning to the glass. I hesitated and looked to her for some sign of what was to come.

"It's okay, really it is," Aunt Sis implored as she smiled broadly. I loved Aunt Sis. She looked over at Mom and said, "I'll tell him." Aunt Sis continued, "The family has been waiting for years to tell you that Tate is your real dad!" Aunt Sis seemed happy, but I felt sick. I already suspected what was probably the least secret of secrets but hearing them say it out loud was a shock. I grabbed the beer and shot it back in one gulp.

Then she added, "The girls are your real full sisters." I had never thought otherwise, but that was good news, and I could see Aunt Sis was trying to make me feel better. So I smiled, said a quick "yes, ma'am," and left for my magnolia tree to clear my head.

The inner conflict about Tate never left me; I feel it even now. But that summer after fifth grade, when he returned to North Carolina, was a time when I got to know him better. He had made terrible decisions, and I blamed him for them. So when he tried to get us together again, he took us to Aunt Warren's lake house. At first, "Dad," a name I was getting used to, spent most of his time with the girls. They adored him and didn't have the anger toward him that I had. I was grateful they were too young to understand what had happened to us while he was gone. Dad rarely said anything to me at first except to tell me what to do. Mostly I kept an eye on the girls, which I enjoyed. Then one day we were sitting out by the lake. He was drinking a beer and I was feeling awkward.

"Are you happy I'm back?" he asked. It caught me by surprise. He sincerely seemed to want to know how I felt about something.

Of course, I said, "Yes," though I wasn't sure if that was true.

"You know, I love you," he said and hugged me. I didn't know how to feel. Frankly, I didn't want to feel anything. I could handle the man when he was angry, but I had longed for a father's love. Now that he was giving it to me, it was overwhelming. I didn't want to trust it or him.

Shortly thereafter, Dad moved us into a small trailer in the Dogwood Estates trailer park. It was small, but we were on our own again as a family. Finally, we would leave Barkley Road. Dogwood Estates was in remote farm country, but aside from waking up to the smell of cow shit, the trailer park was pretty nice. It was a great summer. The trailer was big enough for me to have my own room, and that summer the world's eyes were on Bruce Jenner, who won the decathlon during the 1976 Montreal Olympics. Who could have foreseen that Jenner hid a more devastating secret than mine? I wasn't the only one who was unaware of what the future may hold. The 1976 Olympics inspired me, and I told Dad I wanted to compete there one day. I appreciated that he didn't laugh since I had become pretty fat after spending so much time eating my feelings. Instead, he said, "Then you need to run," so I did. I started running from our trailer down Bell Farm Road to the Beavers General Store on old Mocksville Highway. The first time I ran, I didn't realize my dad was following me in his car. The second time I ran, I spotted him going the other way towards home as I turned the corner. The man had been following me again. I was shocked. After all the times he left us on our own to fend for ourselves, he was showing me some attention. I still wasn't convinced it was safe to love him, but he did get a job with Cory Coffee as a traveling salesman.

When I overheard him tell my mom about the new job, he sounded excited, but we had heard that before. It meant he would be gone. His territory was North and South Carolina, so it might not be too bad, but it might as well have been California with him. Gone was gone. Then he surprised me by asking me to go along with him. That man took me to work with him every day that summer, starting with the textile mills, convenience stores, and distribution centers close to home. He had me dress nicely, with a tucked in shirt and clean shoes.

"People judge you by how you look," he explained. "A nicely dressed man, or young man, breeds confidence. That is half of the sale." He could have been reading me the phone book for all I cared. He acted as if he was trying to become a real dad who paid attention to me, taught me things, and cared that I was alive. Dad was only thirty-seven at the time, so he listened to popular music, and we had that in common. We left early in the morning and, most nights, were home in time for supper and my run.

Dad was working hard as far as I could see. He had the gift of gab, and I loved watching how he could mesmerize people with his voice. People were glad to see him make his rounds and found me to be a novelty. He appeared to be making sales, but we still had precious little money. Dad stopped every day to buy Vantage cigarettes and Miller Lite Beer, but I know, as much as he liked to drink, he held out until late afternoon before breaking into what he called "road beer." He would drink maybe two or three on our way home at the tail end of our traveling day and would also buy me a Tru-Ade, a Cherriwine, or a Mountain Dew whenever he got his first beer.

My Dad drank every day and I never thought anything of it. I can't blame him for my drinking, but it probably didn't help. We were poor, and that is what poor people did. They drank and talked. At least with my dad, he spoke about topics that interested me. It was back to discussions about war, but now more than ever he discussed politics. 1976 was not only the time for the most incredible Olympics, but a peanut farmer from Georgia was causing a rift among the southern Democrats by competing against George Wallace.

There was no doubt we were Jimmy Carter Democrats. However, there remained a great deal of tension among Democrats in Iredell County and the Barkley family. In our own family, the Democratic Party of the South started to break up. The older, seemingly angrier, white folks in our family and the party loved George Wallace, whereas the younger folks, including my father, liked Jimmy Carter. My dad was elated that Jimmy Carter won the Democratic nomination, and we watched the Democratic National Convention together.

That moment watching the late Barbara Jordan give the keynote address while sitting next to my real father was a high point. When she concluded, Dad and I both stood up and clapped in unison. Every time he hurt me in the years to come, I would think back to that day. As we watched Barbara Jordan on our 13-inch black and white television in a beat-up trailer on Bell Farm Road in the middle of nowhere in North Carolina, I felt hopeful and rich.

Jimmy Carter won the nomination, and I got up the nerve to write him a letter asking to participate in his campaign. I knew it would make my father proud, and it did. As the school year began, I received a thick packet of materials from the Jimmy Carter campaign in Plains, Georgia. It included flyers to pass out anywhere and any place I needed. So, my dad drove me around to Beaver General Store and Sharpe's General Store so I could hand out Jimmy Carter flyers. In those days, Democrats surrounded us, so no one objected.

After the summer with my dad, my world became bigger in many ways. First, I became a part of the Barkley family. My kin on my dad's side began to accept me as "Tate's son." It felt good to belong to a real father and have a family. One of my dad's older brothers, Uncle Roy, was a stout man with a big bowling ball belly and a constant smile. He was a Seabee in World War II and now, at age 49, was a potato farmer and a part-time butcher at a local grocery store. I would frequently see him on the weekends and spend the night with him, my Aunt Duree, and my two cousins, John and Scott Barkley.

There was a pond on their land, and my cousins and I would run through the woods chasing rabbits and shooting BB guns. Then, we could swim in the pond when the day's work allowed. We would also help my Uncle Roy. We picked green beans, harvested tomatoes, helped bale hay, and did other chores. One Saturday we were picking potatoes behind the tractor. During a break, I told my Uncle Roy I could not go on anymore because I had a "hernia." I must have heard that term somewhere. My Uncle Roy busted out laughing and said, "Boy, I've seen you eat, the only thing you got is a table hernia." And would call me "table hernia" after that.

John and Scott would fight like brothers, but there was something real about being around them. I was used to being the only boy in a house full of girls, especially when my dad was gone. I admired Uncle Roy and told that to my dad.

"Uncle Roy was a big drinker in his day," Dad said as he opened a can of Miller Lite. "That man could not hold his liquor. He stopped it cold turkey."

The next time I saw Uncle Roy, I asked him if he ever drank.

"I used to," he replied, "but now I am what they call sober." He took a coin out of his pocket and showed it to me. "This coin means I am a member of Alcoholics Anonymous and am an official teetotaler," he said. I remembered how proudly he held that coin, but I never thought it would apply to me. My father made it clear that day that he thought not drinking anything was equivalent to sin. "I don't trust folks who don't drink, except your Uncle Roy," Dad exclaimed.

That summer, I got involved with St. Paul's Lutheran Church. My father wasn't much of a churchgoer, but Ma Barkley was a scion of the church. The Barkley family dominated the church roles with another large family called the Schneiders. It gave my grandmother great pride that the Barkley clan took so many pews at church when we all attended. It especially pleased her that my cousins, Johnny, Scott, and I were the three acolytes on Sundays. I had gone through the communion class to become an acolyte, which meant on any given Sunday, two of us would be lighting candles, and one of us would be bearing the cross. This elated Ma Barkley.

My Dad hated church, and the more I got involved, the more displeased he became. When he was young, Ma Barkley had made him attend all the time and for every event. That meant every Sunday, every Wednesday night, and every Luther League meeting. Now I had him driving me there at least every weekend for Sunday school.

Going to church had always helped me feel I belonged, but I was also, for the first time, becoming very interested in religion. I was interested in the Bible and liked the kids in my Sunday school class. Jesus fascinated me. In Sunday school, we would read directly from the Bible about Jesus. The Jesus I heard about on TV sermons, or the radio seemed different from the Jesus I read about. Jesus from the Bible was kind, merciful, compassionate, and very human. All too often, the God and the Jesus that I would hear about in sermons or on TV seemed angry and condescending. I never understood the distinction. I did know that when we read the Bible in Sunday school, I loved Jesus and wanted to be like Him. It was this loving Jesus that very likely helped save my life when I needed it. My life was finally going smoothly, but my most significant inner conflict would emerge soon, and there was nothing I could do to stop it.

◆ ◆ ◆

When I entered middle school, it seemed that Dad had taken a renewed interest in me. Dad learned that East Iredell Middle School had a football team, and we both loved the Miami Dolphins since we'd lived in Florida. But, of course, I was only a spectator. I had never participated in organized sports.

Dad met me after class on the second day of school and told me that I was going to play football. Before I could object, he had his hand on the back of my neck and walked me up to Coach Chip Myers. The East Iredell Middle School football team was practicing, and as Dad approached the coach, he said, "My son wants to play football." Coach Chip looked me up and down, looked at Dad leading me around, smirked, and asked, "Has he ever played organized sports before?"

"Well, no," my dad responded as if the coach was asking a stupid question.

"Well, I doubt your son's in shape, and we don't need anybody, so I'm not sure he can play." He could see my father was unmoved, so Coach Chip added, "We started practicing back in the summer."

"I bet my son is in better shape than half the guys you have out there. He's been running every day and doing man's work in the potato fields almost every weekend this summer. And he has been bailing hay and plowing."

"We have been learning plays; there is more to the sport than strength," Coach Chip insisted.

I wanted my dad to give up and let me go home, but he said, "My boy is really smart and can learn the plays as fast as you can teach them." I think the coach could see Dad wasn't going to give up, so he reluctantly agreed to let me on the team.

Dad made a lot of promises to Coach Chip that day, but as soon as he got a "yes," he left me alone on the field with the coach and the other boys.

I was staring at the team practicing on the field when one kid approached me and said, "Do you know how to play football?" And I said, "Yes. I watch it on TV, and my dad taught me a few things." He just chuckled at me. I guess I just didn't have the look of a football player at the time.

Coach Chip and his assistant, Coach Foster, handed me a uniform and some pads. Chip said, "Tell your Dad cleats are not provided, so you need some cleats. Now go suit up." There was no changing room or locker room that I could see. I must've looked confused as Coach Chip barked at me, "Go around the corner of the outbuilding and change."

I went behind the building and did what I could. When I returned, the whole team stared and started snickering and laughing at me. I had put the pads on backward. Coach Foster quickly turned me back to the outbuilding and walked with me out of earshot of the team. "Look, these pads are on backwards, and that could give you a great deal of pain, particularly in the groin area," he chuckled, but I didn't feel embarrassed. Coach Foster showed me the proper way so I'd never make that mistake again.

He said, "Now that's how you put your pads on. You must get cleats or Chip will throw you off the team. Let's go back out there." Coach Foster blew his whistle and told me to run laps before I would mix in with the other kids. I was relieved. I already knew how to run but knew nothing about playing football.

It was awkward for me on the team at first, and my dad said he could always find me from the stands because I was on the sidelines swaying back and forth. But my game improved; by mid-season, the other teammates accepted me, and I was getting to play.

I loved playing football at East Iredell. Eventually, I started playing first string, and Dad was there at every game and brought my sisters to watch. Dad's involvement with every aspect of my life helped me stay focused. For the first time, I made straight A's. Dad was grinding me to work hard, but I liked the attention.

It was also the first time I had a girlfriend, Trina Sharpe. Her family owned Sharpe's General Store where my dad would trade and "get credit" when Mr. Sharpe was feeling generous. They were an "important" family and I know, even though we were young, the family was proud of the match. Trina and I would hold hands on the bus and call each other boyfriend and girlfriend. I even had my first kiss with Trina. It felt funny but also right, like I was doing what was expected of me.

There were a lot of firsts that year: My first kiss with Trina Sharpe, my first report card with straight A's, the first time I played football, the first time I got involved in a political campaign. But it was also the first time I stumbled upon the real me.

CHAPTER 11

IT HAPPENED THAT SUMMER

Life is always better when you have a best friend, and I met my first real best friend at the bus stop on the first day of sixth grade. I liked Gerry Schneider the minute he walked up to me and said, "Hi, what's your name." He wasn't shy at all, which was the exact opposite of me. Things had been going well at home and I had my father pushing me to achieve things. Gerry played on the football team with me, but I hardly saw him during the day. When we got home, we were inseparable. He lived in a trailer near ours and the Schneider family made up the second important half of the St. Paul's Church. In those days, and likely today, living in a trailer even in Iredell County immediately designated you as "struggling." His extended family had a lot of land, but his mother and father, Russell and Sandy, were working folks. Russell installed burglar alarms, which was a new thing in those days, and Sandy worked at the textile mill as many hours as she could. Most of the women that worked in my town worked at the textile mills. Russell and Sandy always welcomed me into their home and Russell and my dad became fast friends and seatmates at East Iredell Middle School football games.

At first when I hung out with Gerry, all he wanted to talk about was girls. He was obsessed with them and more excited about my girlfriend, Trina, than I was. I played along but wasn't that interested in talking about sex and what I was or was not doing with Trina. Gerry was on the same football team, and we would stand together on the sidelines. When I began starting games, he yelled his lungs out in support for me, as did our fathers.

When it came time for the last game of the season, I had gotten much better than when I started. This game would be for the championship. I tried not to watch my dad's expressions from the sidelines and focus on the plays, but it wasn't easy. Instead, I listened for Gerry's voice because he always calmed me down.

I was playing right side middle linebacker. With less than 40 seconds left in the fourth quarter, we held a 14-7 lead. Monticello had a huge fullback and a big offensive line. Somehow, we had managed to contain them most of the night. It was fourth down and very short. Monticello was on our 21-yard line. They had plenty of time to march down the field and tie the score.

I suddenly had a burst of confidence or a one-time shot of brilliant intuition and anticipated Monticello's count. I fired out toward the Monticello quarterback the second he said, "Hut!" and blew into their backfield. The Monticello offensive guard responsible for me did not have time to get set and block me. I blew through the gap between Monticello's left side guard and center. I hit the quarterback right as he was attempting to hand the ball off to their big fullback. It was like the world was happening in slow motion; I was as surprised as they were.

When I hit the quarterback, I lost my balance and just fell into their big fullback, stumbling to the ground and landing on my back. But somehow I had managed to dislodge the football and it just dropped right beside me on the ground. At that moment, I instinctively rolled over and got on top of it. I could feel the players piling on top of me. I heard the whistle. When I got up, the ref signaled it was East Iredell's ball.

Our sideline erupted. When I got up, my teammates were hitting me on the helmet, but what I remember most was Gerry running out onto the field as I approached the sideline and literally jumping into my arms. I spun him round and then we hugged in full pads. The hug lingered and I noticed it. I was caught up in the adrenaline of the moment and hadn't realized that Coach Chip was yelling, "Get off the field, get off the field!"

Gerry and I walked off the field together. Coach Chip at that point screamed, "Timeout! Timeout! Timeout! Timeout!" He walked over to me and gave me a brief embrace and popped me on the helmet and said, "Great tackle, but I did not mean for you to walk off the field." He had meant Gerry. I was not only a starter at right middle linebacker, but also a starting left guard on offense.

When the time ran out, my team exploded into celebration on the field. We shook hands with Monticello where we could, but our family and friends were all running toward us on the field. Russell Schneider ran and picked me up and spun me around just as Gerry had done. He said, "I am so proud of you," as if I was his son too.

The moment was unforgettable. Dad, Leighann, and Kairy-Tate had come to the game and saw the win. Coach Foster picked me up and said, "Boy, great job." But I was looking for Dad. When he finally reached me, he and my sisters surrounded me, and Dad said, "Bub, you won the game." I had never seen him look so proud. I walked out to our car holding my sisters' hands. Dad then said, "You're going to go with Russell and Gerry. They're going for pizza, but I can't go on with them."

I was disappointed, but too excited to argue. It didn't occur to me that he may have been concerned he didn't have the money to pay his fair share. Russell said it was his treat, but I knew my dad well enough; he never would have stood for that.

Later that night, for the first time in a while, I said my prayers as Grandma Kirkman had taught me. I included Gerry, Russell, and my coaches right at the top that night. I didn't understand why, but I said an extra special thank you for my friendship with Gerry and forgot all about Trina.

◆ ◆ ◆

As spring began, neither Gerry nor I played any other sports. This meant no practice after school. Every day as soon as I walked Leighann home and changed, I would head right to Gerry's house. Leighann had started kindergarten, so we rode the bus together. Bell Farm Road was full of woods, corn fields, and hay fields. We could walk together, talk, and disappear. Gerry and I spent endless hours in the woods with a BB gun and later with a single shot .22 shooting squirrels and birds wherever we could find them.

As the spring passed, I noticed Gerry looking at me. He was looking at me the way that I looked at him so many times in the past. We were best friends, so I spent the night with Gerry often. Gerry had his own room, so I slept with him. I started to feel something different when we spent a lot of time together. It makes me uncomfortable thinking back to that time, but in the mind of the twelve-year-old boy I was at that time, Gerry was beautiful. I watched him while he slept with only his shorts or pajama pants. His hair was brownish blond and colored by the sun and his skin glowed. What I remember the most were his bright blue eyes and his smile. I can't picture him without a smile that lit up the room.

I knew everyone thought it was so cute when I was "going out" with Trina because they saw it as puppy love, the awakening of the first signs of maturity at that young age. But I was hitting puberty and I knew I didn't feel the same way when I looked at Trina as I did when I watched Gerry.

"What is that under your arms?" Gerry asked, tickling me in my armpit. I started giggling and lifted my arm to show him the small crop of hairs that had been growing seemingly overnight.

"I bet you're growing a bush under your arm," I teased, lifting his arm over his head.

"What are you growing down there?" he asked innocently. "I have hair on mine. Do you?" I moved my shorts away from my upper thigh, revealing the smallest patch of pubic hair.

We laughed and started roughhousing and wrestling. Before falling asleep that night we hugged and lingered longer than usual. We never said anything, but I rolled over and went to sleep on my stomach.

As the summer drew near, I recall a day when I just inexplicably hugged him from behind before leaving for home. After school the next day, we hugged firmly, and our bodies were completely touching. I felt my penis harden and wondered if he felt it too. There was no denying it and no hiding it. He pulled away but pulled my hips closer to his, turning into me. Our crotches were lined up and touching. It was obvious to both of us that we were both hard. It felt electric. We released the hug, and he looked down at my crotch, and I looked at his. He smiled, I smiled, and we walked away.

I became confused because Gerry and I spent much of our time on the bus gaming out how we would meet girls over the summer. Gerry said we just needed to figure out a way to get to parties. We conspired and convinced ourselves we would get laid for the first time that summer if we could just make it to the right places. Gerry had an older cousin named Steven who talked about girls all the time. Steven taught Gerry a game called "odd and even" as a way to get girls to do stuff with you. Steven said you took two nickels and nine pennies. Each player would toss into the air. One player would call out when the coins were tossing in the air, odd or even. It was the same idea as heads or tails. If it was tails and the person had called odd, the winner would take a penny. Whoever had the most pennies won the game.

Before the game, you would set a dare or set a task for the loser to perform. According to Steven, this is how you could get girls to kiss you or take off their clothes. Gerry became a true believer and so did I. As summer began, Dad instructed me that I needed to make some money. Dad also told me that he was not going to take me on the road with him this summer. I was fine with not going on the road with Dad. I knew traveling with Dad would cut into my time with Gerry. I went around the trailer park and signed up yards to mow. The only hitch was I did not own a lawn mower, so I convinced Gerry to come into the business with me. His daddy let us use his lawn mower to perform our yard maintenance business, but we quickly realized cutting grass for a few trailer homes does not fill a full day.

So we would do random things. We would spend a lot of time roaming the woods and shooting. One day, we came upon an area in the woods that looked like someone had built a fort or an encampment there before. We stopped and rested.

"Do you want to play odd and even?" Gerry giggled. I was thinking of some way to encourage some touching without being too obvious that my desire was building. I wanted to know what it felt like to touch him. It was all I could think about.

Soon we were both giggling, and the game began. The first bet was simple: whoever lost had to pull down their pants and show themselves to the other, no clothes! I confess. I cheated during the game. I wanted to see Gerry. I won five out of the first six tosses. Gerry was laughing so hard I didn't know if he was too embarrassed or just thought the whole thing was silly. I was serious about it so I laughed along. I didn't want to break the spell and stop the game. He pretended he couldn't get his pants down, but eventually he complied.

I had never had such a close look at another boy's penis without immediately turning away. I had fantasized about Gerry for what seemed a million agonizing nights. Now it was real. I looked down. Then I looked back up at him. Gerry appeared shy, and I didn't know what to say to make him feel more comfortable, so I blurted out, "It's great. Very, very nice."

We both felt awkward at that moment, so we busted out laughing. Then we both relaxed, and I asked, "Would you feel better, less embarrassed if I showed you all of mine?"

He smiled broadly and said, "Sure."

I said, "Okay, but you're going to have to take it out." I just went for it.

I was in some heightened sense of excitement, and I wanted him to touch me. He reached over without hesitation and unbuttoned and unzipped my jean shorts. He gently lowered my underwear and pulled me out, and we just stood there. We just stood there for a while, exposing ourselves to each other. Neither of us knew anything of what could come next, but we knew something was happening to us.

The next day we returned to our recently discovered encampment and recommenced our odd and even game. This time, the dare was touching, first with clothes on, then with only underwear on, and finally with no clothes. We began touching more and more each time. We would giggle with ourselves about how we "lost" the bet.

Gerry had the trailer all to himself during the summer days. Our days of hanging out in the woods changed to days of hanging out in the trailer. We could spend an entire day together and be only interrupted by mowing grass or helping kinfolk with whatever chores were necessary.

Twice that summer, Gerry and I had to go with his Grandpa Schneider who needed cheap and obedient labor, so we were perfect. That's what boy kids are for in the country: cheap, obedient labor.

For those of you who have never baled hay, congratulations! Baling hay is hard, scratchy, and sweaty work, particularly in the heat of a Carolina summer. Our job was throwing the hay bales up onto the trailer. We would take turns picking up the bales of hay and throwing them on the trailer while the other stacked them high. We did a huge hay field in one day in early June.

Grandpa Schneider allowed us to ride on top of all the baled hay on the tractor on the back. It seemed like it was five stories high. The hay would teeter back and forth on the trailer as we went down the road. We were so high off the road that I think we would have died if we would've fallen over. Grandpa Schneider stopped at Sharpe's General Store and bought each of us a Mountain Dew. Back on the tractor, Gerry and I, of course, immediately talked about when we would get to play odd and even again. He asked if I wanted to play more and I said, "Yes."

Gerry said with what seemed like hesitation, "I guess I do, too." That pause made me nervous, like he was second-guessing our new pastime. I loved everything about what we did during odd and even and I didn't want it to stop.

After work we were walking back to the trailer and our arms kept brushing against each other. The conversation turned to sex as it often did and I asked "Gerry, would you ever suck it?"

And he said, "Only if I lost an odd and even bet, but you would have to do the same if you lost."

And I said, "Sure."

After that day, our physical intimacy escalated. By mid-summer, Gerry and I did not even bother with playing odd and even. We just engaged with each other physically. We expanded the boundaries of our exploration as our comfort with each other allowed. I euphorically loved being with Gerry.

One day we were walking together up the gravel road and Gerry put his arm around me. He asked, "Is what we do together 'homosexual?'"

A wave of fright went through me. I said strongly, "No." Homosexuals "butt fuck" and "French kiss" and we have not done any of that stuff. In that moment of reaction, I realized the spell had been broken. What had been so beautiful and innocent was now something to be condemned. It was clear Gerry was questioning what we were doing. Now I would have to as well.

Gerry said, "Good." There were no gay people in Iredell County. At least none that I knew, nor any that were brave enough to show themselves that I can remember. Every church I ever remember attending denounced homosexuality. It was not spoken of in either of my families other than the occasional demeaning comments from my dad or my uncles. But what little I saw of gay men on TV was demeaning and condescending. It seemed as if gay men were purposely made to look effeminate and silly. I never wanted to be gay because I didn't want to be that kind of man.

Only days earlier, CBS News did a story on what was called the "Gay Pride Parade in San Francisco." Dad and I watched. There were men dressed as women. Guys were prancing and engaging in vulgar acts. Dad with an edge in his voice said, "Fags, it is sickening! Bub, you better never!"

It was made clear to me growing up that an attraction to other men was an abomination, an affront to God totally unacceptable to those around me, a sin, and something for which someone should be ashamed. I knew without question, though I was never told directly, that if I had it, I had to repress it. It was in these days my exquisite ability to repress my feelings, to repress who and what I was, began to manifest myself.

By the end of June, Gerry and I began experiencing some challenges. Increasingly, he would not help me cut yards that we had agreed to cut. As time went on, all we did was sexual stuff. Eventually, Gerry resisted daily sexual interaction. He would still agree, just not every day. But I was craving it every day. Then Dad made the announcement: "We are going to Texas."

When I told Gerry I was leaving, he was visibly upset. I remember he hugged me, not in the way that lovers hug, but in the way that best friends hug, the way we hugged before the summer.

My friendship with Gerry was real. I had never experienced a relationship like it before. We always laughed about everything. I never felt shame, fear, or insecurity with him or from him. I could be truly and completely myself. Gerry gave me a pure friendship, one with no judgments or conditions. My eyes still well up with tears when I think of Gerry and our innocence in that time of our lives. Gerry never wanted anything in return from me. He never asked, demanded, or regulated anything with me. He was simply my friend, and for part of a summer, he was my lover. In that time and place, there was no person I would have tried to explore with other than Gerry. I suppose that's why God placed him in my life. He allowed me to explore and to enjoy with Gerry until such time as Gerry was no longer comfortable. Gerry was one of the many angels that has blessed my life and blessed my life at just the right time.

◆ ◆ ◆

The announcement that we were going to Texas was sudden. Like before, there was precious little time for sentiment. Dad had let it be known during our summer of traveling in 1976 that he had gone to Texas when he left Florida. He liked Texas, Houston in particular. Houston was a place where fortunes could be made, to hear Dad tell it. To me, Houston sounded an awful lot like Florida, so I was not much interested.

Dad came to me again after the initial announcement. We sat down together on the concrete steps outside our trailer one morning. Dad lit a Vantage cigarette, and he took a drink of coffee. He looked at me in a still and genuine way. "Bub, you don't seem too happy about Texas?"

I was honest. "Dad, this place is what I know, our family, my friends."

Dad put his arm around me and said, "I know, Bub."

He saw me roll my eyes, something I tried not to do.

"I can make way more money in Texas," he added. "I think things will be better. More importantly, there is no future here for us, Bubba. Look around town. Farms, furniture plants, and textile mills, and not a damn one pays well. There are some jobs, but not all jobs have a future."

"It's not so bad," I protested.

"I'll be goddamned, Bubba, for you to grow up and work in a furniture plant like my dad, my brothers, and all your uncles. That's not a future. Those plants are not here for long, you can see it happening. They're going to Asia and Mexico. They ain't coming back."

I listened and nodded. This was a new subject for us. The idea of Texas excited me at some level, but I knew that I would lose something very special to me if I left. The past year I had been successful for the first time and still had feelings for Gerry, even if he was pulling away from me.

The truth was my dad was not succeeding at the time. Some days were good, but most were bad. He was not making a lot of money at Corey Coffee. On more than one occasion, I remember being with Dad at Crescent Electric where he would plead for them to keep the lights on at our trailer. Dad hated groveling, it did not sit well with his pride, but he did it. In one particular instance, he and I made it to Crescent Electric late, but lucky for us the customer service representative was walking to his car in the parking lot when we drove up. He was a portly balding man with piercing blue eyes and a good nature. He saw us coming and before Dad said a word, he said, "Tate, there's just nothing I can do! I got your phone message from the front desk—it's three months behind! It's out of my hands!"

Dad immediately said, "I can get two of those three months by the end of the week."

"Tate, I just can't. They're going to make me do it. It's out of my hands."

I could see that Dad was grinding his brain with what to say next. Without even thinking, I said, "What about Brandy-K, Dad?"

The man looked at me with almost a glare and said, "Who's Brandy-K?"

I told him, "Brandy-K is my sister, she's a baby. She has to have a humidifier on to breathe well."

The Crescent Electric man instantly shook his head and looked defeated. He would have had to be heartless to ignore my plea. He turned to Dad and said, "God dammit, Tate, come on!" We followed him back into the building. He turned some lights on, pulled out a form, and said, "Sign here, you got any money today?" Dad gave him $2.00. We owed $92.00.

He said, "Tate, I'm not kidding, I need at least $50.00 on Friday." The man looked at me, and he said, "Don't you go to East Iredell?"

I said, "Yes, sir."

He said, "You play football, don't you?" I said, "Yes, sir."

The Crescent man winked at me. "Congrats on beating Monticello."

As we got into our 1968 Plymouth Fury, Dad looked at me and said, "Where did you come up with that, Bubba?"

And I said, "It just popped in my head." Of course, I learned to think on my feet by watching the best flim-flam man in the world.

Dad paused. "Thank you," he said.

It was evident to anybody that we were struggling. The food at our house was getting less and less, and it seemed like Dad was home less and less too. Dad would take the time to pick me and Leighann up at school on random days instead of having us take the bus. But every now and then, when I had a day off from school, Dad would take me to work with him again. It was late in the school year and we'd been given a day off, so Dad took me around to work. At the end of the day, like many days in the past, Dad stopped by Sharpe's General Store. Time and again, Mr. Sharp had given my dad credit, but on this particular day, Mr. Sharp said in front of me, "Tate, can we talk alone?"

I could see my dad knew what was coming. Dad said, "No, whatever you have to tell me you can say in front of my son."

Mr. Sharp said, "You're already $200.00 into me, Tate. I cannot extend any more credit. There will be no gas, no cigarettes, and there will be no beer, but I will give your son a Mountain Dew."

"No worries, Dad said. "I'm going to drive down to Beaver General Store, and I'll get some credit there." And he was right. We got gas, a six-pack, and two packs of Vantage cigarettes at Beaver General Store that night. I finished my Mountain Dew on the way home.

We were facing extreme financial difficulties as the summer of 1977 approached. For a while we had no toilet paper or paper towels in the house. I recall a neighbor lady had come over to use the restroom because her water was out in her trailer; Mom and I experienced flashbacks to our time in the white house. My mom allowed her to use the restroom, and then the lady left. I remember my mom was so horribly embarrassed because she had no toilet paper in the bathroom. My mom sighed and said, "A good housekeeper always has toilet paper."

There was no money for toilet paper; there was very little food. The only thing we had a lot of in the trailer was Cory coffee.

Dad had often said, "Houston's booming, and things are not booming here, and what you've got to understand, Son, I've witnessed with my own eyes, all things are possible in Texas, especially in Houston." He said again, "Houston's booming." It was July 1977, and my dad was right. Houston was booming. Even a 12-year-old could see things were looking bleak, and Texas could be the answer to our prayers.

We never did return to live in North Carolina. To Barkley Road and Bell Farm Road, I said goodbye and good riddance. But at the same time, I was terribly sad. It wasn't because I wanted to stay, but because I didn't want to leave Gerry. I could never have imagined that I would not have another relationship with a guy for many years.

PART II

Moonshine

CHAPTER 12

NO FRIEND OF BILL W

Thinking about Gerry brought back a flood of memories of how confused I was about my sexuality. But the anger I was feeling as I waited at the hospital felt bigger than that. It wasn't just anger; it was years of pent-up frustration that I tried to dismiss. I was sober for five years and had been working my 12 Steps regularly. I learned from the founders of AA, Bill W. and Dr. Bob, the importance of the 12 Steps of AA. It was a lot of hard work to claw my way back from hitting rock bottom and losing a successful law practice. My finances were in order for the first time in years, I was able to rent a nice place on my own, and I felt like the mature adult I had been working so hard to become—someone respectable. But Dad barking orders at me in the hospital took me back to five years earlier. I felt a familiar knot forming in my stomach.

As much as I hated to admit it, I was still angry at my father for being drunk when he picked me up at the airport as I returned to Houston from spending 28 days in rehab at the Hazelden Drug & Alcohol Treatment Center. It was the beginning of my transition back to the real world trying to stay sober. I knew going home after treatment would be challenging. They take time to prepare you, so I was armed with some tools and tips. For the duration of the flight home, I read my copy of *The Big Book of Alcoholics Anonymous*, the Bible for living a life of sobriety and recovery. I drank four waters, four coffees, and one ginger ale. "Always keep something to drink in your hand," an AA admonition. I was proud of myself. I felt no urge to drink on the flight. But there would be no small group of comrades waiting to support me on the happy road of destiny. When I got off the plane, I expected to see one of my sisters picking me up. It never occurred to me that Dad would be waiting for me, especially not drunk. I had rarely been able to count on him. But this time, I hoped he would think about me for once, and what I might need. While in rehab, I had changed, as tenuous as it was. But I returned unemployed, overweight, and anxious; more anxious than usual. And I was planning to live with my parents because there was no other place to go.

Dad arrived at the airport, he was acting as if nothing had changed. I tried to let it slide, though I had seen it a thousand times before. Dad was unmistakably drunk. His eyes were red and swimming about. The smell of beer was pungent and ripe. It was nauseating. That is probably how I smelled to other people over the years.

"Good to see you Bubba, we missed you," Dad said with a hug. "Let's get your luggage. Mom's cooking a big supper for us." It was as if I had just gotten back from summer camp. This was classic Tate G. But something was different—I was angrier than any other time before.

Alcohol had been in the picture for as long as I could remember. When I was a kid, we never went anywhere without Dad saying, "Mom, pull over. Let's stop at the convenience store and get me a beer." It was common for Dad to drink with all of us kids in the car. Once, Dad slammed into the rear-end of a car while I and my three younger sisters were passengers. When both cars pulled over, Dad said, "Bub, I'm going to meet this guy at his door, you clear out the beer cans while I have him distracted, just in case the police come!" Of course, I complied, as a good son should. No wonder I became such an expert alcoholic and liar.

My sister, Kairy-Tate, was the most involved family member in my recovery at Hazelden. I spoke on the phone with her every Sunday, and with my mom as often as possible. My sister repeatedly asked what she could do to help with my recovery. At first, I didn't know what to tell her, but the counselors at Hazelden advised me to ask my family to attend AL-Anon, a 12-Step recovery program for spouses, partners, family, and friends of an alcoholic.

"Dad, do you know where we parked?" I asked as we walked out of the terminal. He was starting to get defensive. "Of course, I know where we parked, Bub!" We slowly walked to the parking garage, reaching the elevator in silence. He punched three, and when we got off, he looked around and said, "This ain't it." We went back to the elevator and got off at four. I held my breath. "This is it," he finally said. Our hunt for the right floor could have gone on for hours like so many times before. But Dad found lucky number four and there was his beautiful, green, two-toned, extended-cab Dodge Ram truck. I threw my luggage in the bed of the truck and said, "Dad, I can drive. It might be good since it's been a while." I tried to say it just right, in a way where I was making it about me, not his inebriated condition.

"No Bub, I'm driving." New sobriety made me realize how stupid it was to let him drive, but I also knew this was not an argument I could win. I said a little prayer, sat shotgun, and took a deep breath. Once we cleared the parking garage and entered the freeway, Dad asked, "Well, did they teach you how to drink?"

"No, Dad."

He belted out this condescending, dismissive laugh and said, "Why did you go?"

I sighed.

"You know, Bub, I have said this before, you need to learn to drink like me. Just have a couple, two or three or so. I am not an alcoholic! Just have a couple, stop there. For the life of me Bub, I don't get it. You are perfectly capable of doing it."

I wanted to die. My dad was the only person who could make me feel this way. I learned that my feelings were my responsibility, but I also knew I did not have to say anything. Hazelden branded it into my head: "My disease, my responsibility; only I can say I am an alcoholic." Only Dad could say he is an alcoholic. Under my breath, I said, "I can't stop at two. That's why I went. I have a disease. It's alcoholism."

"Well, you didn't get it from me. I do not have this disease and neither do you. I can stop anytime I choose." I couldn't say it out loud, but thought to myself, "You have never stopped at two or three, Dad. You are delusional."

Dad knew just how to flip my switch, then and now. He still had so much control over my emotions. I could repeat all the aphorisms that *I am responsible for my feelings...blah, blah, blah,* but in the moment, I felt like blaming him again.

CHAPTER 13

BLISS ON THE BAYOU

The walk around the hospital parking lot cleared my head and eased my nerves. Yes, Dad could be an asshole, like that day at the airport, but I did love him. I was even grateful to him, especially for bringing us to Texas. Everything changed when we came here. It was also where I started drinking. My mind drifted by again to those early days in Houston.

◆ ◆ ◆

We took about a week to pack for our trip. On our last night in North Carolina, our trailer park neighbor, a biker nicknamed "Deadeye," had a party with all his Harley-riding friends. Deadeye looked the part, with a full beard, a bandana, square-toed boots, and a perpetual scowl. He also wore a gun strapped to his hip like a gunslinger. It was legal to open-carry in North Carolina, but his pistol was the only one I had seen. Dad said he was more bark than bite, which was true. He looked tough, but he was a softy for kids, especially my baby sisters. The whole family went to the festivities, and everyone was relaxed even when an Iredell County sheriff drove by. Everyone except my dad. He hid his head under a cap, and I could tell he didn't exhale until the sheriff passed us.

The next morning, my dad piled us up in his 1968 Plymouth Fury. He was nervous and in a hurry. I should have realized there was a good reason Dad wanted us to leave without a lot of fanfare. To hear him explain it, his ex-wife Martha was a pure evil bitch and had warrants out for his arrest. He conveniently forgot to mention that he hadn't been paying child support for years. I would never have had the nerve to evade the police so openly. It would be a skill I would have to acquire much later. The day we needed to get out of town, Dad rushed to the back entrance of Cory Coffee to grab his final check. Then we went to a seedy part of town to visit a pawn shop that doubled as a check cashing place. Dad rode around the block a few times before parking behind a dumpster. We all waited quietly while he went in to make his transaction.

At this point, Dad wasn't hiding anything from us. "I have to be careful," he said, looking at me and Mom. We didn't confront him but instead knew this meant keeping the girls entertained. Dad returned and announced he had a pocket full of cash. It was about $242, not a lot, but to Dad it spelled freedom.

Dad patted his pocket and said, "Now we're going to Texas."

We didn't even question when he stopped at a convenience store, bought a pack of cigarettes and two Miller Lite tall boys for the road. That was clearly what he needed to get us out of North Carolina and to our next destination. These same items became my go-to road trip provisions in the future. There was nothing like a pack of Marlboros, some tall boys, and the wide-open spaces.

Cars in those days didn't have the same restraints they have now. So the girls and I moved around the backseat and watched the scenery change. I didn't know anything about Texas except what I learned from the television. It sounded bigger than life, at least how Dad described it. All along the way he talked about the Alamo, John Wayne, cattle, gunslingers, cotton, and attitude. I had never seen him so excited, especially when we crossed the state line. He thought Florida was going to be the place to make his fortune, but Texas had taken its place as the land of opportunity.

My dad drove us straight through downtown Houston. I'd never seen anything like it in my life, all those tall buildings. The only thing I could think was, "Wow." I was in awe of downtown Houston the minute we made it there in July of 1977 and I've been in awe of Houston ever since.

My dad belted out, "I have to stop on the Gulf Freeway."

We drove down a freeway that didn't seem to end. I later learned this was I-45 South, also known as the Gulf Freeway. There were people in cars everywhere in this town. Dad stopped at a place called Big State Coffee where he had worked during his disappearance two years earlier. He left us in the hot car for about thirty minutes and came out smiling.

"I start my new job with Big State Coffee tomorrow," he said enthusiastically.

We stopped by at least six motels before Dad found one decent and cheap enough for us to spend the night. We would need a few days to find a place to live and so we squeezed all of us together into one tiny room with two beds.

We lingered in the motel for weeks with very little money. On the first day Dad left us to go to work, he had forgotten to leave Mom money and we had very little food left in the ice chest. The motel room did not have a microwave, coffee pot, or refrigerator.

I'll never forget my poor mother walking all of her kids over to the restaurant next door to the motel. While we were at the restaurant, she looked at the menu and grimaced. She ordered a club sandwich and tea. She took a knife, cut the club sandwich up, and shared it with all of us.

Our waitress, watching the ceremonial cutting of the sandwich, came over and asked if the girls would like a Coke. My sisters looked at Mom and my mom said, "Oh, no, ma'am, no, ma'am, no Coke."

The waitress smiled knowingly and said to my mom, "Oh honey, it's on the house." Not only did she bring us Cokes, but she brought out something we'd never seen before. She brought out a big red basket of chips. She called them "tortilla chips" and something called "salsa" and then a side of green stuff she referred to as "guacamole."

She said, "Here, y'all try this. It's on the house." A sense of relief passed over my mom's face. I looked around and thought, chips, salsa, guacamole, what the hell? We're not in North Carolina anymore!

Here we were in Texas trying to build a new life and if that waitress was a taste of Texas, I knew that I was going to like it here. Dad finally talked Big State Coffee into giving him an "advance." We went to the grocery store and filled up the ice chest that night. We survived off sandwiches and ice from the motel ice machine for the next four weeks. It was not long until my dad said he had found us a place to live, so we all packed up yet again. We landed in a place called the Skyline South Apartment Complex and into a two-bedroom apartment. After the motel room, it seemed like the Taj Mahal.

The Skyline South apartments were teeming with people. We had never lived with so many people in one place. We had lived in trailers of course, and in houses, but never, never like this, in an enormous apartment complex. The apartment was very basic. There must have been a standard that all rental furniture was to be a putrid brown color so no one would think of keeping it. Everything else we had in this apartment was from thrift stores, so it was used and smelled that way. But within three hours of Mom and us working, we had the place smelling fresh and clean as a whistle.

Skyline South Apartment Complex was like the Ellis Island of Houston. There were people from all over the country. The people next door to us, Joey and Sheila Augustino, were from Brooklyn, New York. They had three kids and they had come from New York because "Houston was booming" and they wanted to "make more money." The people across the way were from Missouri. Our neighbors above us had come down from Canada for work. There were four men from North Dakota. They were Native Americans working a piping job someplace outside of town.

Everyone was like us; they were from someplace else other than Texas looking for a better life. The friends I would soon meet at the apartment complex were also like me. They were sort of wide-eyed, hoping to figure out what in the hell was going on with their lives. None of my friends had any real experience in Texas and no one seemed to be a native.

There were a lot of kids my age in the complex and they took the first step to invite me to be a part of their group. The first person to knock on our door was a girl named Kitty from Ohio who simply asked, "Is that boy here? If he is, tell him to come to the pool." That was all it took. I was identified as being someone around their age and when I got to the pool, the area was full of kids having fun.

I waded into the pool and didn't have time to have anxiety because right away Kitty introduced me to everybody. At the time, I was 12 years old and in seventh grade, and glad I was making friends who would be going to school with me. The only problem was one of the boys named Ralph was very good-looking and I found feelings rising up in me. I knew deep down that I was attracted to guys by this point, and it wasn't going away. I was never sure if Gerry was playing doctor and experimenting, but I knew that for me the feelings and desires were real. I needed to stop being attracted to guys, so I did my best to avoid getting close to Ralph.

My other new friend was a guy named Troy whose dad was a mortgage broker from Wisconsin who had fallen on hard times. Troy was yet another hot guy that I had an attraction to right out of the gate. My friend Leanne's family was from Missouri. Leanne's mom was a waitress. Her Dad had been laid off at a factory job somewhere in Missouri, so he moved them to Houston and then promptly abandoned them once they got here. These kids seemed to struggle the way I did.

When I started classes at South Houston Intermediate School, I realized quickly I was in the minority. As early as 1977 the school had a majority of Latino students. This was an abrupt and awesome change. The hallways of South Houston Intermediate School were filled with brown kids, most of whom spoke Spanish. I met kids who had recently immigrated from Mexico and had not been in the United States for very long, and other "Mexican kids" that had been here for generations and whose English was better than mine. It was an interesting mix of folks. Seventh grade is also where you learn "Texas history," which I found fascinating. This began a lifetime of fascination with the history of my newfound state. But it was also where I discovered the dangers of being gay in Texas. I couldn't hide in the hayloft or run through the fields of wilderness like I could in North Carolina. I was filled with raging hormones that were unfortunately drawn to guys.

It didn't take long for the shower after PE class to present a terrible problem for me. Seventh grade in general had less supervision than my small-town middle school, and we never had to take a shower with other boys. The worst part was I developed a fantasy attraction to the exotic Latin guys, many of whom seemed much further along in their adolescence than I was. They looked like men, and one in particular, Anthony Benevidez, became a secret obsession.

Anthony was tall and muscular. He always undressed beside me in the gym, even though we rarely spoke. I would do the most awkward things to steal a glance at him as he undressed or as he dried off. Often, he and his other insanely hot friends would linger in the shower, and I would just stare at them whenever I didn't think that they were looking. I was so embarrassed to feel myself growing erect as I stood near him taking a shower. I couldn't help but stare at him but thought I was being careful, only glancing his way for a few surreptitious seconds.

One time I cut my shower short because I was afraid of getting an erection in the open where I couldn't hide it. I was horrified that my body was betraying me. Somehow, I was able to prevent what would have put me in a terrible situation. I knew that if I ever got an erection in the shower during gym class that I would be labeled a "fag." And once you were labeled a "fag," they would proceed to beat the shit out of you for the rest of the year.

I struggled with these desires, with a mixture of terror and awe, as I went through seventh grade. I ached to have someone like Gerry again. I found myself thinking about sex constantly. My friends also talked about sex all the time, but they had no idea I was thinking about guys when they were fantasizing about girls.

After school, I started hanging out with another guy named Gary who may have had the same tendencies as I had. He started the school year later than the rest of us. His family had moved down from Pittsburgh to find work. Gary was an anxious guy who was quick to smile and talk shit. He had green eyes, jet black hair, and looked like an old-fashioned Hollywood movie star. He and I became fast friends. Our friendship was also constantly strained by a very real, palpable attraction for each other that both of us resisted. We never spoke about it; I joined in with everyone else spewing hate about "fags and queers."

I quickly learned that urban schools were different from the schools that I had attended in Florida and North Carolina. There was a real edge, constant friction, and fighting with fists, knives, and brass knuckles. I wasn't about to bring any attention to myself if I could help it. You had to be vigilant in Houston. This was the first time in my life that I was around real troublemakers. Half of my friends were truants on any given day, and many would be in detention or suspended from school at various times.

If any of these kids were struggling like we were, it was understandable that they would vent their rage in school and upon each other. My dad's job at Big State Coffee was not going well. That fall he became devastatingly sick with an ear infection and had to stay home for over a month. At first, he just tried to beat it with rest because we had no money for a doctor. By the time a neighbor lent my dad some money to go, the infection had nearly reached his brain. The doctor all but begged my dad to go to the hospital, but he wouldn't do it. There was no money for such things.

Big State Coffee fired my dad. The rent fell into significant arrears, and the world closed in on us. My Dad cut a deal with Joyce, the property manager, to do work around the apartment complex, and became the handyman for Skylane South. I was proud that he was being resourceful rather than leaving us high and dry again.

This job proved to be one of the best things to ever happen to Dad. No one passed judgment on me, and no one passed judgment on him. We were living with working people no different from us. They understood what was happening to us. They realized that Dad had been sick and that we were struggling financially. Never once did anyone in the complex make fun of my father, me, or my family in any way. What happened, though, was they would come out and talk with us, give my dad beer, make his lunch, and one neighbor even gave him a new pair of gloves, while another brought him a new pair of sunglasses. People helped each other and we made friends with people from different cultures.

A man named Baker was one of the most interesting people we met at Skylane South. Baker was the epitome of cool and everything the seventies fashion had to offer. I never knew much about Baker, other than he played football at the University of Alabama. He talked rapturously about how he played football in the "early days" for Bear Bryant. Baker had a white wife named Lynn. The two of them were both expert card players, but I think they were hustlers. Almost every night Baker had six to eight people playing poker at his dining room table. They were not playing for fun, and inevitably, he and Lynn wiped them out. I asked Dad why he never played, and he explained in no uncertain terms that Baker was a professional and he could lose money without any help from the cards.

I know Baker and Dad were friends and liked to shoot the shit over beer. My Grandma Tevepaugh died in the spring, and my dad did not have the money to carry us to North Carolina for the funeral. He went to Baker, who said, "Brother, you don't even need to give it a second thought." Baker lent him the money and never asked for anything in return. I'm sure he knew it would be impossible for Dad to pay him back any time soon. But he didn't care. He just lent him the money. The more surprising thing was Dad let him do it.

The Boulevard Methodist Church was packed full for Grandma Tevepaugh's funeral. North Carolina looked different to me now. After seven months in Houston, my view of the world had already changed. The families were all happy to see us, but something inside me was different.

But Dad had let his guard down during this trip, and Martha heard we were back in Statesville. She alerted the sheriff, and my dad was arrested the day of the funeral for back child support. Dad now found himself in the Iredell County jail. We were broke and stranded in North Carolina, just like old times. Ma Barkley cashed a life insurance policy to make bail for Dad and Dad called Baker who wired us more money so we could afford to get home. The day after Dad made bail, we tore out of North Carolina in a dash. Not a lot had changed in North Carolina, but a lot had changed for our family. Personally, I felt like I was going home when we left North Carolina and headed back to Houston.

When we returned, Dad figured out a way to pay Baker back. One small loan was okay, but this larger loan didn't sit well with him. A few days in jail were also humiliating.

More importantly, at least for the future of our family, Dad found a job at the Arco Lyondell Chemical plant in Mont Belvieu. Dad had no experience in the refineries, but he knew an opportunity when he heard one. All it took was a guy telling Dad there would be a "shutdown" at the Lyondell Plant and that he could get him a job as a "laborer." Dad knew how to fit in and learn as Texas refineries became our mainstay.

Dad's buddy picked him up daily, and they would perform maintenance on the plant. My dad was always looking to get ahead, and in short order, he became a Foreman at a chemical plant in Pasadena, Texas. Dad had a natural aptitude for all things mechanical, and it wasn't long before he made his way up the chain of skilled labor. Despite his lack of experience, he excelled at the refineries.

There was a bayou that ran behind the apartment complex, which became the perfect place for the kids to hide from the world of adults. We had graduated from pool games like "Marco Polo" to Spin the Bottle and experimentation. We became a close-knit group.

Our friend and neighbor, Bruce, worked at Putt-Putt, next door to the complex, and not only did he help us have fun without funds, but he did something that would change my life forever. Bliss's common definition is "perfect happiness and great joy." I do not find that definition too strong or too expressive for what I experienced on the muddy bayou that night. I had experienced something like it with Gerry, but now Bruce scored a box of Miller High Life beer. Some of us had gathered on the banks of the bayou when Bruce introduced us to these small seven-ounce beers. The commercials billed Miller High Life as the "champagne of beers." The beers weren't cold, but I didn't care. So that night, I was with my friends Troy, Bruce, and Ralph, all of whom were a little older than me. They encouraged me to join in because it was not their first time drinking. Ironically, Dad had forbidden me to drink even though he did constantly. He had also forbidden me to smoke, but I would smoke a cigarette whenever I had the chance. But there was something about drinking that gave me pause. Bruce twisted off the cap and he handed me a beer. He was a lean 16-year-old with curly, wiry hair, and a Midwestern "aw shucks" persona.

Bruce swigged back a beer and smiled. My friend Ralph soon followed suit, and I said, "What the hell." For the first time in my life, I drank a beer. I drank one, then I drank another, and I lost track at three. But the one thing I do remember is that I'd never felt greater peace and ease in my life than when I fell into this buzz on the banks of that bayou.

It was the first time in my life that I felt relief, I felt free. I loved the courage that coursed through me as I eased into my first deep beer buzz. I felt totally separated from this oppressive place and my problematic life. That night on the banks of the bayou, Miller High Life, the champagne of beers, gave me my first taste of bliss. Frankly, I've chased that feeling the rest of my life.

There was a water pipe that ran across the bayou. I had always been afraid to walk across to the other side. On that night, I actually ran across the pipe. It was like I was Superman; I ran across and then I ran back. I had no fear and total confidence.

Ralph and Bruce were laughing. I remember Ralph tackling me; he was buzzing too. He began to wrestle with me, his body touching mine. He was Mr. "I'm not a fag" but now he was fondling me, touching me, and holding me like never before. I loved every minute of it. The guys gave me the last beer out of the bunch as they left to go home. I laid back, alone, drinking the last beer. It was like I was floating away, separated from everything, experiencing peace. I guess I drifted off, but Ralph came back and shook me awake. He said, "You need to go, it's late." I followed him back to the complex. He walked me to Apartment 2 and hugged me. He had never hugged me before.

Flash forward from that night on the bayou, through all the self-loathing and failed relationships, and I wish I could have told my younger self to put down the beer and go home. I wish I could show that innocent boy it is better to sometimes feel pain than the nothingness of advanced alcoholism. That's what I felt when I hit bottom: nauseating nothingness.

Twenty-one years later, there was nothingness, not bliss. You lose track of time in a semi-blackout. I had no clue how much time had passed, my whole body ached, my head was killing me and I was lying on my back in my mom and dad's garage with no idea how I got there. Then I felt a grotesque wetness in my sweatpants. What I feared was true; I had pissed all over myself.

In my haze, I realized, "I can't live with or without alcohol." It was destroying me. That moment not long in the future was a far cry from that night on the bayou when everything was silly and fun. Alcohol was a solution and made me feel invincible. The water pipe that I ran across over the bayou was my proof. All the boys in the complex would walk across it easily, but until that night, I was always too scared to try. But with my beer buzz, I was a new man, no longer a boy.

CHAPTER 14

THOSE DAMN SHOWERS

I was pacing the hallway near the waiting room, debating whether to go out for another smoke. The nurse from the heart Cath Lab told us Dad came through fine, but it would be a little while before we could see him.

When she finally took us back to the recovery room, Dr. Patel was there to explain the results.

"It went perfectly, as expected," he said. "You did not feel a thing, did you?" It took a minute for Dad to understand the joke, but then he smiled with a groggy grin.

"You will get a breathing treatment soon and I will check on you in the morning," Dr. Patel added. "If there are no complications, you will be out of here in a few days!"

I followed the doctor out of the room as the others waited behind.

"Is he going to be alright?" I asked, the implication being there was something he was not telling us.

"Your Dad is a lucky man," he said. I remembered all the times Dad said he was "God's Baby Boy" when something broke his way that probably shouldn't have. "From what I understand of his lifestyle," Dr. Patel continued, "his heart could be a lot worse, and I wasn't here to discuss his liver. He needs to stop smoking and drinking so much to avoid future events. Next time he may not be so fortunate."

I got the message and thanked God for my sobriety, but I was pretty sure any advice the doctor would give would bring out Dad's desire to be oppositional. No one could tell him what to do, not even a doctor.

I didn't bother to tell him what the doctor said when I visited him in his room. I was already exhausted, and I didn't want an argument. Dad was tough, but we all knew he would be expecting someone to stay with him, so we decided to take turns. I volunteered for the first shift.

Dad was still sedated and looked so much smaller in his hospital bed. Seeing him so helpless made me see him as a man rather than Tate G. Barkley, a bigger-than-life hero, despot, and disappointment. As he drifted in and out of sleep, I felt my heart open with a love for him I had been pushing down. He was my father, and I would have been devastated to lose him. At that moment, I vowed to do more to spend time with him, forgive him, and learn to be more patient.

Several hours later as I waited outside Dad's private recovery room, a formidable male nurse moved him to his bed and organized his IV, pillows, and bed tray.

When I strolled in, I asked, "What are you boys doing?" I was trying to make light of Dad's situation, especially with my newfound compassion for him.

Dad barked, "I wish I knew Bub. I thought I was fine." I could see some of the sedation was wearing off, and he was becoming aware of his situation.

The nurse looked at me and said, "Hi, I'm Edwin. You must be the son? I've already heard all about you."

I couldn't imagine Dad talking up a storm about me, but people do say odd things when coming out of anesthesia.

I watched as Edwin tucked Dad in nicely. He must have done it with a bit too much flourish as the minute he left the room, Dad said, "Thank God, Bub, you saved me! My big ole nurse there is sweet on me. I didn't think I could fight him off!"

I said softly, "I guess he likes you." I hoped Dad would leave it at that. My life was different now as an openly gay sober man. The only one who didn't know the real me was my dad; I still hadn't told him. He shook his head and said, "He's a big ole boy, Bub, and he's queer as a three-dollar bill."

Dad had used that expression many times, but now it cut me to the quick. It was apparent that Edwin was gay. He was what the gay community would call a "Big Ole Queen"—he was effeminate and didn't try to hide it. But of course, these characteristics were arbitrary, and since I had just met him, I would hesitate to say anything more than I knew he was gay. I felt a bit envious that Edwin was comfortable in his skin, but as AA teaches, "Never measure your insides by someone else's outsides." For all I knew, Edwin may have had a father as disgusted by him as my father would be by me if he knew who I really was.

It was time for a shift change. I needed to leave the room to center myself.

"Dad, I'm going to grab a quick cigarette, but I will wait until Mom or someone else comes to sit with you." He weakly tried to protest, saying, "I don't need anyone," but at that moment, he seemed like the neediest person I knew, though I wasn't far behind.

I left the room. Edwin waved as I walked past the nurses' station. I smiled, wondering if he could sense I was part of his tribe. Dad had called Edwin "queer as a three-dollar bill." I always hated that phrase; I hated it almost as much as I hated "fag." These phrases had haunted me since middle school and could still affect me 25 years later.

◆ ◆ ◆

Dad was promoted to Journeyman Millwright when I entered eighth grade and moved us into a nicer, newer house in a neighborhood called Scarsdale. Ours was working class, but the surrounding area zoned for the Thompson school district was more affluent. I knew it would be a significant change for me, and when we registered, Dad insisted I find out about football.

"It will make you tough to continue playing football," he implored.

When I asked the administrators about the football team, they were dismissive. I knew my dad wouldn't want me to accept an immediate "no," so I kept asking. And they kept blowing me off. Finally, they said I should have my dad talk to the coaches. Of course, they said this right in front of my mom. They probably thought they could reason with my father and explain why I couldn't join the team. I signed up for speech class as an elective and was interested to see where that would take me.

Thompson was a first-class school with a good football program. Football had already begun when I arrived on the first day at Thompson. The eighth-grade team had four weeks of summer training, with camp before I even showed up. I understood why they wouldn't want me on the team. It was hard enough in the sixth grade when I didn't know how to put on pads. I was indifferent, but my dad insisted.

The coaches reluctantly agreed. I am sure Dad told Coach Oakley and

Coach Renfro what a great football player I was, completely overselling my abilities. So many kids wanted to play that they had an "A team" and a "B team." Although I likely didn't deserve it, the coaches put me on the "A team" before they saw me play.

From the beginning, I knew the "A Team" was way out of my league. The team had already learned plays for the year, and they were calling defenses. Also, these kids were big, tall, and fast. In sixth grade, we just lined up in an ancient five-two formation on defense and hoped for the best. This "A-Team" had different defenses called in response to various offensive formations. Thompson football was the real deal.

The coach made me the second-string middle linebacker, which I survived for about three weeks. Then Coach Renfro encouraged me to try to get faster, and he moved me to safety in the secondary position. I was shorter, not as solid as some of the other kids, and I was not as talented. Football was not just a sport to these kids. This team was their future, and they had been playing and learning for a long time. My history of the winning tackle against Monticello didn't win me any points on this team.

Another thing I immediately noticed about the students at Thompson was they reflected their parents' success. These families had parents working at NASA or in management positions in the chemical industry. Their kids were white and solid upper middle class, different from my friends at South Houston, who were predominantly Latino and working class. There were only a dozen black students at Thompson. The school was diverse-ish, just enough diversity not to be lily-white. Here, there was a presumption that you could afford to go to the movies or play putt-putt, and they took for granted that you could afford to buy a uniform for football or a cheerleading outfit.

If I hadn't been so self-conscious, I might have walked the halls of this new school with my mouth hanging open. All the kids were beautiful, well dressed, well groomed, and involved in their education. They cared about it. It seemed I was behind in Math, English, and everything else. I had never cared about clothes until coming to Thompson. I began to covet what the other students could afford. They went to summer camps, beaches, and the mountains. I had never heard people talk about the places they went.

I wish culture shock was my only problem at Thompson. Before coming here, I had developed an attraction to Latinos. They were a minority at Thompson, but one guy caught my eye. Jorge Lascano was on the eighth-grade football "A team." We would often practice late and had to shower together. His locker was close to mine, and I could practically feel him before seeing him walk into the room. I tried to avoid eye contact with Jorge, who was close friends with a macho slender white guy on the team named Justin Mencer. Justin Mencer oozed what people today call "toxic masculinity" even at an early age. I saw him as a potential bully and didn't want to draw his attention.

I got through most of the season without any incidents, but with only a few games left, the coach asked Jorge Lascano, myself, and several others on the team to stay late to work on some things. By the time we made it to the showers, most of the rest of the team was gone and it was only Jorge and me with a few stragglers. I tried everything to resist, but the old feelings of desire were overwhelming me. Jorge was walking around in a jockstrap, laughing and "razzing" the other guys as he usually did. I could not resist looking at him. He and I undressed at about the same time; on this day, I had stupidly made a point to pace myself to track Jorge. We wound up showering next to each other. I thought I was being covert and clever. I was looking for a quick glimpse of him, nothing more. I must have hesitated a few seconds too long while looking at his penis. I only wish I had turned away to make it seem accidental.

Jorge looked over and caught my glance. I watched his eyes widen as he realized what was happening. I tried to look up at his face, but as if I had lost all control, I wound up looking down at his penis again.

"Barkley," he said, catching my attention. I immediately felt flushed and tried to look away, but it was too late. I only became more aroused and started to develop an erection. My body had completely betrayed me, and there was nowhere to hide.

Then Jorge asked, "Barkley, are you a fag?" He started to laugh. "Barkley, up here," he said, directing me to look him in the eye. "Are you looking at my dick? Are you a fag? Are you a fucking fag?"

He had caught me, and even though I denied it, I still couldn't stop looking at him. I think I was having an out-of-body experience or a non-alcohol-related blackout. Everything was in slow motion; it was surreal.

"So Barkley, you like my dick!" he said, louder for anyone within earshot to hear. This had turned from curiosity to harassment.

"So you want some of it?" he said, waving it at me. "Are you a fag that wants some of it?"

Bile rose in my mouth, and I wanted to wretch. "Jorge, shut the fuck up," I shouted. "I was not looking at your dick!"

Jorge looked at me up and down, hesitated, and grinned. What I thought was beautiful about him changed into something weasel-like. I wanted to run away, but now the entire locker room was listening and moving closer to us.

"I thought you might be a fag," he said. Then he said it. The words I had been hearing all my life, "Boy, you're queer as a three-dollar bill." Jorge left the shower. I did not follow. I lingered in hopes it would all just go away.

Jorge must have gotten bored with me that day or had somewhere to go because he stopped the harassment. But from then on, any time after practice, if I dressed near him or we showered at the same time, he would say, "Are you looking, Barkley? Are you looking?"

One day he was walking around in his jock strap, calling me a fag and asking if I liked his "tighty whities" as we got dressed, when his friend and fellow asshole, Mencer, walked in. Jorge decided to involve him in the fun as we walked out the door.

"Hey, Mencer, guess what? Barkley's a fag. I caught him looking at my dick while we were in the showers. Barkley wants my dick, the little fag!"

Mencer walked over and thumped my ear. "Are you a fag, Barkley? Oh my God! We got a fag in the locker room!" Mencer was a mean-spirited bully who loved to harass and insult everyone. Now I was in his sights as the worst thing possible, a fag.

I lost hope of fitting in at Thompson as Jorge and Mencer told the news about me to the football team and anyone else who would listen. Aside from what happened in the locker room, I had been so careful to act like any other straight guy. If anyone said anything to me, I denied the event ever happened. But like any gossip, no one cared whether it was true. I was done for. Damn my hormones.

Whenever he could, Mencer would do things to show off. He would frolic around naked or in his jockstrap near and around me and whisper to me, "Barkley, do you want to see it?" Had I not been so ashamed, I might have seen through Mencer's continuous efforts at intimidation. I honestly think it bothered him that I showed no interest in him or his dick. But unfortunately, this inattention made him angry, so he kept upping the ante.

Mencer didn't know he and Jorge had already won. I withdrew into a shell and went through the day detached as if I wasn't there. That must have made it more challenging for him because he became relentless. He took every opportunity every day to thumb my hair, flick my ear, hit, touch, and push. Twice he pushed me down and seemed frustrated when I didn't react. I wasn't being brave. I felt empty and didn't have it in me to do anything about it. I thought I deserved it for looking at Jorge, wanting to look at Jorge, and being someone who desired other guys. Others on the football team occasionally called me "fag" but eventually got tired of the whole thing. But Mencer never forgot.

Finally, one afternoon after football practice, I was waiting for my dad to pick me up. Mencer again started on me. He flicked my ear, and I felt a ball of anger rising into my chest. I felt just like when Tate had taken my savings. It wasn't anger; it was pent-up rage. But I told myself to calm down.

Then Mencer did it again. I grabbed his hand and said, "Don't do that." I was emotionless. And he said, "What, fag?"

"Please, stop," I said, and I honestly thought he would.

At that moment, he flicked again and then took his fist and pretended to land a punch on my chin. I don't know what came over me. I'd had enough. I pushed him back and kicked him as hard as I could, right in the balls!

Mencer curled over in pain, but before he hit the ground, I popped him right in the nose with my right hand as hard as I could. Kids started running toward us to watch the fight. But I wasn't aware of how many there were. Instead, I was laser-focused on Mencer and pushed him down onto the concrete. I am frightened to think what I might have done to him had Coach Oakley not come over to break things up.

"Barkley, what the hell is going on?"

"Coach, he keeps bugging me. He flicked my ear. He pushed me down twice and kept calling me a fag." I could hardly get the words out. I wanted to cry, but I couldn't. I knew I could not cry in front of the guys, especially not Coach Oakley.

Coaches Oakley and Renfro were now surrounding Mencer and helping him up.

"You motherfucker!" Mencer shouted. Coach Oakley ignored the cursing and asked him if he was okay and needed to go to the doctor. He said no and stormed off.

I waited for it, but Coach Oakley and Coach Renfro did nothing. Either they knew Mencer was a bully, or they considered calling someone a "fag" the ultimate Texas insult. I imagine they didn't think it was true about me but rather a mean-spirited way for Mencer to haze the new kid. Finally, my dad pulled up, Coach Renfro screamed, "Barkley, your ride is here," and I left. The coaches never mentioned anything again, nor did Justin Mencer. Texas justice at that time meant taking care of things in your own way. Today, I imagine we would've been shepherded off to the counselor, expelled from school, and then sent to some violence mitigation training. But in 1978 Texas, boys whipped each other's asses and hoped for the best, ignoring the rest.

Like with football, I was struggling to be average in academics. Athletics was my only "A" the first trimester, and everyone gets in an "A" in football. Thompson seemed to be so much farther along than South Houston. I was almost failing Math and had a "C" in all my other classes. When the second trimester began, I went to speech class. I credit that class and my speech teacher for bringing me back to life.

Ms. Moreau was a Cajun from Louisiana. The Cajuns descended from the earliest French settlers in Canada but were later expelled because of conflict between France and England. All I knew is Ms. Moreau was different, colorful, and took a liking to me. Her class was my oasis from everything else, where I felt capable, special, and confident. We learned persuasive speech, informative speaking, debate, and performed T.V. commercials. I realized the benefit of a school district that could afford something so sophisticated. Football and being called a fag became irrelevant.

Every year Ms. Moreau sponsored a talent show. I was still withdrawn and somewhat shy, but she chose me to be the Master of Ceremonies. The MC is the person who introduces the acts, warms up the audience with jokes, and keeps things moving. Ms. Moreau didn't even have me audition for the role. She decided I was the right person for the part. I was elated and scared to death.

I was shaking backstage before I had to go on. My thought was this is too much for me! I didn't want to make a fool of myself. I had enough teasing at school to last me and didn't want to give anyone reason to single me out. But the minute I got on the stage and looked at the audience, something changed in me. It was as if someone switched on a light in a darkened room. Electricity ran through my body every time I made people laugh. They not only laughed at the right places; they applauded. When I handed flowers to Ms. Moreau after each show, she smiled and gestured for me to take a bow.

Shortly after the talent show, a guest visited our class during one of my speeches. I noticed her taking notes. The woman, Ms. Copeland, was from the high school where I would be going the following year and oversaw a competitive speech team. She and Ms. Moreau were friends, and Ms. Copeland was scouting for the upcoming year. She asked me if I was interested in speech tournaments, and I didn't hesitate to say "yes."

Ms. Copeland took me out into the hallway and said, "Well, if you want to debate, I recommend that you learn to debate properly. It takes commitment if you want to win."

She anticipated my next question by telling me I needed to go to debate camp.

"The best debate camp in the state is Baylor University in Waco," she explained. "They hold a two-week debate camp every summer at the University." I know my eyes must have widened with excitement.

"You go to Baylor University," she continued, "and you stay there while they teach you how to debate, help you pick a topic, help you research the topic, and get you ready for the competitive season. If you want to be on my team, you need to be able to hit the ground running when you come to me in the fall. Do you think you would like to go?"

My excitement stopped when I realized something this great could not be free. The other students at my school didn't worry about such things as fees for extras, but we were still just scraping by.

I stood silently and then asked, "Does it cost?"

And she said, "Yes, there is a cost, and it can be a little expensive."

My heart sank as it had so many times before when something I wanted was out of my reach. We were doing better, but thoughts of going without were not far behind me.

The debate camp would cost four hundred dollars, which might as well have been a million. I left Ms. Copeland feeling excited but discouraged. I felt good that she thought I could be a competitor, but my status as a working-class kid was never more apparent. Kids like me would not be Olympic runners; we couldn't even afford to go to Baylor debate camp.

Later that day, Ms. Moreau called me to the front office and handed me a note to give to my dad. She had sealed it in an envelope so I couldn't read what it said. I gave it to Dad as soon as I got home. I watched Dad read the note as I waited in the kitchen.

Dad read it a few times, looked up, and called me into the living room, where he was sitting smoking a cigarette and drinking a beer. "You know what this is about?" he asked. I had trouble gauging his reaction. He seemed surprisingly calm but may have looked troubled; Dad had a good poker face.

"Your teacher says you got a shot at winning some competitions on the debate team next year," he said. "That true?"

"I guess so," I replied. I didn't know how to feel or react.

"You guess so?" he said sternly. "If you only guess so, I guess I won't call her."

I took the bait. "Dad, she says I got a good chance as a competitor. But she says I need to learn to debate properly to hit the ground running in the fall. She said at Baylor, they will teach me what I need to know about everything." Then I let my true feelings show. "Dad, I am good at this. I think I can be a winner."

Dad smiled slightly and told me to get in the car. Unfortunately, we still did not have a phone of our own. Dad said it was too expensive for something so inconvenient, but it was also a way to avoid creditors, so we had to go to the payphone at the convenience store. I waited in the car while Dad used the phone with his back turned to me so I couldn't see his expression or read his lips. I had no idea what my fate would be.

Dad returned to the car with a Miller Lite tallboy. We sat in the parking lot for a few minutes when he said, "You know, this teacher of yours wants you to go to this debate camp. So does the high school teacher, but it costs over $400 when you count the extras they will probably add." My Dad did not say anything else but drove home. I figured the conversation was over, so I dropped it.

Two weeks later, my dad came home and said, "I have to go to the phone again to call that lady, Ms. Copeland. She sent me a letter wanting me to call her, so I will."

When Dad returned from the payphone, he motioned for me to sit with him. He didn't say anything immediately, which made me wish he would get it over with.

"Do you want to go to this Baylor Debate Camp?" he asked. Of course, he already knew the answer, but he seemed to be testing my resolve. It wouldn't have been the first time I lost interest in something, like the Spanish guitar he bought me in sixth grade.

"Yes, Dad," I answered enthusiastically. If there was any chance at all, I wanted to take it. "I want to debate, and I want to go to debate camp," I added.

"Okay. If that is what you want, I've managed to save some money, and even though it will take it all, I'll do it." I practically gasped. "Besides, Ms. Copeland and Ms. Morrow are kicking in what I can't scrape up. Those two women believe in you as much as I do, so you are going."

For the first time in a long time, or maybe since I could remember, I spontaneously threw my arms around my dad, and he embraced me back.

"Okay, okay," he added. "Just do a good job and we will all be happy. You know Dad loves you, Bub."

The kids at Baylor Debate Camp were unlike any other kids I'd been around. They were intense, confident, and highly competitive. You would never have known they were 14-year-olds. There were moments when I felt I was not even in the same league as them. The attendees were from as far away as El Paso and Amarillo, but most kids were from Dallas and Houston.

The practice competitions were challenging, and I did not distinguish myself, but I thought I might be a regular guy for the first time since my time with Trina. I met a beautiful mixed-race fourteen-year-old girl named Beverly who pursued me, making it easy for me to overcome my shyness. I liked her and was impressed with her intelligence, but the best thing about her was her experience. We walked together by a creek on the Baylor campus and she grabbed my hand. I had held hands with Trina and even shared a few pecks on the lips, but this felt different. We sat by the water and she kissed me, held her lips on mine, and opened her mouth. When she slipped her tongue past my teeth, I felt like it was touching my penis. I had never had an erection because of a girl. After that day, we hung out together every night, but we never got much beyond French kissing, even though she was sending me clear signals that she wanted me to touch her.

I had a crush on Beverly, but I think the appeal was the comments the other guys would make when they saw me. I am sure they figured we were doing much more than kissing and holding hands. Beverly was beautiful, and any fourteen-year-old would love to kiss her. The reality was I shared a room with a handsome straight boy, and I was nursing a big crush on him. I was terrified to even look at another guy unless I was positive no one would catch me. I wanted to start high school with at least the debate team thinking I was the guy who had scored with the beautiful Beverly rather than the repressed and confused homosexual whose only outlet was fantasy and masturbation.

Baylor debate camp was run by the university but relied upon the speech and drama teachers to chaperone. Rodrigo was a speech and drama teacher from South Texas, and David Reina was Clear Lake High School's speech coach, both of whom were chaperones on my floor. When I met Rodrigo, I felt unsettled because when he introduced himself, his handshake lingered, and there was something odd in how he looked at me. The chaperones would check the rooms each night to ensure we were all inside by a 10:00 p.m. curfew. Rodrigo, not David, always came to ours. He would sit on my bed and ask questions about what was happening with my assigned debate case.

One night, he insisted that I come by his room to pick up an article he said would be helpful for me. Although he made me uncomfortable, I did not think anything of it. After all, he was a teacher and a responsible adult. Rodrigo opened the door slightly after my knock. I could see that he had a towel wrapped around him.

"I just got out of the shower," he said. He quickly added, "But it's okay, you can come inside," when he saw me turn to leave. Before I could say, "I'll come back later," he reached over to his desk for the article with his right hand while his left hand allowed the towel to drop. He brought the paper closer to me.

At this point, Rodrigo was naked and didn't acknowledge the inappropriateness of what was happening. He continued talking as if nothing was wrong and said, "I want to help you. Here's the article I told you about." Rodrigo put the article in front of me and placed his left hand on my shoulder, gently and firmly, and pulled me to him. He was totally and completely naked. I could not help but look at his naked body and his erection. I didn't know whether to be frightened or aroused. As he pulled me closer, he said, "You can come by anytime you like."

I felt my mind going into a tunnel. Adults frightened me, to begin with, and I had never seen a man his age naked and hard. I didn't feel disgusted, but I did feel paralyzed and entirely out of control. My mind raced as his arm grew tighter around me.

As if God intervened, we both heard loud talking outside his room. Rodrigo shared a room with the other chaperone, who walked in before Rodrigo could completely cover himself with his towel. The other chaperone, David Reina, saw what was happening and seemed to glare at Rodrigo. Maybe this had occurred other times at other camps, but all the coach said was, "Son, it's almost curfew. Go to your room, please." I bolted out of there like lightning.

I felt sick after what happened with Rodrigo. It was one thing to experiment with Gerry or to sneak a peek at some guys in a shower, but this made me feel vulnerable and gross. It felt like I had been violated, and I didn't understand why.

Before I returned to my room, I went to the payphone to call my dad. I wanted to go home even though I had met Beverly and was learning a lot about debate. I had to call a neighbor to get Dad, so it took a while. By then, I was almost in tears, and I am sure he could hear it in my voice.

"What's the matter, Bub?" he asked, very concerned. Of course, he would have killed Rodrigo if I had told him the truth. But I also felt ashamed that he might figure out my tendencies and think it was my fault.

"Dad, I want you to come to get me," I said.

"You know I will always help you if you need it, but everybody has a bad day now and then," he said. I am sure he thought I was frustrated with the challenges and hard work.

"It's important that you be there and do these things so that you can be ready for the fall," he said. "But I will come to get you if you want me to come to get you. Do you want me to come to get you, Son? I will do it."

I calmed down knowing my dad would be willing to get me even though we had spent all that money. Suddenly I felt stronger with him on my side. I was never going to tell him the real reason I wanted to leave. For now, he would think I was having a bad day, and he had succeeded in making me feel better, safer, so I decided to stay.

The next day Coach Reina announced, "Coach Rodrigo had to go home because of some 'personal matters.'"

CHAPTER 15

FAGS AND FAIRIES

After a fitful night of memory flashes, I returned to the hospital to visit my dad. It was his second day of recovery, so he was more rested and alert. When I entered the room, he was holding a pillow up to his chest and coughing.

"It's nothing," he said. "Just clearing my lungs, Bub."

"Are you in pain?" I asked, placing my hand over his.

"Not too bad," he said, gesturing to his IV. "They still have me on some good drugs."

He looked better but worried. I was not sure what was troubling him.

"Bub, you know, no one knows you better than Dad. You have a lot on your mind lately." I laughed silently to myself at the thought of how little he knew.

"Well, you damn near died of a heart attack, Dad!" I said. Of course, I was devastated that he could have died, but my thoughts were more about me than him if I was honest with myself.

"It's something else," Dad added. I wondered if the drugs were giving him an added sense of empathy. Suddenly I felt vulnerable and tempted to share everything on my mind. He was giving me a perfect segway.

I breathed in hard and said, "I'm just thinking about our time here in Texas. Everything changed when we moved here. Today just reminded me of our history and some unfinished business."

Dad's face turned serious. He scowled and said, "Unfinished business?" My mind raced and put a halt to my gears. This discussion would have to wait. It wasn't the time or place.

"Yes, Dad," I said. "But don't worry about it. Just legal stuff for you and Mom. We can get to it when you are home." I had bullshitted my way out of a confrontation once again but I did not feel triumphant. I felt cowardly.

At that moment, Edwin walked in. "Your dad is a strong one. If all goes well tonight, he should get out of here by tomorrow."

"You mean I will be sprung?" Dad said sarcastically. When Edwin left the room, Dad made a face that reminded me how much he didn't like gay men, especially if they were effeminate.

There were so many close calls during high school that I was surprised Dad didn't figure out I was gay for himself. The situation with Coach Rodrigo was certainly not my fault, but it made me concerned about how much people could assume about me. I didn't want my dad to know I was gay; I wanted him to be proud of me. Of course, that would be more difficult now that I wasn't doing what he thought would make me a "man."

The Baylor debate camp changed me, and I was excited about the competitive debate season. High school would allow me to start over by doing something that gave me confidence. J. Frank Dobie High School had a very competitive speech and debate team, and I knew it would take up my time. The speech and debate team were taken to tournaments almost every weekend in the fall and early spring. This schedule directly interfered with Friday night high school football, making it impossible for me to play even if I wanted to. But I wanted to do something where I felt like I could succeed, where I could win. I knew that football wasn't for me anymore.

Breaking it to Dad wasn't as easy as I thought. Even though he paid for debate camp, I don't think he realized it would become an either-or proposition.

"Bub, you're a good football player," he said with genuine disappointment. "You're disciplined and smart."

But I stood my ground. "Dad, I wasn't first string in eighth grade, and I won't be in ninth. I want to focus on where I can be a success, and that's not football."

Dad said nothing, which felt worse than if he had yelled at me. I couldn't tell him that I also didn't want to face another season of showers with the boys. I needed to play it straight and thought the debate team would make that easier.

I couldn't have been more wrong.

At first, all I focused on was winning. My first medal was third place in Novice Speaker Points in debate, but it might have been a gold medal at the Olympics. Walking across the stage to applause was thrilling.

I went to debate and speech competitions every weekend. Some of my teammates also competed in drama events such as prose reading, poetry, and dramatic and humorous interpretation as well as duet acting. They were a different crowd than those of us called forensic debaters, as we mainly focused on persuasive arguments and research topics. One of the "drama people" was an effeminate-behaving junior named Tony. I am unsure if he pronounced his "gayness" to anyone, but he didn't try to hide it either. He was flamboyant and emotional and had stereotypical gay mannerisms. I wonder if I sent off some pheromone of gayness because Tony immediately decided we would be friends. I was intrigued and repulsed at the same time.

I knew he had a crush on me and took advantage of it, but I never hinted at a reciprocal attraction. There wasn't one. Tony wasn't my type. People are under the misconception that all gay people like each other just because they're gay. What I liked about Tony was he gave me rides to the tournaments. He could be fun and liked to drink and smoke cigarettes. It was with Tony that I tasted Boone's Farm apple wine and got drunk for the first time since the bayou.

Tony had a driver's license, a car, and a fake ID, which made him a good friend to everybody. He smoked Benson & Hedges menthol cigarettes and didn't mind buying me a pack of Marlboros when he bought them. Tony always had the money for beer, sickeningly sweet Boone's Farm, or something even cheaper and nastier. He was a perfect friend, except for the constant sexual flirtation he sent my way.

Tony also made me uncomfortable if we were around other people because of his persona. I didn't want any guilt by association; I was still fighting my attraction to guys. Seeing Tony behave the way he did made me more resolved to be heterosexual, even if it killed me.

One day, in April 1980, I asked Tony to take me to a Ronald Reagan rally at the Hyatt Regency in downtown Houston. I had never been to such a fancy hotel and was surprised to see at least 800 people waiting for the presidential hopeful. The crowd differed from the people I remember campaigning for Jimmy Carter back in North Carolina. These people were wealthy looking and seemed successful. Reagan's message was patriotic and upbeat and I was swept away by his persuasion. The crowd cheered when he walked to the podium. The room was electrified with enthusiasm and applause as he said, "Now is the time to realize we don't care if the world likes us or not. We've got to do what's right for us." At that moment, my loyalties totally shifted. I decided, "To hell with Jimmy Carter; I'm a Reaganite now."

Reagan represented all my aspirations. I was interested in politics and government and felt I was a proud patriot. I wanted to go far, and he would be my role model.

The crowd was ecstatic, and so was I. Then came the question-and-answer section of the night. After several innocuous questions, a quintessential Texas woman with big frosty hair approached the mic. Her makeup was perfect, and her perfume wafted through the air as she walked by.

She said, "Guv—enor, what is your feeling on homosexuals teaching children in the schools?"

I immediately felt kicked in the stomach and self-conscious. I knew I could pass better than Tony, but I always had the irrational feeling that people could know my gayness by some beacon emanating from my aura. It would only be visible to bigots, religious fanatics, and straight people.

Reagan didn't hesitate before he replied, "I do not, nor will I ever condone the homosexual lifestyle. I can assure you that no administration of mine will ever provide 'special rights to homosexuals!'" Then, as if that wasn't enough, he said, "That culture and lifestyle is harmful to our people and our country."

I wanted to run out the door, but I knew that would be the ultimate admission. So instead, Tony and I walked silently to his car. I could see he was hurt by what he heard. I tried to believe it didn't apply to me and strengthened my resolve not to be gay.

Finally, Tony said, "I would not vote for him."

"I would," I said.

Tony just scowled. I believed Reagan was right. The gay lifestyle was not good for America. A guy being with a guy was an abomination in the eyes of God. He was right; it said so in the Bible, at least how they taught us at church. I just had to get past these feelings. I had to get past these desires to be with a guy. I needed to get over it, move through it, get past it!

My support for Reagan didn't deter Tony from making overt sexual advances on me the next time we drove together and stayed overnight for a tournament. The school set us up as roommates and I couldn't tell the coach why I had objections. When we were alone, Tony tried to seduce me. Of course, I resisted by acting like I had no idea what he was doing. I knew I liked guys but did not want to be involved with Tony, even behind closed doors. I had decided not to be gay and did not want him to think I was. I had it all figured out.

Tony was also the kind of guy that I did not trust. It was no secret Tony wanted a lover and an ally. He was looking for someone to have sex with and to point to as "also gay."

If I told Tony I was attracted to guys, he would tell everybody. So not only did I need to ignore his advances, but I also had to keep my secret. We couldn't be friends beyond the superficial. Another good thing was although I was a teenager, and my hormones were going crazy with desire; I did not want Tony. I wasn't attracted to him. There was no chemistry, so it helped me stay straight around him. After a while, I think I had him convinced, so he backed off a bit.

During that first year of high school, Dad proudly secured a job at ICI chemical plant in Pasadena, Texas. ICI manufactured paraquat, which is a toxic chemical widely used as an herbicide. Paraquat is similar to Agent Orange, the chemical weapon used in Vietnam. Most places have banned paraquat as it's toxic and harmful to humans. Dad was oddly proud he made a dangerous chemical about to be banned. It was hazardous work, but the job was steady, and so was the pay.

Dad was busy and had lost interest in my activities since I wasn't playing football. It was just as well. I did encourage him to attend a joint parent-teacher night for members of the speech and drama clubs. Although it was for the parents, a few students were selected to perform a duet acting scene, a poetry presentation and a mini-debate. I did not attend as I was not one of the performers but I thought he would be impressed. I wanted him to take an interest in what I was doing.

When Dad returned home from the parent-teacher night, he grabbed a beer, lit a cigarette, and sat in his chair, shaking his head. I couldn't determine if his expressions were amusement, confusion, or pride.

"Bub, I just don't know what to say," he finally said with a grin. "That little parent-teacher night you sent me to was a circus. I mean a fucking circus!" He took a short drag, "Bub, I met two teachers; I couldn't tell you their names. One was Looney Tunes, and the other one was a dingbat. Bub, a dingbat!"

"What do you mean?" I tried to interject. Dad talked over me.

"Bubba, all the boys up there were fairies or fags. I'm not sure which. I'm a little worried about that place."

I had gotten used to seeing Tony, but many other performers and teachers were equally flamboyant even if they were straight. It went with the creative territory. At that moment, I realized my dad had been a sheltered man from small-town North Carolina and hadn't had much exposure to the different types of people in Texas. He used to complain to Mom and anyone who would listen that he longed to get away from the small-mindedness of Statesville, but he now seemed to be their representative.

"I guess you just met all the drama people," I told him. "That's not the speech team."

Dad just looked at me, "I hope that's the case, Bub, because tonight was concerning!" That was all he said. After that, I was never able to interest him in any speech or debate activities again.

◆ ◆ ◆

I was 15 years old and that summer, I developed an intense sexual fantasy life. As the heat and humidity of the Houston summer escalated, so did my desires. I reasoned it was okay to fantasize about guys if I didn't act upon those feelings. I could still be an upstanding American, successful, strong, and good, as defined by Ronald Reagan. Not an easy task when I walked past construction sites in my neighborhood and saw shirtless Latin guys glistening in the sun. I was going nuts!

Tony dropped by my house with his mother during the first month of summer. He introduced her to my dad, who had come outside to see who was at the door.

"I overheard you say you were looking for some summer work," Tony said. I wasn't sure when he would have heard me, but it was true. I was always looking for ways to make money when school was out.

Tony's mom spoke to my dad. "I manage some apartments near the university, and my son Tony is going to paint for me. It is too big a job for one boy, so he recommended your son."

Dad looked skeptically at Tony, someone he had probably seen perform at the parent-teacher night, but his mom seemed nice and normal enough, so he agreed. He hated to see me idle, and it paid well for three or four days of work.

The next day, Tony picked me up and we drove to the apartment. The place was huge. The first day went fine, but the fumes got to me on the second.

We were not ventilating correctly, and I felt dizzy and nauseous. Finally, it became so bad that I needed to lie down. There was a bed in the apartment, so I went to lie down to stop the room from spinning. I dozed off into a light sleep and then felt the bed move.

Tony had crawled in next to me as I pretended to sleep. I thought about how in a bear attack, you play dead until the predator goes away. Instead, Tony drew close and wrapped his arms around me. I cringed as I felt him place a small kiss on my ear.

Then I heard him whisper, "Michael Tate Barkley, please love me." I could feel his erect penis against me. I was wearing my clothes, a tank top, and light shorts, but I could feel him. I stayed still, not wanting to become accidentally aroused. I moved away from him and feigned waking up. Tony was completely naked and just looked at me and smiled.

"Tony, come on, man," I said, pushing him away. "It's not going to happen; I am not gay," I protested. "Let's just go paint."

Tony gesticulated a "So-rr-y," put his hands in the air, and backed away. I hoped that put an end to it.

About two weeks later, around midnight, a car drove by our house, and someone yelled, "Barkley's a fag." I knew it was Tony as I caught a glimpse of his fender as he sped away. He had enlisted a friend to help him cut up a bunch of paper to dump in our yard as he proclaimed my sexual orientation, sounding like a scorned lover.

My Dad was livid. I was only grateful that I had trusted my gut about Tony and stood my ground with him. Even though I was not attracted to him, my hormones were vulnerable and might have given in had I not decided to stop being gay.

I went to Tony's house the next day to confront him. I must have looked furious because he seemed genuinely frightened.

"It was just a stupid joke," he insisted. "A prank. I didn't mean anything by it. No harm done."

"You're lucky my father didn't come here to straighten you out," I said. "He didn't think it was so funny."

Much to Tony's credit, he went to my house and apologized to my dad.

Tony said, "I was teasing Michael Tate. I don't think he's gay. I'm sorry for the embarrassment."

My dad was surprisingly gracious, but I think more than anything he was relieved.

CHAPTER 16

ROB AND RAPTURE

"I'll be here tomorrow, Dad," I said as I left his hospital room. "Maybe I can drive you home. Won't that be great?"

"Sure," he said. I could see he was getting restless but needed another night to recuperate. I'm sure he didn't want to admit it, but despite his feminine ways, Edwin was an attentive nurse who ensured Dad had everything he needed. Dad had a huge scare, and nurturing and reassurance was what he needed. I was grateful to leave for the night because my feelings were too mixed up for me to have patience with him. I was afraid I would say something that would open a conversation I wasn't ready to finish.

As I drove to my house, I thought about calling my sponsor but decided not to. I wasn't feeling like drinking at that moment, but I felt sentimental and close to tears. In therapy and the program, I learned about sitting with feelings and looking at them objectively to see what they might tell me. So many memories were emerging, but not all were bad.

❖ ❖ ❖

During my sophomore year, my dad had fewer opportunities to make sideways comments about the people on the speech team because I stopped hanging around with Tony. Dad never suspected that I had fended off Tony's advances only to meet a guy from another team who became my lover. We met as adversaries, but I immediately noticed a look in his eyes. Rob was an enigma, which only made me more attracted to him. I had no real "gaydar" at the time, but there was something I sensed in him that made me wonder.

Rob and I were thrown together for the last competition of the year.

Although we were in different high schools, we shared the same school district, which had us all travel together to other parts of the state. So Rob invited me to spend the night and ride with him to the competition. Dad showed no concern because Rob looked like a regular guy. That night I had my answer when we shared a bed. The attraction was palpable as we caressed each other's hands with our fingers. I was nervous and excited and grateful that nothing further happened that night.

At the beginning of summer before my junior year, Rob asked if I wanted to go to the beach. We went with a group of friends, but it didn't take long for us to find a private spot. I am sure the others noticed, but no one seemed to care. Rob and I lay in the sun on the same beach towel with our bodies touching one another as we soaked up the sun. We drank from the same Coke can and smothered each other in suntan lotion. Every movement was a sensual act of seduction that I didn't want to resist. We drank Coke, smoked cigarettes, listened to the transistor radio, and played in the water.

The ocean became a blanket of privacy where we could touch and explore. We held each other closely under the water, our bodies intertwined in ways others could not see. The intimacy was different than it had been with Gerry. Rob was gay, and our foreplay was beyond two twelve-year-olds in the first blush of puberty.

Rob invited me to spend the night again; this time, I knew what might happen.

We ate an early dinner with his family, and Rob helped his mom clean up while I went to take a shower. I let the water flow over my body and took extra care to wash while I fantasized about Rob with me in the ocean.

As I imagine anyone does before a hot date, especially a forbidden one, I washed and brushed my teeth, using mouthwash and a slight amount of aftershave. I thought it ironic that the aftershave was a gift from Trina from a Valentine's Day long ago in North Carolina. When I had finished and dressed, Rob popped his head into his room, smiled, and said he was taking a shower too. I liked the way he smiled at me.

There were a lot of people in Rob's house that evening. His sister was home from college with a friend also spending the night. They tried to engage us in a game of Monopoly, but I casually mentioned I had a sunburn, which allowed Rob to move us into the bedroom. He had me lay on the bed with my shirt off and rubbed lotion on my back. Then, when Rob was sure no one could see, he moved his hand down to my lower back. When he slathered me all over, he said, "Your turn," and took my place on the bed.

Rob was on his stomach, and the door was mostly closed. I squeezed the lotion in my hand and gently spread it across his shoulders and down his smooth, tan back. Before I could finish, there was a knock on the bedroom door. We both jumped and put our shirts on even though no one other than us would have thought we were doing something wrong.

His sister gave us one last chance to join the board game fun, but Rob said, "No, not for me. The beach has worn me out. I'm ready to go to bed soon, but thanks for the invite."

She said, "It's only 8:30! But, okay." I always wondered if she figured out why we wanted to be left alone.

After politely saying our goodnights, we returned to the bedroom and chatted about the day and the upcoming speech and debate season. In my head, I was getting frustrated because we were in that undefined place of will we or won't we. However, I didn't want to face rejection if I had misinterpreted his intentions, so I put my head on the pillow and drifted off to sleep.

I realized Rob felt the same frustration because he gently shook me awake and asked, "Are you awake?" We were touching.

I put my arm around him, "Are you okay?" Rob then pushed me from my side to my back and kissed me passionately. It happened so fast I hardly opened my mouth.

As I felt his lips on mine, I could feel his hand on my now hard penis. He held it in his hand, outside of my underwear. I wasn't ready for his kiss, so I was hesitant. Finally, he pulled his hand away and started to roll over so I grabbed his hand, put it back on my body, and whispered, "Rob, I want to," and placed his hand inside my underwear. It was heaven!

Soon after, I gently moved on top of him, "Shh, they're just in the next room. I don't want them to hear us," he said. We both laughed softly and continued caressing and kissing. Then we decided to go to sleep. We hadn't made love, but we had explored each other.

As we drifted off into a relaxed and satisfying sleep, he nudged me and said, "I forgot to kiss you goodnight."

He rolled over and gave me a long, slow, and sensual kiss. We rubbed against each other until we both felt me ejaculate. I was in rapture and wanted to stay that way, but Rob quickly turned the lights on, so we could clean up and hide evidence of our sins. Then, as I expected from a fellow Texan, he said, "Mike, we can't tell anyone about this."

"I know," I replied, hurling myself back to earth. I saw the look of stress on Rob's face and said, "Please, let's just not talk about it."

The following day I felt unsettled. I didn't feel ashamed, it felt right, but Rob was so worried. It reminded me how much we each had to lose if word got out. I trusted him to keep our secret, but I also knew the secret would prevent us from being together again.

Rob was very dedicated. He wanted to go to college and then law school. He was intelligent and ambitious, and so was I. We both knew you did not get out of Pasadena Independent School District with great recommendations as gay boys. That was just reality.

That first time with Rob was one of the only times I had sex without any alcohol involved. He would be the only man I would have sex with without alcohol until I got clean in 1999.

Four days after that Saturday night, Rob still hadn't called me, nor had I called him. I was going nuts! I did not want to seem too eager like I was some desperate horny homosexual, but I was dying to know if he wanted it to happen again. So finally, Wednesday night, I broke down and called him. We chatted about bullshit for several minutes.

Rob went silent, and I could hear the upset in his voice.

"Are you okay?" I asked.

"I know we said we wouldn't talk about it," he replied, "but I can't stop thinking about it."

"Do you want it to happen again?" I asked.

"Yes, but I'm scared," he answered softly.

"Me too."

We hung up the phone. I couldn't sleep that night thinking about Rob and weighing the risks. When I was sure everyone in the house was asleep, I looked at myself in the mirror and talked to myself out loud.

You can't lose yourself in this. You can't lose who you are. You have to balance all this, Michael Tate. I stepped back and looked at my reflection. I had been taking good care of myself and was no longer the chubby little kid I was in Statesville. I was becoming a man. But my thoughts would not let me enjoy the moment.

"Don't lose yourself," I said aloud. "Don't you tip over into being gay."

I believed I could be a little bit gay and not give in to my natural inclinations. All I needed to do was be disciplined and cautious. My dad got me a car that summer, and he also got me a shit job at a tool grinding shop. So I had some extra money, transportation, and a secret boyfriend. Rob and I came up with excuses to spend the night at his house, but we made sure it wasn't more than every other week.

I also decided it would be a good idea for me to date a girl. I was elected class president my sophomore year and was planning on running for re-election my junior year. Expectations were that guys like me needed a girlfriend. So I pursued a girl named Jodie before the end of the school year. Jodie had won the honor of "Valentine Dance Princess," and as girls went, she was cute and very smart. I also heard she had her eyes on becoming class president, so as ambitious as I was, I introduced myself in the hallway and asked for her number.

I asked Jodie out on a date, and we went to a popular place called Luther's BBQ. When I took her home, we made out in her driveway.

Jodie lived in a single-parent home, and her mother preferred Jodie's friends gather at their house even if they were doing things they shouldn't. She knew we would find a way to drink and smoke but felt safer if we did not drink and drive. So if any of us was too wasted, we were always allowed to crash at her place.

Although I desired Rob, I liked Jodie. I loved her intelligence and humor. Once we were dating, Jodie regularly invited me over to hang out and party with her friends. They were a group of cool nerds and heavy drinkers. I was drinking more and more and fit right in with this bunch.

Everything worked fine with my clandestine visits with Rob and my dates with Jodie until one week when Rob asked me over and I told him I had plans. I was dating Jodie and trying to get physical. I wanted to be with Rob but made up my mind that I could not succumb to just homosexual sex. I couldn't. I might get lost. I told Rob that I could not spend the night that weekend, and I was truthful that I had a date with a girl. There was a pause, and Rob said he had to go.

I died when I heard him hang up the phone without a "goodbye." I thought he understood why I was seeing Jodie and didn't think about how it would make him feel. I wished I hadn't told him, but then I would be a liar. I ached, hurt inside, and questioned if I had done the right thing.

The following Sunday evening, Rob stopped by my house. There was nothing odd about it to anyone else, just two school friends getting together, but we were uncomfortable as we sat in some lawn chairs outside. It was a typical sticky, humid Gulf Coast night. Rob looked down at first and then looked up at me. "I know we said we were not going to talk about this, but I have to talk about it, because I'm dying on the inside. Do you like this girl? Are you two going to be a thing? Are we done?"

I felt awful, but I told him, "I need to date girls! I cannot give up on that part of me, Rob!" He turned away. "You know I am right, but that does not change us."

I reached over and held Rob's hand in the dark. My sisters had gone to bed, Dad was watching TV, and Mom was cleaning inside the house. I knew no one would come outside, so I took a chance. I said, "Rob, you are so important to me, the most important thing to me. She has nothing to do with us. Nothing!"

Rob looked at me, "Okay."

I stood up and pulled him close, and at that moment, I didn't care who might see. I did what was in my heart. I gave Rob a long, sensual kiss right in my driveway. I was making a statement to him.

Jodie and I tried to date, but we both knew it would never be more than friendship. I don't think she questioned my sexuality. She and I just worked better as friends.

Daydreaming about Rob was a dangerous distraction from the job Dad found for me at a tool grinding shop. My job was to take a sanding brush to the burnt portion of various machine tools, soak them in acid, and put them in soda water. Then I would dump them into a super-hot wax to provide a coat of protection around the precise drilling ends. This way, the edges would be safe and remain sharp for shipping. I cut and burned myself so many times that summer that I couldn't count. Nevertheless, the job helped me maintain the image of a good little redneck, and I even hung out with my dad and his friends, all of whom were good old boys.

I smoked cigarettes when my dad was not around, and I dipped Copenhagen snuff when he was. For some odd reason, my dad let me dip, but he wouldn't let me smoke. My dad would let me drink beer with him and his friends every now and then, but that was a rarity. I usually worked and fetched beer for him and his friends when they were hanging out in the driveway. But when I was not around Dad, I drank beer all the time on the weekends. I made friends with some of the young guys at work who were old enough to buy alcohol. They had no qualms about buying beer and cigarettes for me. This additional source allowed me to drink during the week too.

Even though I made a statement to Rob, I was still determined to not allow my increasingly intimate and growing relationship with him turn me into a gay guy. I was hell-bent on acting the part of a straight, masculine good 'ole boy. I had convinced myself Rob was an aberration for me. He would be, for this moment in time, a summer fling.

I also rationalized that our physical relationship was just a manifestation of our special friendship, nothing more. Rob understood me. Like me, he was a young Republican who wanted to be an attorney, who wanted to be a great success. We both wanted to rise above the refineries and the jobs available to people like us. We both dreamed of affluence and possible political careers in Texas, so being gay was not an option.

I would have kept things low-key and occasional, but then my Aunt Sis died. Dad decided to drive us to North Carolina for the funeral, but I didn't want to be away for two weeks. As sad as I was for losing my dear aunt, I didn't want to go back to Statesville and Barkley Road for any length of time. I also sensed an opportunity. I told my Dad I didn't want to be away from work for so long, so he let me fly back home right after the funeral. That meant I would have the house to myself for a week, including an entire weekend.

When I returned, Rob and I schemed for him to stay with me. He would come over after work in the evenings, but we both knew we had a weekend coming up with no interruptions. By Friday, Rob came straight to me after work. We had the house, just the two of us, and the intensity and the escalation of the sex had hit a heightened pace and forged into new territory. It was great, but overwhelming.

When Rob woke up that Saturday morning, we talked. I was in my dad's recliner, and he was on the couch. After 30 minutes of chatting, I got up and headed to him to be affectionate. But he caught me off guard by holding his hand up to stop me.

"Can we be friends the rest of the weekend? I'm afraid we're doing it too much."

Since I had deluded myself into thinking I was the good 'ol boy and straight guy, I said, "Sure, Rob." I felt embarrassed and a bit rejected.

I was still horny. I wanted sex. Everything felt weird now, and I didn't know what to do.

In the early afternoon, Dad called. He told me that my cousin John, Uncle Roy's son, had fallen on hard times, and he would be coming to Houston soon. I asked, "When?" All he could say was a vague, "Later in the week, I think." John was a heavy drinker like all the Barkley men, with a DWI or two, along with the job losses. He was coming to Houston and staying with us. I cringed. Three separate relatives had lived with us and used my room to "get on their feet," and now it was John's turn. Dad was now a supervisor at the ICI plant and could get people a job on his crew or another part of the plant. John was next.

Putting John out of my mind, I made every effort to respect Rob's feelings and have fun. We went to the movies, picked up a pizza, and talked. Saturday night, Rob went to my room to sleep, and I hesitated to join him. I had a small bed, so it was an effort not to touch him. I wanted to respect his feelings. I laid down, and I gently whispered good night. Rob leaned over, kissed me, and said, "We can at least kiss goodnight." I said nothing.

Rob made the next move, which led to a night of passion. We fell asleep in each other's arms, and at 7:00 a.m. I heard a pounding on the door. I was confused and answered the door in my underwear. My cousin, John, excitedly walked into the house, ready to start his new life. I explained that I had a friend over, hugged him, and apologetically ran back to the bedroom where I knew Rob was still naked in my bed.

I guess I wasn't thinking because Rob and I both walked out of the bedroom without shirts and in our underwear. John said, "Morning."

Rob and I quickly excused ourselves and got dressed. When we went back out to visit with him, John looked at me with a puzzled expression. I figured he didn't know what he didn't know. When Rob left, John and I went to the convenience store to get a 12-pack of Miller Lite and a pack of Marlboro Reds. We lifted the garage door, pulled out the lawn chairs, iced down the beer, cranked up the country music, and sat in the driveway drinking.

After about three beers a piece, John looked at me and said, "Bubba, thanks for making me feel welcome. I didn't mean to mess up your good time!" John grinned at me and hit me on the arm, just like when we were kids. I wasn't fooling anybody. John knew what was going on. I was lucky he was a good 'ole boy with a talent for keeping secrets.

Nothing was the same with Rob after that.

As the summer ended, the conflicting emotions in my relationship with Rob became more evident. Rob's rejection or pushback against sex during our weekend was a decided shift in our relationship. My guilt became too strong, and coming so close to getting caught made me swear to myself I wouldn't act on my impulses again.

Increasingly, we were dismissive and passive aggressive with each other. It seemed everything was getting complicated. But as a 16-year-old boy, I vowed to repress my desires thinking that would resolve my conflict.

I always knew I had to focus on getting into college. Dad wanted me to go, and all my friends would be going. By my junior year, I knew I wanted to be a lawyer. But first, I would be facing the PSAT and SAT. Sadly, when the time came to take the PSAT, I drank heavily the night before and did not do well. This was a mistake I would repeat the night before my SAT. For some reason, I didn't see the connection between my choices and the outcome. Even in high school, my drinking was getting out of control. I was so afraid of failing, so afraid I couldn't get out of my dad's house and our incessant cycle of financial deprivation I was overwhelmed with anxiety. Alcohol was the only thing that I knew with certainty would calm my nerves.

No matter what I said in my head or proclaimed to the world, I always made an excuse to drink. By the close of my junior year, I was doing well in every respect except alcohol use and authenticity.

My grades were good during my senior year, enabling me to rationalize that my escalating drinking habits in high school did not affect them. I made straight A's for the first time in high school, mainly because I took no math or science classes. In addition, I received my SAT score: It wasn't great, but it was good enough to get into the University of Texas at Austin.

I was tired of being poor! I didn't want to follow in my father's footsteps. I needed to go to UT. I was going to major in business and go to law school. I had a plan. My high school honored me as a "Trailblazer," one of the top 20 students in the senior class. The students elected me "Most Likely to Succeed" on prom night, though for many years I loathed myself and looked at that trophy with disgust. I was always drinking and fantasizing about guys, but the fantasies were my secret.

◆ ◆ ◆

At the end of my senior year, I was selected by the school administration to be the commencement speaker. They demanded I be a good foot-soldier, and stick to an upbeat, patriotic script. On graduation night, the assistant principal said, "I have a .30-06 pointed at your head, boy. Go off the approved text and I'll put a bullet in you." I think he was half serious. You see, Pasadena ISD didn't like people going off script, and they certainly didn't like people with loose ideas.

"Are we heading in or heading out?" I opened with this quote from Bob Seger, asking my fellow classmates if we were looking to our past or anticipating our future on that night. As with all my speeches in those days, this one was filled with ideas of American exceptionalism. I assured the crowd that my classmates and I understood what was expected of us. In an escalating cadence, I spoke louder. "We know that duty, honor, freedom, country, and love are not mere clichés of generations past, but real responsibilities and precious rights." The crowd roared their applause. Ending the speech, I shouted, "To all my friends and classmates, 'Damn the torpedoes, full speed ahead,'" With that, 6,000 people rose to their feet and erupted in applause. I was in heaven.

I received three standing ovations that night. My high school principal slapped me on the back, saying, "Damn, boy, that was the best speech we ever had in this place!" I felt rapture, as good as the feeling that washed over me when Rob touched me for the first time. I'd performed the speech of a lifetime, but that's what it was a performance. I was an excellent foot-soldier and gave a rousing patriotic address that would not soon be forgotten. I loved the feeling of thunderous applause but knew the only way to continue along this path was to make sure no one ever found out who I was. So I became a divided self, with one side soothed only by alcohol and the other by self-deception.

CHAPTER 17

BURNT ORANGE HAZE

When I got home from visiting Dad at the hospital, I took out one of my early notebooks from the first time I tried to get sober. I read my notes from when I had taken myself to a local rehab facility because I had been drunk through most of New Year's Eve and the day after. Typically, I would've just considered this a good time. But when I'd woken up at noon, I was naked, and when I went into my kitchen to make coffee, I found beer cans strewn all over the house and MTV blaring on the television. The front door was wide open and my car was parked sideways in the front yard, with tire tracks torn through the lawn. I remembered nothing.

I put on some clothes and poured Bailey's Irish Cream into my coffee. I vowed to stay sober the rest of the day so I could be ready to go back to work, but I figured a bit of the "hair of the dog" would help. By this time, I was a successful lawyer with a thriving practice. I had my own beautiful house with a gym, an eight-person hot tub, and nice furniture. I was making a lot of money but decided maybe I needed to get my head straight.

I relaxed in front of the television, and although I had just told myself I shouldn't, I cracked open a beer. After all, it was a holiday. What was one beer going to hurt?

One beer turned into a six-pack, and a six-pack turned into a trip to the convenience store and two twelve-packs. When I returned to the television, there were ads about drinking. At first, I ignored them, but during an old movie, there was an ad that said, "Do you think you have a drinking problem?"

Two days later, I drove myself to Charter Hospital, an alcohol dependency treatment facility. I didn't believe I was an alcoholic, but I knew some things had become unmanageable. I figured a few days away from temptation would help me clear my head and make a plan. I went there knowing what I wanted to get out of it and I negotiated a fifty percent reduction on the cost for a seven-day stay. I wasn't like the other people I expected to meet there. I just needed to get away for a little while and do a reset.

I spent seven full days at Charter. It was like a mini vacation, and I felt physically better with a short detox. I got my head straight and wrote out everything I needed to do for my law practice during the times I was supposed to write about what brought me into the program. I set goals for my cases with timelines and wrote out plans for marketing and revenue growth. I loved being institutionalized and enjoyed the process of sharing and endlessly talking about myself without guilt or shame. I reasoned that I wasn't going to see these people again and never realized that I completely missed the point of being there.

At the end of the seven-day detox, many stayed for an additional 28 days for their sobriety program. I decided when I got there that I wouldn't. As I was leaving, one of the counselors stopped me.

"Detox is only the beginning," he told me, handing me a copy of the *Big Book of Alcoholics Anonymous*.

"I don't need this, but thank you," I said, trying to hand it back to him.

"Please take it as my gift," he insisted. "Alcoholism is a devious disease. If you ever feel out of control, this book has the answers. And we are always here for you."

I appreciated the gesture and his sincerity but knew I wouldn't even crack open the book. So I took it anyway and threw it in the trunk of my car where no one would see it. After that, I decided to try to stay sober to prove I could do it.

◆ ◆ ◆

Thumbing through the journal I wrote at Charter, I re-read one of the first exercises they gave us: "Write about your history of drinking." What stood out to me was how much I drank at the University of Texas. My friends tried telling me to slow down, but I couldn't. I was edgy and nervous if I wasn't drinking.

I began my journal by writing about my college friend Greg. When I first met Greg, a former high school baseball player, he was quiet and shy. But he was also strong, well-built, and intelligent. I wrote about him because of the countless times Greg would save me from my drunkenness and insanity. Greg could drink responsibly, but I could never stop at a few.

That is what I remember the most about college. Drinking was more fun because it seemed like every guy I met drank. There seemed to be parties everywhere, even during the week, but especially during football season— tailgates were one big party! I smoked cigarettes freely in the hallway, the lounge areas, and even in the classrooms. I felt like I was an adult.

Mom and Dad drove up the weekend before Thanksgiving my first year, and the three of us went to the Texas Tavern. Dad and I drank two pitchers of beer together, which was the first time he acknowledged me as a drinking buddy.

My reputation was building as a guy with an incredible capacity to drink and laugh. Sometimes the guys would call other people over to watch me chug. I loved the attention for something I already loved to do.

But my grades weren't great that first year and I knew I had to improve to attend law school. Still, the following year, I started doing crazy things while drunk. One of the guys in our dorm, Cowboy Bill, fancied himself a rodeo rider. We all used to laugh at him until he and his buddy invited us to enter an amateur rodeo down in Giddings, Texas. The entire floor of my dorm agreed. We all entered the Lee County Sheriff's Posse Amateur Rodeo. Cowboy Bill, me, and a bunch of the guys on our floor drove out there, got drunk, and signed up for the event. I rode my first bronco bull, I got 4.8 seconds on it until it threw me to the ground face-first and busted my lip, but somehow or another, based on metrics that I still don't understand, I got to ride again! I was too drunk and stupid to say no.

I rode again and got thrown in less than three seconds by a bull named "Lightning," landing smack on my face again, this time my forehead required stitches. I also had a small crack in my right wrist. There was a Country and Western dance after the rodeo. Despite my injuries, it was a hell of a party, but I don't remember much after that. That entire year was a blur.

Reading my journal brought back good memories. It made me miss some of my more exciting days before sobriety. But then I turned the page to something more embarrassing. I wished I hadn't written it down. I was compliant for the first few days at Charter and tried to do as they said. They wanted me to look closely at when things got out of control, so I did.

I had grown fond of whiskey at UT. I blamed it on my heritage and my great-grandmother, the moonshiner. Everyone knew her for the shine she made in the stills she kept on the Barkley land, but she wanted to be known for her high-quality whiskey. It was the best in Statesville, and people came from far and wide to have some. She would guard her whiskey and shine operations with a shotgun, so if she didn't know you or your kin, you were in for it. She was a hard woman and didn't tolerate fools. I liked to think I was celebrating my heritage even as I made a fool of myself.

I figure it must have been in my blood because I developed a taste for Mr. Jim Beam and had a bottle to myself during one of our keg parties. The music was loud and the people were everywhere. The next thing I remember is when I was shaken awake by an obnoxious guy who looked like a troll in my haze. He kept shaking me. I tried to hit him back but didn't make contact.

"Dude, you need to get up," he insisted.

As I roused myself, I sensed something caked on my face. The smell was horrific. I realized that I was waking up in my vomit. It was all over me, all over my bed. My door was open, and several guys were looking in to see. As I woke up, I was beyond embarrassed. I had also pissed in my bed for all the world to see. That had never happened to me before.

My roommate had passed out earlier, and the noise woke him up.

Worried and confused, he said, "My God, you okay?" He jumped up, pushed the other guys out, and quickly shut the door.

I got up, stripped off my soiled clothes, and washed myself in the shower. It took me all morning to air out and clean the room. It was the first time I was concerned about how much I drank.

Later that day, several guys dropped by my room after I had everything cleaned. The guy who had pushed me awake said, "You could choke to death on your own vomit if you drink like that. It might be best if you just stick with beer."

I also blamed the whiskey. This was my first complete blackout. I knew there were likely times I'd lost track of what was going on, but nothing like this. It scared me a bit, but it didn't scare me into not drinking.

Another time that concerned my friends and me was when we all went to Night in Old San Antonio. NIOSA, as it's known, is a San Antonio tradition. Every year, Texas has a fiesta in the Texas-Mexican style with music and dancing celebrating the uniqueness of Texas. I know that I drank Corona beer and margaritas most of the night. I remember an excellent Tejano band. But nothing else until I was face down in the grass with my hands cuffed and a big old black sheriff's deputy saying, "Settle down, son."

The deputy asked if I had someone to call. I don't remember what I said. I later learned I had entered the San Antonio Police Department recruitment trailer and made quite the scene. I have no idea why I picked the police recruitment trailer to be an asshole. I was cuffed face down on the ground. One of my friends came upon the situation and managed to talk them out of arresting me for public intoxication, resisting arrest, and being a drunk asshole.

My sophomore year in college was defined by the same trend of ever-escalating drinking. Before I went home to Houston for the summer, I went to one more party with Greg. It was great until I passed out on the sidewalk. A middle-aged woman woke me up and said, "Why don't you go to the party and get some food?" So instead, I got a beer and walked back outside.

The next thing I remember, a security guard woke me up on the folding table in the washeteria at the same apartment complex. Greg had left because he could not find me and assumed that I had gone home with somebody. Fortunately, the security guard lent me a quarter, and I found a payphone. I called Greg, who again came and picked me up.

I wrote in my journal about that summer. I couldn't find a job until I worked at a call center selling *USA Today* newspapers. I had a delightful time speaking with people on the phone, but I could not sell a subscription to save my life. Finally, on my fifteenth day of work, I sold a subscription to a gentleman from Arizona. When he confirmed the subscription on the phone, my supervisor quipped, "You must be Michael Tate's Grandpa, right?"

My supervisor at *USA Today*, a far-gone raging alcoholic, became my drinking buddy after hours. I wrote about him in my journal too, but I never put together that my future could be the same as his if I didn't stop drinking. I was just a kid, and he was 41 with linear cracks all over his face and a Lucky Strike filterless cigarette constantly hanging out of his mouth. With a raspy voice and standing at about 5 foot 4 inches weighing about 200 pounds, he had an unkempt, shaggy salt-and-pepper beard, hair to match, and his teeth were a hard yellow, turning brown. I thought of him as ancient, and with his hard living, he was. Since I was broke, he would always buy the beer.

I got a second job to pick up extra money on the side, calling people to sell piano tuning services. I would sit in my employer's spare bedroom that smelled like cat urine and use his phone to call people randomly and ask if they had a piano. The odds were one in three people did, and most of them needed their piano tuned, so this became my chief source of income. It was an awful summer, working two dead end jobs and continuing to repress my sex drive as best I could. It made me sad reading about this in my journal.

Before heading back to UT, Dad invited me to take a road trip with him to North Carolina. That summer, there was so much possibility for me to open up to him. We sat in the lawn chairs in the garage, and he said, "Bub, Dad can tell when you're down, you've been down for a while."

We both popped open a fresh Miller Lite. I lit a Marlboro for Dad and one for me. He had stopped giving me a hard time for smoking, another acknowledgment of my growth.

"You're not yourself, Bub. You haven't been home long, but I know when my son is not right."

We both took a couple of tugs from our cigarettes, I said, "Dad, I feel odd, a little down. I can't give a particular reason, but I do."

As I read the journal entry, I could see how much my younger self struggled. I wanted to come out to Dad and not keep up the charade. The sadness had been overwhelming because I still didn't have the guts to tell him the truth.

The following day I quit both of my little jobs. My drinking buddy boss at the call center was disappointed, as was the piano tuner. Dad was on furlough from his job at the time, so Mom and the girls were grateful I was getting Dad out of the house.

He and I became great travel companions, especially now that I could join him in his drinking. We packed up his 1976 Chevy El Camino with racing stripes and headed to North Carolina.

Dad and I road-tripped across the South, and we eventually made it to see my Uncle Phil's family in Elizabeth City, North Carolina, on the coast. I wrote about this in my journal because we all stayed up late drinking on the first night at Uncle Phil's. Uncle Phil loved his Kentucky Bourbon, so I loved some with him. Later, I was sleeping on a Baptist palette, a makeshift bed, on the floor in his front room, and I pissed all over myself during the night. I was mortified.

My Dad and Uncle Phil were very gracious. Yet again, I washed myself, my clothes, and the linens.

On the drive home, Dad said, "Bubba, I love you, but you can be a little scatterbrained. You've always been that way. It's okay, but it makes drinking much more dangerous." He promptly added, "I'm not scatterbrained, Bub, but you are."

During my junior year of college, I decided it was time to get off-campus and live with my friends, Greg and Steve, in a three-bedroom apartment. All our parents gathered to help us move into the new apartment one day in late August. Steve's mom Linda was an awesome lady; she cooked for us that night. Greg's dad was a part-time rancher so we had lots of meat that he would always give us. In fact, that was Greg's contribution to the household account other than his share of the rent.

It was a weird year, living with Steve and Greg. I was in an odd place. I kept feeling like I needed to change. No matter where I went, I was unsettled. Something had to give because deep inside, there was like a drip, drip, drip of corrosive acid on my self-esteem. My constant yearning to be with a guy wasn't helping matters.

I was aching on the inside, wanting to be who I was, and daydreaming about all the beautiful guys I saw on campus. I would constantly think about Rob and Gerry, my only two sexual experiences, and fantasize about them, that is, when I wasn't fantasizing about food, which became my go-to when I was trying not to drink. The longer I went without being with a guy, without being true to myself, the harder it became. I went through all of college without any real sexual experiences. I just felt this need to repress it.

By 1985, the AIDS crisis was rearing its head and it was clear that gay men were being struck down by this disease that they were calling the HIV Complex. That just bolstered the feeling that I needed to continue to repress my desires now more than ever.

My drinking did ease some, but I continued to party. Living with Steve and Greg off-campus was what I needed. It helped that I was with responsible people. Steve and Greg did not drink as much as my friends in the dorm, so I wasn't drinking during the week like the year before. I had rallied physically and academically going through my junior year and Greg was looking out for me the whole way. He and I grew closer as friends, and my disastrous GPA began to improve—I had to get into law school.

I knew I would not get into the University of Texas or other top law schools. Still, in an interesting twist of fate, I received a packet from a place called Willamette University in Salem, Oregon. It looked like a nice place, but what caught my eye most was that Oregon had a reputation for being liberal and open. So I became fixated on the idea of going to Oregon for law school.

CHAPTER 18

WILLAMETTE, DAMN IT!

It seemed like all these years of frustration, triumph, and confusion rushed me all at once. As an openly gay man, five years sober, I still had not come out to my father. No wonder my sponsor told me to look closely at why I had to hide. It was a constant internal battle to be myself inside and out. I was not drinking, so I figured I was well into recovery. I didn't listen to the warnings about the aptly named the "dreaded five-year mark" by the old-timers who knew too well of its danger. My sponsor was trying to warn me, and perhaps the angels brought me to this place of my father's illness to test my resolve and help me over the hump.

The five-year mark is when feelings are said to return with a vengeance. Maybe it isn't as hard for people living honestly, but any alcoholic is likely just a few steps ahead of a trail of lies. That is the life of an addict. We lie to ourselves, we lie to others, and we certainly lie to God. We say the serenity prayer, but if we are not addressing our buried feelings and the causes of our drinking, we use it as a default mantra with little meaning.

Alcoholism is a progressive disease with many factors. But it never occurs in a vacuum. I wanted to look at my sobriety as the final marker of success, but this five-year mark was another beginning. I had to face myself and how I got here. There's a saying in the AA rooms: "It's not the change that's painful; it's the resistance to change." I decided not to resist that pain, but to instead mine my memories for answers.

I had such high hopes for Willamette University Law School. My entire decision to go there was to live life as a gay man out in the open. It wasn't entirely irrational. I didn't believe I could come out around my family, friends, or frankly the entire state of Texas. When I announced my move to Oregon, everyone looked at me in utter confusion. Like a well-practiced alcoholic who has trouble telling the truth, I lied and said Willamette Law School was giving me a job as a part-time debate coach, providing six hours of free tuition each semester!

I also believed it was my sexual repression that was causing the drinking, so if I moved to Oregon to come out, the drinking would work itself out. Finally, I would be free.

My dad drove me to Salem, and I knew he could sense my stress. He started asking questions to make sense of why I was moving from Texas to Oregon.

"Your Uncle David doesn't live too far from Oregon if you need a place to go," he said. "Is that what is bothering you?"

I was quiet.

"Bub, I know you, son. You always go quiet when you are worried. Dad will pay to get you set up! Didn't you tell me the financial aid money will be ready when we get there?"

I exhaled, "It's not that." I could feel everything rushing to my throat. I was anxious; my mind said, *tell him. Just tell him. If you tell him, we can just turn around and go home. It can end this lunacy. What the fuck is in Oregon?* I could feel myself starting to pant. I was tired of hiding and nothing about this move seemed right.

Dad must have sensed my sudden onset of stress, so he laughed his cynical laugh. "Bub, I confess I thought you had lost your mind when you said you were going to Willamette. I had never heard of the place. Why Willamette, why Oregon? For fuck's sake, none of it seemed to make sense. But now I get it."

I got nervous that somehow, he'd picked up on what was really on my mind.

"I know you are nervous, but moving from Texas is best for you, Bub. Right now, at this time in your life, it is the best thing."

My hands started to sweat. The truth was bubbling up.

"Bub, you come from a restless tribe. It would be best if you were totally on your own. But, as a man, you must build something uniquely, all yours. You're restless and proud, and there must be something to do, so go do it. You know Dad is with you. I will come to get you if it all falls apart, or if you fall apart."

I wanted to cry but didn't. I almost resented this man who had caused me so much disruption, chaos, and pain, who could know me so well and yet know nothing about me!

"I know, Dad," I said. "I know you will come to get me." And then I said nothing.

The silly thing was, if I was brave enough to come out as a gay man, I could have stayed in Austin. Austin had become open and liberal with a great LGBTQ infrastructure. There were gay people around me, and the type who didn't frighten me either. A guy my sophomore year lived on the same dorm floor as me. It was clear he was bisexual. He came on to me twice, touching my groin and rubbing against me, whispering in my ear. I wanted to, but I did not react. Another time, a friend from high school named Ricardo, a hot Latino, pulled off his clothes and came to me, trying to seduce me, but I pushed him away. He must have known in high school I was gay, but he couldn't be open about it any more than I could. Again, I wanted him, but I pushed him away. I still didn't understand my fear.

I simply could not come out. I kept finding a reason not to, but even worse, I demeaned the community even though I desperately wanted to belong.

I think I was still hoping somehow, someway, I could be straight. If I'd had the guts, I would have come out in Austin, but instead I was running away, thinking things would be different. I just didn't want to be gay. My dad often just up and left when he needed to get clear headed, so I suppose that's what he figured was happening with me.

All the planning and thinking was of little consolation. After visiting my Uncle David in Seattle, I dropped Dad off at the Portland Airport. I felt isolated and lonely. I didn't realize I would miss my dad so much. He had given me no pushback about going to Oregon. He declined a potentially lucrative project in Pennsylvania so he could take me. He had done all I could ask for and more. As I sat in my cheap apartment, I felt depressed, a poor start to my big plans of liberation in Oregon. So I did what I always did: I walked across the street to a bar known as Boone's Treasury and bought a six-pack of cool-looking beer in a green bottle called Henry Weinhard's. This beer would become my new favorite. I took it home and popped the top, feeling the familiar calm. I reclined in my rented chair, lit a cigarette, and realized that all had not been lost. Maybe it would be a new beginning.

◆ ◆ ◆

On the Friday of the first week of law school, my neighbor in the apartment building, Bill, who was also a first-year law student, invited me to his place to have a beer. One of the second-year guys was having a party in our building and invited us to hang out. Bill had asked another guy, William, to come along, and now I officially had a group. I brought a six-pack of beer, and William and I sat on the couch drinking and chatting with Bill and a few other people when a tall, handsome guy walked in. John had deep black hair and a mustache and was from Kalispell, Montana. We all told stories about surviving the first week of law school, what it took to get there, and wound up sharing a keg.

A guy named Bruno joined us, and when the beer ran out, he told us of a place where we could shoot pool and drink until almost dawn. We were all law students living in a rickety apartment building, drinking away our anxieties and concern for our futures.

Beer had always been my dear friend. No one noticed how much I drank. With a constant beer buzz, I could be a social animal and fit in anywhere. All these guys were good-looking, straight, social, and loved to party. I immediately eased into the same life I had at UT. I was drinking, stressing, and trying to stay straight.

People who experience first-year law school are a unique club. No matter where they attend, there is unspoken respect and understanding for what it's like to have your mind turned inside out. The first-year professors purposely try to weed out those students who don't have the heart and stomach for the law through the Socratic method. They seem to have a sixth sense of who is unprepared or struggling. That is invariably the person they call upon to answer questions. Some professors are more sadistic than others, but I don't know of any who have not at least made one or more students cry out of sheer humiliation.

One of the things that kept first years like me going was the obscene amount of money I was spending on an education I wasn't even sure I wanted. The Willamette financial aid office kept the cash flowing, but eventually there would be a reckoning. I hadn't forgotten why I chose Willamette over Texas, where I planned to practice law. But as the weeks went by, I got too used to being the good-natured, straight guy from Texas who loved to drink. I mastered that part of heterosexuality so well that I almost believed it myself.

I hated law school! I found the material boring and the competitive dynamic among students distasteful. I would have much preferred to study politics, journalism, or sociology. I'd graduated from UT-Austin with a Bachelor of Arts degree in Government, even though I seriously considered changing to Broadcast Journalism. But when you decide as a teen to go to law school and talk about almost nothing else, it's a lot of pressure to walk away from it. I also knew it made my father proud to tell people I was going to be a lawyer.

There was another problem. At UT, everybody drank almost all the time. The undergraduate keg parties were notorious, so even though I drank more than other students at unusual times, it never seemed to be an over-the-top issue. I never thought of myself as drinking like an alcoholic Instead, alcohol and I appeared to coexist; it helped me think better. At least, I reasoned that it did. I could abstain when I needed to focus on finals or a paper or hit just a couple of beers when I needed it to steady my nerves. It all worked out well at UT.

Law school proved to be a different animal. Besides the legal research and writing class, there was only one final exam in a law school course. Then, of course, there was the ever-present fear of being randomly called on by the professor. But taking after my father as a first-class bullshitter, I seemed to navigate that well, even if I had only marginally studied the material.

Having only one exam for the entire class at the end of the term was not good for an alcoholic. Law students are supposed to form study groups, outline the class material to study methodically, and then review it before the finals. Alcoholic procrastinators don't work that way. In the beginning, I made it a point to study and prepare, but as the semester wore on, I spent more time at the pool and beer hall and less time at the law library.

Since I lived alone, I studied in my dank basement apartment, but that soon grew old. Then I tried to study in the law library, but that was no good as too many of my classmates were there chit-chatting. Their chit-chatting made me nervous. Even the slightest noise could be a huge distraction. Their apparent familiarity made me feel inadequate. If they were talking about what they were doing to study, it could derail me until I had to leave to find somewhere else. I also didn't like how dark and foreboding the Willamette Law Library felt. The paintings on the walls of long-dead professors and judges seemed to be saying, "You don't belong here."

Eventually, I found a cubicle on the second floor of the Willamette

Undergraduate Library that became a hideaway until I decided I needed to eat and drink while studying. Once again, I couldn't focus, so it was back to my dark, dank apartment where I could study with a six-pack. Sometimes I would study with my friends who didn't know I had already downed a six-pack earlier in the evening. It was easy enough to convince them we deserved a night of pool and partying after mastering the work for the day.

It was here that I began to integrate alcohol into my daily life. I wasn't drinking to party or let off steam. I was drinking to function. There is a line an alcoholic crosses that is apparent only in hindsight. There were a lot of brilliant and personable people in law school, but I only hung out with people who drank a lot. I did not have the patience to hang out with non-drinkers. I would get impatient and anxious if I went too long without drinking.

Our favorite place to meet was called the 50/50 Tavern, a beat-up bar and pool hall on Salem's West Side. It was on its last legs until my dear friends and drinking buddies, Bill, John, Bruno, and a few others, made it our home away from home. It had cheap beer, a jukebox with old Country and Western songs, and a couple of pool tables—and no one scolding us for wasting many nights drinking until closing time.

Fred, the owner, liked all the new business. He was a hard-smoking and drinking man who seemed surprised to see new life in his little place. He shot the shit with us, asked about our lives, and started a cheap spaghetti night on Sundays to ensure we all had enough to eat.

The night before my first big contracts law final, my friend John and I drank and played pool at the 50/50 Tavern until 2:00 a.m. I barely remember how I made it to the exam and was shocked when my grades came out. By some miracle, it was my highest grade in my first law school semester. To this day, I don't know how I did it, and I think the alcoholic in me misinterpreted my luck. Rather than thanking God for looking after fools and drunks, as the saying goes, this made me feel invincible, like my drinking wasn't a real problem at all.

During that year, my friendships became crucial to me. Although I ached to be myself, I didn't want to risk losing the respect and camaraderie of my buddies. I simply couldn't justify coming out. Further, I could not identify one gay person in the entire first-year class. No one was gay, or at least no one was out and gay. I would have been the only openly gay guy if I had come out, and I didn't want to take the chance of being ostracized. The world was not a friendly place for gay men in the mid-1980s. There were pockets of liberalism, which was why I wanted to go to Oregon, but the AIDs crisis made even liberal people suspicious of anyone they thought was homosexual. I could not bear the thought of being the only gay guy in class. So, I drank, drank, and drank some more.

I want to think the reason I chose to not be openly gay during that time was all the controversy surrounding the AIDS crisis. HIV/AIDs swept through the gay communities and was in the news. People were dying, giving more reason for onlookers to think of gay people as "other." While it was not limited to homosexuals, calling it a gay disease helped people feel safe. I didn't want to be gay. I knew I was attracted to men, but I had already had a small taste of stigma and now could be risking my life.

On two occasions, I left bars with girls to have sex. I made sure everybody saw me. The first time I got one back to my apartment, nothing really happened. I just could not successfully get aroused with these girls. I am sure my pickups were confused. On the outside, I looked like any other healthy male. The second time I picked up a girl, she was particularly free-spirited, and even tried all kinds of creative maneuvers to turn me on. She even bit me all over. I think she thought I just needed more kink, and it worked—we actually had sex—but a bite on my chest eventually became infected, requiring outpatient surgery during Christmas break. Playing it straight wasn't working, and I realized it was unfair to lead a girl on knowing you were gay.

I managed to rank in the upper third of my class at the end of the first semester, and my friend Bill and I decided to leave our rickety apartment complex and become roommates in a better place. We moved two blocks from our favorite drinking hole. We shared a love of drinking, me more than him.

Early into our second semester, I followed Bill to a new bar further from where we lived. We took two cars in case one of us got lucky. It would certainly not have been me. On the way to the bar, the weather turned to rain and sleet, which can create black ice in an Oregon winter. That didn't deter us from accepting the bartender's suggestion that we drink the special, a concoction called a Prairie Fire, which was a shot of tequila with a hit of Tabasco sauce. It went down hot at first but later seemed like nothing. I lost count after downing four. We followed that with straight tequila shots and Tecate beer to stay in tune with the night's Mexican theme. We drank, we partied, we laughed, and we left.

Bill was in front and going fast, and I followed close behind. I was concentrating hard to ensure I didn't swerve. Still, when we entered the cloverleaf bridge that crossed the river into West Salem, another drunk driver was headed the wrong way. Unfortunately, we never saw him until it was too late, and he hit Bill head-on. I was driving so fast I could not stop the El Camino in time, so I rear-ended Bill. Then my car spun out. When I finally stopped, I shoved the car into park and struggled with my seatbelt.

I scrambled out of my car and saw a large man stumble out of the driver's side of a blue four-door Ford sedan. He was making a run for it. He raced to the middle of the cloverleaf bridge and jumped about 20 feet to the ground below. I shouted and ran after him, but then I saw Bill slumped over his steering wheel. Blood was pouring from his forehead. He was unconscious, and I smelled the distinct odor of gasoline.

When I realized the danger, I began to sober up. I started to freak out. A passerby had stopped to help, who I hadn't even noticed up until then, and said, "We've got to call the police." It's hard to imagine a time before cell phones, but this person had to drive off to find help. God only knew when someone would arrive, and the gas smell was getting stronger. Acting on drunken instinct, I got Bill's car door open and pushed on him as gently as possible to see if he would wake up. I was sure he was alive but knew there was no time to waste.

"Bill! Bill!" I said over and over. I had been working on his seatbelt when he finally woke up.

"What..." he started to utter, but I told him we had to get him out of the car. His eyes were glassy, and he was bleeding profusely from his forehead. I was trying to get him out before he could realize what had happened.

Finally, I got the seatbelt open and slipped my arm under his. I didn't know the extent of his injuries, so I pulled him out and dragged him as far away from the car as possible. We walked backward about fifteen yards before I felt it was a safe enough distance to put him down on the ground.

It wasn't long before the police and an ambulance arrived. The EMTs went to work on Bill. Then a young cop grabbed my arm and pulled me aside.

"Were you involved in this accident?" he asked, gesturing to the smashed cars. As drunk as I was, I was thinking on my feet now. I told him mine was the El Camino but that I hit my friend Bill in the rear after the head-on crash.

Then I redirected the officer's attention to the blue Ford and walked him over to it. "I saw the guy get out and stumble away," I said emphatically. "I am sure he was drunk. First, he was going the wrong way and hit my friend. Then he got out of his car, jumped down the embankment, and ran."

The officer was writing down my version of the facts, and just as I suspected, when he opened the car door of the Ford, which was already partially open, a bunch of beer cans fell out. He told me to stand back so I wouldn't mess with any evidence.

The officer finally got around to asking me if I was sober. I answered curtly, "Of course, sir, I am a law student, and Bill is my friend. I am very worried about him."

He looked at me suspiciously and said, "How do I know you're sober?"

And I replied, "Well, you tell me."

He decided to give me a field sobriety test which I passed. He then said, "I am not convinced. Can you recite the presidents of the United States?"

It did not seem like a fair test, but I liked history and politics.

"I can recite the presidents of the United States and their secretaries of state backward," I said. "Would you like me to start?"

I was a bit of an asshole because I was anxious to get to the hospital and be with Bill and knew that I was still drunk. But once I had recited backwards to Franklin Delanor Roosevelt, the officer said, "Okay, you can go."

My El Camino was drivable, so I went to the hospital, and thankfully Bill's injuries were minor compared to how his car looked. Eventually, they caught the guy who was going the wrong way on the cloverleaf. He had a history of drunk driving and drug dealing, so it wasn't a shock that he would do something like this. Once again, I could look at the man's behavior and see no connection to my own.

I was probably as drunk as he was or even more. The drinking slowed my reactions, and the impact of my crash into the back of Bill's car could have killed both of us. Nevertheless, I thought I was clever, diverting the cop's attention from me and my responsibility, and I even deluded myself into thinking this would make me a good lawyer.

By the next week, I was back at it, drinking and spending what little money I had from financial aid on partying, beer, and cigarettes. One of the things I learned about the Willamette Office of Financial Aid was you could get four emergency loans there each semester. I used up all four. My life was an emergency. I was well into the early stages of alcoholism with no desire to turn back.

When the year ended, I decided that even though I didn't live out my goal of "coming out," it made sense for me to return the following year. Since I was going to take this trip back to Houston alone, I promised myself no drinking and driving. It seemed something had changed during this past year at Willamette. I had come to the realization that if I drank a beer, I would need at least five more after that one. At the time, I didn't understand that alcoholism was a progressive disease.

I was nervous about taking the trip and didn't understand the anxiety and OCD disorders I had brewing. Driving from Salem, Oregon to Houston, Texas, is truly a long road home. To make myself more comfortable, I planned out every part of the trip with small rituals. If I drove a certain distance, I would stop at a motel, replenish my ice chest, and allow myself a six-pack at night. I played whatever local country station I could get at each stretch and would only change it when it became nothing but static. I tried to make as few stops as possible and would only pull over to fill up the gas tank when I was almost on fumes. If I hadn't made my distance, I mentally punished myself and sat in the car until I dared to get back on the road. Only the promise of the six-pack I had chilling in the ice chest kept me focused on my next destination.

After two days of driving, I broke the Texas line. I let out a whoop that would have made a Texas A&M Aggie proud! I was home.

By the time I made Amarillo, it was turning dark, and I was tapped out. I saw a red vacancy sign for a motel inside the Amarillo city limits and pulled over. There were 18-wheelers everywhere and a noxious smell of fumes, but I didn't care.

When I got to my room, I cranked up the AC unit and didn't bother to unpack. I walked to the convenience store and bought two six-packs of Miller Lite and two packs of cigarettes. I was proud for not giving in to the cravings that dominated my thoughts during the day and couldn't wait to pull the tab off the first can. I savored the crisp, clean taste with a hint of sweet malt and hops. Nothing like it!

It felt good to relax. I didn't want to think about my life and gnawing loneliness. Maybe I wasn't gay after all. I had good male friends and didn't see any of them as potential lovers. All I knew was that drinking usually stopped the noise in my head. That night I tossed and turned and when I woke up, I counted eight empty Miller Lite cans strewn across the room.

I felt ragged but figured it was due to lack of sleep. After a long shower, I began my routine of filling up the gas tank, purchasing a bag of ice, two coffees to go, a day-old sandwich from the convenience store, and a cold can of Mountain Dew, the nectar of the young in North Carolina.

I got back to the El Camino and chugged the Mountain Dew. I checked the air in the tires and all the car's fluids. I liked everything to be perfect before heading out on the road. I was sweating like a bandit at this point. Finally, when I was squared away, I took a big sip of coffee and lit a cigarette.

Texas is a big state, and it was ambitious to try to make it from Amarillo to Houston in one shot. But that was my goal. I couldn't wait to get home. The first country station I found was playing the song "Good Ole Boys Like Me." That is how I wanted people to see me. That was the only natural way to fit in with the people I grew up with. Working class Texas was pool shooting, beer drinking, country music listening, hunting, and talking shit. I was not in "Ag" like many of my high school friends, and I did not "skin bucks and run trot lines," but I appeared to be a good ole boy among many good ole boys. My dad drank and carried on with his friends, and now I could keep up with the best of them. It would be okay, even admirable, for me to rise above the working class and become an attorney, but there were still certain expectations I had to honor.

As I hit the lonely road for this last leg of my journey, the cold cans of beer kept calling me. I had all kinds of rationalizations. I was now a veteran drinker, I thought, so one little beer wouldn't hurt. I would never admit that, despite so much evidence to the contrary, I couldn't stop at one. Finally, I thought, "What the hell? I'm in Texas and almost home." I reached into the ice chest and rubbed the cold can on my face before I popped the top. I held it between my thighs and figured I still had four beers left from the night before. I would only need two of them before making it to Houston.

I cruised through West Texas and watched the oil pump jacks and cattle as I relaxed and listened to music. I looked at my watch and saw that I was lagging behind schedule, so I picked up speed. I swigged down another beer and felt on top of the world. I should have known better.

Somewhere south of Big Springs, Texas, I heard the unmistakable noise of a police siren and then noticed his lights. I had no idea how long he had followed me before I finally paid attention. I looked down at the speedometer and saw I had been blazing at 85 miles per hour on a Texas State Highway. As nervous as I was, I still managed to finish the beer and put the empty can in the ice chest with the others.

There were many things Tate G. Barkley didn't give me while I was growing up, but he made sure to teach me the essential things, like what to do if you get pulled over while you are drinking. "If you ever get pulled over by 'the cops', don't mess around," Dad told me one night while we were drinking beer in the garage. "If you keep Hall's menthol lozenges with you it masks your breath, and Old Spice after shave also hides the smell." I always kept Halls's cough drops and Old Spice handy just for this reason. I popped one in my mouth and put on my flashers, slowly pulling over onto the sandy side of the road.

While the Officer was fixing his uniform and checking my plates, I dabbed on some Old Spice. I stayed calm and greeted the man with a calm but befuddled look and a "Yes, sir?"

The minute I heard his voice, I could tell this boy was not originally from Texas, so I couldn't pull the familiarity routine. The man looked like what you would expect in those days. He was white, square-jawed, and overweight with a buzz haircut and no sense of humor. He asked for my license and insurance card and studied them for a long time.

Then he sarcastically asked me if I had a "medical emergency" to explain my speed.

"No, sir," I replied. "But I do need to piss like a racehorse." He did not even crack a smile. Instead, he leaned inside my window and said, "Boy, is that marijuana I smell?"

Now I knew I was in for it. I wasn't smoking marijuana, but my El Camino was packed with stuff, including a loaded .38 revolver underneath the passenger-side seat. My father insisted that we travel locked and loaded.

I tried to stay calm. "No, sir, there is not nor has there ever been marijuana in this car. However, you may smell cigarette smoke." Then I told him, "I'm on the third day of a three-day road trip from Oregon to Houston, so no doubt this car is a little stuffy."

He looked at me with a scowl. "Are you permitting me to search your car, or do we need to wait until I get a search warrant, which will likely take me until tomorrow?"

I told him, "I consent," and then advised him, "Before you begin your search, there is a fully loaded .38 caliber revolver and 50 rounds of ammunition underneath the passenger seat."

I got out of the car very slowly and moved away as the officer reached under the seat and pulled out my gun. My ice chest was on the floorboard, so I figured it was better to tell him about it.

"Officer, you'll also find four empty beer cans in my ice chest. I drank that beer last night." I was sure he knew I was lying, so I shut up.

While holding my gun in his left hand, he opened the ice chest and pulled out one of the empty beer cans. The Officer looked at me in disbelief, "Boy, have you been drinking while speeding with a concealed weapon under your seat in my county?"

I looked at him and said as innocently as I could, "The empty beer cans are from last night, and I was not aware I was speeding."

He called me to the car and asked if the gun was "registered."

I said, "No. This gun is a gift from my dad. Dad doesn't register guns."

I finally got a rise out of him. The Officer laughed and said, "I don't blame him."

Now that I realized he was posturing, I asked if I could walk over to a mesquite tree to relieve myself. He still thought I was lying about the drugs, so he insisted on going with me.

Once I zipped up, and he was happy that I didn't have a stash hidden on me, we went back to the El Camino. The officer promptly began to pull and yank everything out of the car. As he made his way through the stuff in my car, he saw my "Battles of the Civil War" calendar. I always hung that on my wall and each year I sent away for a new one. Just by chance, I had it flipped to the battle of Vicksburg. I could see a change in the officer's expression. He asked, "You interested in the Civil War?"

I told him, "I'm a Civil War buff, as you can see."

He then asked me, "Do you know much about the battle of Vicksburg?"

"Yes, more than most," I replied honestly. It was true that I'd been there twice and read about the battle of Vicksburg at least a thousand times. He told me he was a native of Vicksburg, Mississippi. Now I could place his accent. In a real twist of luck, the officer and I began chatting about Vicksburg, the siege of Vicksburg, U.S. Grant, and his entire Mississippi campaign. Like me, he was a dedicated Civil War buff. He decided he only smelled cigarettes, gave me a minor speeding ticket, and sent me on my way.

This incident should have been a warning and lesson for someone with the compulsion to drink. But unfortunately, I didn't interpret it as a warning but rather as good luck. Someone was watching over me, and I again got away with something. If only I weren't so good at getting away with things, my life might have stayed more manageable.

I tried to stay sober and within the speed limit as I headed toward Houston, but I continued to feel excited and anxious. The next time I filled the tank, I bought a 12-pack of Miller Lite. With the day I already had, I rationalized that a few beers wouldn't hurt on the last stretch on the road home. I do not remember how I made it back to Houston, but I know I did.

CHAPTER 19

GOD'S BABY BOY

In 1988, Texas had not fully recovered from the oil bust but things were improving. I was staying with Mom and Dad for the summer, and I needed money right away. I learned the Olive Garden restaurant was hiring. I'd never waited tables in my life but figured it would be better than working hard in the oppressive Texas heat and humidity. At least the Olive Garden would be air-conditioned.

I dropped by the Olive Garden and filled out an application. I got the job on the spot even when I told him that I'd never waited tables before. The manager told me I would do fine and that "with three days of training, you'll learn everything you need to know." I left feeling pretty good. I drove home and picked up a six-pack to celebrate.

True to his word, I breezed into waiting tables after three days of training. I hated the side work like rolling silverware and cleaning the salad station, but I loved meeting people, bullshitting, and socializing with the customers. Before I started the job Dad told me, "Bubba, make the bartender your friend and it'll pay off." This proved to be true. I became buddies with all the bartenders. They got a piece of my tips by custom, but I always paid them more. They took care of me and my tables.

I became an expert at upselling liquor and wine. The managers made it clear the money was really in selling booze. The bigger you pumped up the bill's price, the more you were usually tipped. Liquor and booze were the fastest ways to pump up a bill while waiting tables.

I learned that waiting on smokers was always more lucrative. In those days, restaurants had smoking sections. The smokers were my people. Smokers seemed to drink more, a lot more. They laughed, joked, and tipped twice what nonsmokers did. Over time, the bartenders prioritized my drink orders, and it was not unusual for them to have a shot ready for me when I picked up my customer's drinks at the bar.

Being a little bit lubricated helped me wait on tables. I wasn't particularly graceful in getting the food out to the tables, but I always had their drinks ready and on time. The people I worked with at the Olive Garden loved to party, and the kitchen crew were hardcore party animals. More particularly, I met a fellow server named Mike. Mike was a recent college graduate from the University of Texas and was about to start law school.

Mike and I took an instant liking to each other not only because we were both from UT and going to law school, but because Mike loved to drink. Mike was smart and fun and smoked cigarettes like me, which made our drinking trips much easier. He and I went to Bennigan's Bar and drank a couple of times after the evening shifts. There was no doubt we were two peas in a pod. One evening in early summer, a friend told Mike about a rave in the warehouse district in downtown Houston. I'd never been to a "rave," and I wanted to go.

Mike and I bought a 12-pack of Miller Lite and a fifth of Jack Daniels to start the evening. Then, as a pre-function to the rave, we drank with some of Mike's friends in Pasadena. By the time we took off to downtown Houston in Mike's Delta 88, we were both shit-faced drunk. Mike and I got to singing to the radio so intently that Mike took his eyes off the road, and his car veered off to the shoulder and scraped the concrete divide on I-45.

Mike yelled, "Whoa, Nelly!" and quickly veered back onto the roadway. We both looked at each other, busted out laughing, and started singing again. I swear, getting drunk certainly makes you think you are bulletproof. We eventually made our way into the warehouse district. The warehouse district in Houston at this time was just a bunch of old abandoned warehouses from back when the rail line ran through downtown Houston.

When we walked inside the venue, there was a live band on the west side of the building and a DJ with a large makeshift dance floor on the east side. And the booze was flowing. All you had to do was pay a formidable cover charge, and then you could drink, dance, and meet whomever you wanted. People were selling and dropping acid, Ecstasy, and every party drug you could imagine. I'm unsure what I ingested that night or how long we were out. I know that I partied, danced, and sang, and eventually, Mike, who was clearly drunk, pulled me off the dance floor and said, "We got to go."

I wasn't sure how we decided that Mike should drive home, likely because it was his Delta-88. It took an eternity for us to find where we parked, but when we finally found the car and hopped in, we could not find a way out to the freeway. The streets were dark, and we couldn't read the street signs, so it felt like we were feeling our way through a labyrinth. As we finally rolled up on what appeared to be a freeway entrance, we saw at the very last second it was closed. Mike had to adjust very quickly to avoid slamming into the barriers. As he changed direction, his speed increased, and we ran up over a curb and entered the freeway underpass. The engine roared and we climbed at what seemed like a record pace up the concrete hill, coming within inches of careening into the underbelly of the freeway.

Mike turned hard to the left, over-adjusted to the right, hit the accelerator, and we came within an inch and a half of slamming into a concrete pillar. Mike slammed on the brakes, the wheels screeched, and finally we came to a stop. Everything was silent then except for our labored breathing. We looked at each other, and with my hands shaking, I lit us some cigarettes and said, "Mike, let's take our time."

We eventually made it home.

That summer I also got into fitness training with a friend of mine. Despite all the smoking and drinking, I was probably in the best shape of my life. I would brag that working out gave me "a greater capacity to sin." My friends thought it was a funny joke, but I knew I was only half kidding.

It was a good summer. I was buff, toned, and fit. I partied like a maniac, earned a pocket full of money schlepping drinks, and found a new friend in Mike. I hadn't forgotten about my disappointing life in Salem, Oregon, but a summer of fun, fitness, and making money had done a lot to take away the sting. Despite myself, I realized that I had missed Texas, and I had missed it an awful lot!

As I got ready to head back to Salem for my second year of law school, I kept thinking about whether it was the place for me. After going round and round, I realized that I'd already had a successful first year at Willamette. Somehow, I managed to finish in the top 30% of the class. I had also made a lot of friends, so I felt compelled, almost obligated to go back.

When I returned to Salem, I managed to secure an apartment that didn't feel right, but I took it anyway. I had enough money in my pocket for a deposit and the first month's rent, but I was quickly running out of money. I spent as fast as I earned at Olive Garden, though I did save some. This apartment was more antiquated than my first, with no shower, only a bathtub, no dishwasher, and an old 1950s refrigerator. But I didn't have much of a choice. The place was available and cheap.

As I drove around campus, my body knew before I did that this was not the place for me. I felt constantly nauseous and couldn't shake the feeling that I wanted to go home.

All my dreams and plans for Salem had essentially crashed and burned. I had a fun time in Texas, but nothing had changed there either, but at least it was home, not to mention it was where I intended to practice law.

I knew it was the right decision to leave Oregon, but I worried what my dad would say. I was afraid he would think I was quitting. I had sleepless nights rehearsing how I would tell him so he wouldn't disapprove. After all, I spent so many days and nights extolling the virtues of going to law school in Oregon. When I finally got the nerve to call him, I had an entire speech prepared. I was practically disassociating with worry. My head felt like it was underwater when I dialed the phone. He answered. I said, "Dad, I need to talk to you."

I'd laid out the plan of what to say in my head. But before I could tell him anything, he said, "Bub, do you want to come home?"

I stammered. Sometimes he was clueless, but there were times when my dad knew me better than I knew myself.

"I do, and I will be going back to a Texas law school," I said.

"That will work. You know best."

"Can you take the drive with me, Dad?" I asked.

"I would love to help you out," he replied. "But I am out of work for the time being and broke."

"I'll pay for your ticket out here if you share the drive with me." I offered. I figured I could get an emergency loan from the financial aid office and say I needed a leave of absence in case I wanted to return after all.

I arranged for a flight for Dad on Delta Airlines and said my goodbyes to my not-so-shocked friends. They knew I was thinking about returning to Texas even at the end of the first year.

My dad was set to arrive on August 31, 1988, on flight 1141. I had spent the past few nights at parties and going away dinners, and before picking him up at the airport I was at a goodbye lunch with some friends.

While I waited for Dad to arrive, one of my friends ran in entirely out of breath. He kept saying, "Dude, have you heard? Have you heard?"

"What?" I said.

"Come on!" We turned on the television in the bar, and all over the news was the announcement that Delta Flight 1141 crashed, killing 14 people. My heart sank. I wasn't ready to lose my father just as I was getting to know him. We were drinking buddies! I was supposed to be going home! In the face of tragedy, all kinds of strange thoughts cross your mind. I thought about Sunday dinners with Grandma Kirkman and attending church. I hadn't been to a church in years. I thought about how Dad hated church and hoped God didn't hold it against him. As the news sank in, I thought, "Not Dad, he won't die."

I called Delta Airlines, but all the lines were busy. I called Mom and she was in tears. She said Delta Airlines had called her to say their records showed Dad was on Flight 1141, and it had gone down leaving Salt Lake City. I felt this incredible ache inside of me. My friends Bruno and John sat with me until I finally said, "Let's go."

Bruno volunteered to drive me to the airport, and I ran right to the Delta Airlines counter. The Delta representative was there with a clipboard. We were surrounded by other people crying and demanding information. When the Delta representative made it to me, I asked about my dad, he said, "We have not confirmed whether your father was one of the fourteen killed."

He also said there was another flight out of Salt Lake City, originating in Jackson, Mississippi, not Houston, scheduled to land in Portland within the next 30 minutes. I prayed my dad was on the second flight even though he was supposed to be on the other one.

Dad claimed to be the luckiest man alive. I hoped this was one of those times. He used to say, "I'm God's baby boy." So, I thought to myself, could it be possible? I made all kinds of promises that I hoped I could keep. I would be good; I would slow down my drinking and stop thinking about men. I wanted to see my dad again. Just like in the hospital decades later, it took the fear of losing him to help me realize how much I loved him.

John, Bruno, and I waited outside the gate for the other Delta flight from Salt Lake City. But the plane had landed early. As we walked to the gate area, my dad walked toward us with a big grin. I ran to him like a little kid and threw my arms around him.

"Good to see you too, Bubba," he said, sounding confused. "I was hoping to get here quicker, so I jumped to this flight. I just walked up and said, can I switch? They said sure and waved me onboard. "

"Dad, didn't you hear?"

"Hear what?"

Dad had no idea that he could have been a dead man.

"That flight you were supposed to be on crashed." With the usual Tate G. deflection, Dad was wide-eyed but said, "I told you I am God's Baby Boy." At that moment, I believed him, and I hoped that would continue to be true.

We decided to stay over in Salem before hitting the road. The night before we left, there was a big party at the 50/50 Tavern, and Dad told the story of his close call all night with flourish and just a bit of spin. He and I got drunker than "shithouse rats," as Dad liked to say. It was a good night.

CHAPTER 20

NOW I GET IT

We woke up at about 7:00 the following day, showered, loaded up the ice chest and my few clothes, and filled up on gas. Dad went to a parts store and bought Freon to fill up the El Camino's AC. We chose to drive through California, only stopping for gas, restrooms, and cigarettes. Very little was said the first day because we both had vicious hangovers. We spent the night in Stockton, a big "cow town" that reminded me of Texas and smelled like cow shit. Once we adjusted to the smell, Dad and I ate, split a six pack and went to bed. Early the next morning, we blazed through Modesto, Merced and Bakersfield and entered Arizona. As we left a gas station in Arizona, I felt compelled to say something more to Dad. I touched his arm and said, "Thanks for coming, Dad. I did not have it in me to do this drive alone."

There was silence. Then Dad said, "Bub, you've done it alone twice, but the first time and this time, you needed company. I know when you need me, really need me, so there was no question about me coming to get you."

I felt the shame of quitting erupt inside me. He didn't know what a disappointment I had been and my real reason for wanting to run away to Oregon. I hurriedly said, "I am going back! To law school, that is, I hope, in Houston. It will happen, Dad!"

Dad looked over and lit a cigarette. He cracked the window on his side and said, "Bub, I'm not worried about it. I want you to do what you feel is best for you. You know Dad always wanted to be a commercial pilot. I had the chance several years after you were born. You were little. I had an opportunity to go to Australia to train and fly for Qantas Airlines, but I turned it down. Ma Barkley was almost vicious in her opposition to me going. Your mom felt the same. Everyone else in Statesville just smirked when I told them of the chance. Everyone but Pa Barkley. He said, 'Go, Son, go! If that is what you want, go as quickly as you can!' I remember it to this day; we were sitting on the porch having a cigarette at the home place. Bub, your Pa Barkley had tears in his eyes when he said it to me. He knew if I didn't go, I would regret it, but I had all that yakking in my ear about 'the family is here, moving the kids, blah blah blah.'" Dad exhaled his cigarette smoke and said, "I did not follow my dream. Think about it, Bub, we could have had a life in Australia. We could have seen the world together."

We remained silent as we drove through the darkness of the Arizona desert.

It was one of the most revealing conversations we ever had, but it didn't make me feel better. Although Dad didn't know it, I had crashed and burned my dream with cowardice. I was in the very act of fleeing my dream and letting my dad drive while I was doing it. I slid down into the passenger seat and tried to hide.

For a long time, I blamed my dad for everything. I saw him as bigger than life and felt his love was conditional from the early days when he would disappear on us, swoop back in, and start ordering me around. But it wasn't his fault my life turned to shit because of my drinking and my inexplicable inability to tell the truth, to come out and be me.

When I returned to Houston, my friend Jodie, who was in law school at the University of Houston, helped me get a job as a law clerk at the firm where she worked. I also entered South Texas College of Law in Houston as a transfer student. I announced to the world that I wanted to be called "Tate," not Mike or Michael. I was reunited with my drinking buddy, Mike, and we became roommates. We lived in an apartment complex with many older people, but there were also two gay couples. We all became friends, and I enjoyed observing how comfortable they were with each other. But I made sure never to drink around them. I was ignorant about gay people and thought I was frightened of them, but I was really envious they had the courage to be their true selves.

I knew Houston, Texas, the fourth largest city in America, had a substantial gay and lesbian population. Houston, like Austin, had an excellent gay and lesbian infrastructure, a place for gays to go no matter where they were in their coming out process, but I didn't see myself as like them. It was the same reasoning I used about my drinking. I didn't appear gay and was not acting upon my desires, so I wasn't anything like them. I was also functioning and not on skid row, so consequently, I was not like other alcoholics. I just liked to drink.

The schedule at South Texas allowed me to work eight hours during the day and go to class at night. I usually returned to the apartment at about 8:00 p.m., put on my running clothes, and jogged around the neighborhood. Then I showered, ate a TV dinner, drank two beers, and watched the 10:00 p.m. news. After the news, I would go to my room, turn on my desk lamp, and study cases while finishing the rest of the six-pack. It was a routine that worked for me until the six-pack eventually became close to a 12-pack every night.

My second year of law school passed quickly. Mike eventually met the woman who would become his wife and left me alone in the apartment most of the time. Soon after finals, a new partner joined the firm where I was clerking. My original boss had taught me a lot about civil litigation and gave me a lot of autonomy. This new boss was a medical malpractice lawyer with an impeccable reputation. He was also difficult to work with because he didn't see the law clerks as people. On more than one occasion, he said, "Do you work here?" He was also extremely critical and didn't mind dressing you down in front of the entire staff. Eventually, they reassigned me to another new partner whose background was in divorce, even though our cases were primarily insurance defense and medical malpractice. The new lawyer, Mr. Wince, was not fond of the details, so they were essentially left to me. It was very nice to be able to run a docket as a third-year law student, so I never complained. Besides, work became my safe place. I was sick of law school and hadn't taken any breaks since I started at South Texas, even during the summers.

By now, all my studying involved alcohol, and I had also started drinking at lunch from time to time. I couldn't shake the feeling of constant sadness. I was in the midst of an existential crisis, denying my true self and hiding it with drinking. I finally had enough and decided to take a trip. I needed to clear my head. I was looking for something—an answer, peace, my father's validation, something. I hadn't been to North Carolina for a while. I thought seeing my family where it all began might help. With some reservations, I decided to stay with Ma Barkley.

Ma Barkley was waiting on her front porch when I arrived. She looked older than I remembered, but that wasn't the biggest change. Instead, she seemed softer and actually happy to see me. I felt genuine love from her. I suppose she had always loved me, but the Ma Barkley I remembered was acerbic and bitter with few kind words for anyone.

After a surprisingly warm hug, Ma invited me to sit next to her on the porch. She was stringing green beans and gave me a bowl of my own so I could help. I got up to grab a beer out of the ice chest, but she stopped me.

"Michael Tate, you don't need a beer. I got some nice, fresh sweet tea waiting for you." I knew she was worried I had the same habits as my dad; of course, she was right. The tea would have been great if I hadn't been craving alcohol. I figured I could grab some at night while she slept.

Four in the afternoon was our official tea time each day, and since Ma had been losing her eyesight, I read her the newspaper every day I was there. Then I read her two stories from Reader's Digest after supper.

One night, after our supper, Ma and I sat out on the porch particularly late. After all these years, I had questions in my mind. Ma had spoken of her childhood in an aristocratic and idyllic way. So, I wondered, how had she ended up in a log cabin off a dirt road at age 17? At least, that was what I could surmise from the bits and pieces of family lore I'd heard over the years.

I remember looking at Ma as she sat in her chair, shelling peas. She was a large woman, about 92, with a graceful face, cherubic cheeks, and surprisingly stylish reading glasses. She liked to keep her hands busy even though she could no longer knit or crochet

"Ma, how did you get here to Barkley Road?"

There was a long pause, and Ma looked off into the distance as if watching a movie of her life in reverse. Her hesitation made me realize this was not an easy thing to explain.

Ma rocked her chair to help hoist herself upright and said she would make us some hot tea. I took the chance to run to the car and chug a can of beer. I got back to the porch just in time to help her with the cups. It was a cool summer night, and I remembered all the sounds of the woods and the big magnolia tree that had been my refuge when I was younger. It was all the same as it must have been when the Barkleys first made this part of the state their home.

When Ma settled in, she said, "I know Tate, your dad tells you some tall tales. That boy had it good. If he wanted something, we were usually able to get it for him. If Roger, your Pa Barkley, or I couldn't, his brothers and sisters could. That boy didn't know hard work like the rest of us did."

I almost spit out my tea when Ma said that. Dad was always so hard on me about working and not being idle that I pictured him working the farm from dawn to dusk.

Ma didn't notice my expression since her eyesight was so poor and just continued talking. "Christ the Lord, farming is just hard work. By the time Tate came along, we didn't have the whole 150 acres to worry about. We just had Roger's little 17.5 acres. That was it after years of backbreaking work. Anyway, Tate did not know the work like we did. If I only knew what I was getting into here the day I left my father's house. This is our home now." Ma paused, drew a full breath, and whispered, "17.5 acres."

"I don't understand," I said. The home place seems plenty big to me. "What about the rest of Barkley Road and Third Creek?"

She held her head down and said, "You really don't know the story, do you?" Then she continued, "When we were courting, you would have thought Roger was Rockefeller when he rode to our place out near Troutman. My dad was the superintendent of the brickyard. We had a good name in that town. Your Pa Barkley, Roger, would come straddled upon a pretty morgan horse with a nice Sunday suit and full head of hair combed and greased perfectly. My dad would let him visit on the porch while he sat inside close enough to listen. Things were very different back then. Good Christian folks were chaperoned. I was mesmerized by his appearance; he was a good-looking man in his day with great prospects." That was not the Pa Barkley I knew.

I liked watching Ma as she reminisced. It was the first time I could see that, at one time, there was love that she felt for him.

"Roger let me know he had 150 acres of fertile farmland he worked," she continued. "It was the land of his people. He said that since he was doing the farming, he would inherit the farm, as none of his brothers had any interest. Two of them had gone to college, one was becoming a plumber, and the other was a near invalid from being gassed in the war."

Ma got silent for a while. Finally, she sipped her tea and said, "He could be charming. That is where Tate got it, certainly not from me. I knew so little in those days. Surely, 150 acres could provide. The truth started the day we married. We moved to this land. There was not a home. We had to build it bit by bit. There was only a log cabin that he and his brother used as a playhouse. That's right, Michael Tate, we moved into his playhouse from when he was a boy. I was picturing a palace and what I got was less than a mud hut." I winced remembering some of the worst places we had lived.

"Roger told me a week from the wedding that there was no time for a honeymoon," Ma continued. "Cotton had to be planted. I loved Roger and wanted to be a good wife, so I made do. But there was no running water in the log cabin. We had to pack our water from the creek until Roger found time to dig a well, which would be two years, two years mind you, to get a water well. That creek is a good half a mile away. My father took me aside on one of my visits home, and asked if I wanted to leave, but I said, 'No.' That was not how he raised me. I admit I was tempted, but Roger made all kinds of promises of what life could be like for us."

Ma put aside her now empty teacup. "We slaved on that farm. When our children were old enough to stand, they helped with planting corn, picking cotton, plowing, and pulling. With our hands bleeding and backs aching day in and day out, we had to turn any money we earned over to his mom and dad. Roger's dad was ill. We worked the land for him because he had a stroke and could not do any of the work. The promise was always that the farm would be ours one day.

"We worked and worked with rarely a supportive word from Roger's mother. She was a Sharp before she married Father Barkley. The Sharps are mean. I suppose she had her reasons. I was fearful every time I went over there, especially during prohibition. She was a tough old bird and made whiskey and moonshine money. Lord have mercy."

I stared at Ma, wide-eyed. "We were a moonshine family!" That was something I already knew but I had never heard the history. Dad had told me proudly, and the cousins had shown me where she kept her stills on Third Creek. At least I came by my love of drinking honestly.

Ma glared. "Boy, shush about that. Roger's Ma was no one to be proud of."

"What do you mean? I heard she made the best shine in the county and her whiskey was what made her proud."

"Yeah, but that woman also disgraced the family and could have had us run out of town. While her husband had a stroke that incapacitated him, we worked our fingers to the bone, and she would gallivant and spend her time with a young Negro man. The whole county knew she had taken up with the Negro."

Seeing the look on my face, she explained, "That's what people called them or colored in those days, and the KKK was very active. I know Roger warned her to stop being so flagrant. He didn't care that the man was Negro, but his mother was humiliating the family by showing no shame. So, the woman got meaner and more defiant, and the poor Negro man got lynched just as Roger predicted. We felt bad about it, but his mother didn't even seem to care. She didn't even flinch when she heard the news."

I had to take that in for a minute. I remembered seeing the remnants of the Jim Crow era when I lived with Grandma Kirkman, but it disgusted me to realize there were lynchings so near my home. "I can see why you had a grudge against Great-Grandma, but why are you bitter about Great-Grandpa? I have never heard you say anything nice about him."

Ma took a deep breath, "Father Barkley gave Roger his 17.5 acres when we got married," she replied. "That was the agreement. Roger's brothers all said he could have the farm after Father Barkley passed because none of them wanted anything to do with it, and Father Barkley agreed. Roger always spoke about how we would change things when we got the rest of the land. My grudge against Father Barkley is when he eventually passed, all of the children got equal shares of the land promised to us. Roger never said a word or fought for us. Two weeks later, he got a job at the Statesville chair factory."

"Was Pa Barkley told that he would get the land when Great-Grandpa died?"

Ma scowled. "Every planting and picking season."

"He must have been disgusted!" I exclaimed.

Ma looked down and said angrily, "He did nothing! Your Dad doesn't want to know the truth about his father. But Roger was never much of a husband. He was nothing like my father, Lewis Tate Holler. On the contrary, my father was exceptional in every way. Roger drank, dipped, smoked, and jerry-rigged everything he put his hands on. But I had rules for your dad so he would grow up to be a good man like his Grandad Holler, not like his trifling Dad."

I didn't want to add to Ma Barkley's disappointment by bringing up my dad's past. Things were good with Dad now. He had a steady job, stayed in one place, and we were getting along. I thought a lot about Ma and Pa Barkley and Dad growing up in an environment fraught with dashed expectations and shame. I also convinced myself that I had broken the pattern of the Barkley family.

I had a day to spare before returning home, so I bought a six-pack and drove the back roads of Iredell County, jamming to music and drinking. I wanted to see these places that were the origin of my family. My dad talked about these places while I was growing up, but we never took that trip together down memory lane. I drove by the old movie theater, Cool Springs High School, the football field, and even found the tree from where my Great Grandma Barkley's rumored black lover was lynched. I wasn't completely sure that I stopped in front of the right tree, but it looked ominous enough. I said a prayer and imagined how horrible it must have been. I apologized to the man for the inexcusable racism of the time. Then I made a final stop in the clearing by Third Creek where I knew Great Grandma Barkley stood guard with her shotgun. I took a moment and breathed it all in and realized that disappointment and shame had followed my family for generations.

When I returned the car and got to the airport, I started drinking and didn't stop until we landed in Texas. I was tired and spiraling down into a pit of depression and sadness. I was dying on the inside in a million different ways. I wanted to be free of myself but had no energy or courage to change anything.

I had scheduled a few days off before returning to work, but when I called in to inform the receptionist that I had returned, she told me a client we had been expecting and that I had been working with had come in early. So instead of waiting another day to go in, I showed up for work still drunk from my trip and burst into the conference room while the attorney and another law clerk were prepping the client for a deposition.

I introduced myself to the client without even saying hello to the others and tried to hijack the meeting. I thought I was doing the right thing. That is how unaware I was at the time. Finally, the other law clerk gently touched my elbow, and we walked into the law firm's library.

He said, "Tate, I know you've just come back from your trip, but one of the things you don't do is bust into a meeting reeking of alcohol and being disruptive. We got this! You don't need to be here, and you especially don't need to be here drunk. So, why don't you just go home and sober up?"

I was stunned. This was the first time someone who was not my friend had called me out on my drinking at work. One of the things that I was never able to understand during my entire drinking career was how so many people knew I was drunk when I felt contained and sober. I thought I covered it up quite well. Now I realized that I wasn't fooling anyone.

As an alcoholic, I never smelled alcohol on my breath or emanating from my pores. If I think I'm sober and capable of functioning, then goddamn it, I am!

I spent the next several days trying to fix things, especially with my friend Susan, the attorney who was in the conference room that day. One night I walked into her office, plopped down and said, "I've not been to class for two weeks."

She looked at me with shock. "Are you telling me that you've missed the first two weeks of your last semester of law school?"

Tearing up, I said, "Yes. The mere thought of going to another class just makes me feel sick."

Susan sighed and gently explained "Tate, there's likely more to this than just hating law school. Many of us hated law school, but we finished. You've come too far to let whatever is bothering you stop you from getting that JD." She hugged me, and said, "I'm driving you to school, and that's that." The next two days, Susan drove me to school. It was what I needed to get back on track.

Somehow, I managed to complete my law degree. Dad was ecstatic. He always joked with his friends that he needed a lawyer in the family to keep him out of trouble. If only we kept each other out of trouble. We were closer than ever, but it was the kind of camaraderie reserved for drinking buddies— from hanging out in pool halls, ice houses, beer joints, and a garage full of neighbors and friends. I felt respected and like an equal. I left Texas practically hating the man, but during this time, it was like we were best friends rather than father and son.

CHAPTER 21

TATE, ARE YOU SOBER?

On the day of my law school graduation in December 1990, a rare ice storm gripped Houston. Although it was treacherous and maybe an omen, I did graduate. Dad threw a festive graduation party for me with barbeque and margaritas. I had never seen so many people at our house. I was filled with such gratitude for all these folks celebrating this moment with me.

Now I had to buckle down for the Bar Exam. I did a prep course to make up for the gaps in my class notes while maintaining a dedication and commitment unlike any other time in my life. I did not want to have to take the Bar Exam twice. I had neither the money nor the patience for it. After Day One of the exam, I decided I needed a drink. It was ridiculous to try to pretend any studying would be productive without some alcohol. So I strolled into the bar in the hotel where I was staying near the exam location, and promptly ordered a Miller Lite and a shot of Jack Daniels. I quickly fired back the Jack Daniels and drank my Miller Lite with intention, and then I had a second Miller Lite. I felt better, a lot better—more balanced, more settled, and less uptight. I was proud of myself for showing the measured discipline required to effectively study for the exam. After drinking my fill at the bar, I drove to a convenience store where I bought a 12-pack of Miller Lite, a pack of Marlboro Reds (fuck "Light Cigarettes") and went back up to my room in the hotel where other students were staying during the exam. Everyone looked at me as I walked into the lobby, probably asking themselves, "Why does he have a 12-pack?" I remember thinking to myself, *I have a 12-pack because I need a fucking 12-pack.* The final two days of the exam were made easier since I lifted the prohibition not to drink.

While waiting for the Bar results, I applied for a job as a law clerk at a personal injury plaintiff firm. They called me in for an interview, making it very clear this would not be a job for an attorney. That was a relief because I wasn't even sure if I wanted to practice law, but I needed the work.

I told them I was asking for a clerk position even though I graduated law school and had taken the Bar because I was waiting for a spot in the Navy JAG program to open up. I had twice discussed the Navy JAG program with a recruiter. He'd said that I qualified, but it would be a year before he could formally approve me since there was a long waiting list of lawyers applying to the program. I never really intended to go back in a year, but it seemed a plausible excuse for why I didn't already have an attorney job. I just did not have the capacity to search for a job and study for the Bar Exam at the same time.

The firm hired me as a clerk, and I was glad to be there even after I learned I had passed the Bar. I knew somehow or another when I first got the job as a clerk that I would prove myself to them. I'm not sure that I ever impressed them, but as with most folks, they seemed to like me. I also knew how to push the limits. When I passed the Bar, I told them I can't be a law clerk because I am a lawyer now and asked what they planned to do with me. I simply made the whole thing their problem.

The lawyers met behind closed doors and debated whether to hire me as an associate. I wasn't qualified, my grades were mediocre, but they decided to create a new staff attorney position, somewhere between clerk and associate. That suited me just fine.

The lawyers gave me enough responsibility to challenge me as I learned the ropes. One time I stayed up all night at the office to help them prepare for mediation in a challenging case. My work was excellent, primarily because one of the associates helped me. I was always able to get more competent and experienced people to help me through tough situations. I pulled an all-nighter to complete the presentation, but it required a six-pack of beer while I worked to settle my nerves.

The next day, after a very successful mediation, the partner's elation with me turned into anger and disappointment. The office manager had advised them that I had left beer cans everywhere for the staff to see when they came into the office the next morning. I was usually more careful about covering my tracks, but I had forgotten to tidy up.

Strike two came when I stumbled into the office intoxicated after a particularly long lunch with some office staff members. They probably should have fired me then. The senior partner had a clear and specific policy about lawyers fraternizing and socializing with staff. She said it interfered with the "clear lines of authority," and it was too confusing for the staff. I was more comfortable with the staff because they were more like me. I felt like I didn't belong with the attorneys. Returning to work intoxicated didn't help either.

About a month later, there was another incident, and it became my third strike. The attorneys had begun to rely on me to help with trial prep and motions, and one night I stayed up finalizing some replies for motion hearings to be held the following day.

Yet again I had left beer cans in the copy room trash can. I thought, *at least I put the beer cans in the trash can this time.* By some grace, they did not fire me, but they made it clear I needed to consider that I had a problem, and it better never happen again.

The other senior partner said, "Tate, I like you, but the drinking up here has got to stop. I don't know if you may have a problem, but I know that you can never have a drink up here again."

The writing was clearly on the wall, especially when that same senior partner came into my office each day and asked, "Tate, are you sober?" Eventually, I turned in my two-weeks notice before things could deteriorate further. We ended on good terms. I could not yet fully see how badly my drinking was progressing. Even though I wasn't admitting a drinking problem to myself, my gut knew things could get even worse if I stayed. After I collected the few things in my office and said my goodbyes, I walked out the door with a sad feeling. But at the same time I felt liberated!

◆ ◆ ◆

Among my closest friends, the occasional gripe about my drinking was now becoming a cacophony. I even started avoiding Jodie, whose concerns were the most vocal. This led to a confrontation with our mutual friend from high school, Liane.

I went to visit Liane at her house, and as always, arrived with a six-pack. Liane remarked, "Michael Tate, you cannot travel without a drink anymore."

"I can, but I don't want to," I said, putting the beer in the fridge and following Liane to the living room. As if synchronized, we both lit a Marlboro Light. I took a swig of a beer and said, "Honey, why is Jodie on my ass all the time?"

Liane took a drag and exhaled. "Because you're becoming an ass. We love you. You're a part of our DNA. We all love to party, but you don't party anymore. You're abusing the booze and abusing those around you."

She continued, "No one can complete a sentence around you anymore. The more you drink, the louder you become, and worse, anytime anyone reasonably asks you to stay the night or offers to drive you home, you harshly reject it!"

Stunned, I sat in silence.

"What does that mean?" I said weakly.

Liane crushed out her cigarette and said, "You need to quit or cut back. Jodie is close to being done with you. She is tired of worrying. Our fear is that you are going to kill yourself with booze."

There was very little to say after that, so I left with the rest of my six-pack. While I was saddened by my conversation with Liane, I still had a few friends who didn't have a problem with my drinking. I reconnected with Burk Morris, one of my few friends from law school, who helped get me through an oil and gas class. Burk was a refugee from the oil field and a good drinking buddy. Our study sessions usually consisted of Miller Lite and talking about his days in the oil field. I was fascinated by Texas oil history and stories about oilmen. Often, I'd drive up to Arlington, Texas, just west of Dallas, to party with Burk and his brother A.J. Dr. A.J Morris owned two medical clinics, Industrial Medical Associates, and Little Road Medical Center.

One night A.J and I were drinking a lot of Mezcal. He confided, "You know, I helped Burk get his law practice started. And I refer clients to him all the time. I think his law practice can thrive." Then he stunned me. "You need to come up and be Burk's partner."

Despite our history, when I had to make a decision, I knew I needed to talk with Dad. He was on the road working when I called, and I was sitting in my apartment with all the lights out drinking a beer.

"Bub, what is going on?" he said, sounding a little concerned.

I took my time answering. "Dad, things are just not right. I'm not making enough to pay my debts. But that's not all. I feel trapped. I want to leave."

Taking a long pull on my Miller Lite and lighting a cigarette, I told him about Burk and all the possibilities with A.J.

When I was done, Dad said, "If you feel trapped, leave. Never feel trapped Bub. I do not wish that life for you. Never." I could hear Dad take a swig of his beer. "I got you out of North Carolina so you wouldn't be trapped by a furniture plant or a cotton crop, Bubba. I took us from that life."

I sat in silence and listened. Dad continued, "I ache when I think about your Pa Barkley. He was trapped, all his life, by his mom's withering demands for more and more, by his father's illness, and by life in a chair factory. Bub, he was a fine man, but you wouldn't know from the way Ma Barkley puts him down. He was a dreamer. He wanted to travel, sail and see. Pa endured a life of suffocation, but he had no resentment, Bub! Do not endure your life, never become trapped." There was silence and Dad continued, "You don't need my permission. You will not disappoint me by busting free of this feeling. Dad loves you and I'm happy for you, Bub."

"I love you too, Dad. I'm leaving in about two weeks," I told him, feeling a weight lifted. I had already made the decision; I just needed my dad to validate it. He had never shared so much about Pa Barkley before. And even though Ma Barkley's story differed, I now had a better perspective on my dad's early family life. I felt relieved.

What I didn't realize was how much he was showing me his real feelings. I was focused on my own and couldn't take in that he was opening the door for me to be myself with him. In the long run, I would always underestimate him and how much he loved me.

So, it was decided. I would move to Arlington, live with Burk and use his spare office. We would call our new firm, Barkley & Morris. I needed a fresh start to try to be me again.

CHAPTER 22

HERE WE GO AGAIN

Arlington was the perfect geographic cure, and it was a Morris family affair. Burk already had a solid docket of personal injury and insurance bad faith cases. A.J was constantly referring injured clients to him. Burk's sister, Julie, worked with us and helped A.J at his medical practice. And they all loved to drink and party. I moved in with Burk on a Saturday with only my clothes and started my life at Barkley & Morris on Monday.

As our practice grew, I handled medical collection against insurance companies, personal injury, and insurance bad faith cases. Within two years, I was making real money and gaining a reputation as a litigator. I liked working for myself and Burk placed no obvious expectations on me. He was a good roommate and a great drinking buddy. But it was obvious he was not as interested in building a law practice in Arlington. He preferred his first home in Archer County where he had been elected County Attorney.

At the close of 1992, my two biggest issues were still money and sex. Believe it or not, the money part bothered me the most. Burk handled all the money, and I would "get" money from him as needed. My dissatisfaction with this arrangement and his desire to practice in Archer County led to the ultimate dissolution of our partnership. So I began my solo practice. Despite the dissolution, I was and remain deeply grateful to Burk. If not for him, I may have never stood on my own.

North Texas had given me another shot at being me. But my desire for male companionship was drowning me. One day I was so overwhelmed by a wave of intense sadness that I locked my office door and sobbed. I was drinking heavily, but I was overly cautious when I went out with male friends because I was terrified I would lose control and do something inappropriate. I was afraid if my clients, referral sources, or colleagues knew I was gay, business would dry up, and so would the money. I hated, truly hated, being poor and vulnerable, and I was not going back. But trying not to be gay wasn't working.

One afternoon I had a bout of sentimentality and combed through my address book for Rob's phone number. We hadn't spoken in years, but he immediately answered when I called his office. I got straight to the point. "Rob, if I come to Houston this weekend, would you have time for dinner? I need to talk with you, please."

Rob did not hesitate; he agreed. A few days later, we met at a Mexican restaurant. He looked good, more mature. We made small talk as I played with my food. I wasn't looking for an affair, and I think he sensed that. I needed compassion from someone who knew the real me.

He said, "Mikey, how are you doing?" Mikey was a nickname Rob used when we were lovers. It made me smile, as I am sure he knew it would.

"Rob, I don't know; I mean, okay."

Rob looked at me, touched my arm, and said, "Is there more here?"

"I'm just trying to cope, you know," I said as my eyes filled with tears.

Rob quickly paid the check and said, "Let's talk in the car where it is more private."

When we got to the car, he said, "Are you still struggling?"

After he said that, I couldn't control the tears. He held me, and it felt so good to have someone know what I was feeling at that moment. I hadn't cried or expressed real emotion in what felt like forever. When I stopped sobbing, Rob kept his arm on my shoulder, and I said, "I'm just so tired."

Rob said, "I know. I know the feeling and, Michael Tate, it has been long enough; it has been long enough." After that, there was a long silence.until he added, "You know, I am completely out now."

"You are?" I said, "I didn't know that."

"It will be okay, Michael Tate. I am living proof. I never thought I would have the courage, but now I'm free."

I was shocked and encouraged at the same time. Rob hadn't even left town; he was out and thriving in Houston. I said, "I am still afraid of what I might lose."

"People love you," he said. "It will be okay."

"None of my friends know I am gay," I protested.

"At least one of them does," Rob said, laughing. "I am more concerned about what you will lose if you continue this charade. I am afraid you will lose yourself and your chance at peace and happiness. I will support you. I know it is scary." Rob paused for a moment. "I started with my friends. My best girlfriend went with me to my first gay bar because I was scared to death. It went fine. Mike, where you live is a big place with many gays. You will not be alone." Rob said, "It took me a while to build up to family, especially my mom. Everyone adjusts and accepts it in their own way and time."

I sat there a bit, and then said, "Thank you."

Rob hugged me again, "It will happen. It may not happen perfectly, but it will happen. You be who you are because you deserve your truth."

I couldn't stop thinking about that day with Rob when I drove to pick up my father at the hospital. That was years ago, and yet I still had not worked up the courage to be myself with my dad. I still had too many resentments. He was there for me when I needed him sometimes, but it was only on his terms. He liked me when I was drinking, and we could relate on that level. Now he seemed to be further away than ever, and I wanted to be closer to him.

Dad was happy to be home and settled into his own bed. After a few weeks, he would be good enough to return to work, and he promised to stop smoking and maybe exercise. I almost believed him.

I hadn't had any gay interaction since being with Rob as a teenager, so meeting him for dinner when I was at a low point opened a Pandora's box for me. He made being out seem okay.

Often in the early 90s, I traveled to Austin for hearings. Austin was a liberal, gay-friendly city. They even had a free magazine called "Fag Rag" with places and events of interest to the gay population. What interested me were the ads in the back. Not only did they have personal ads of males seeking males, but they also had listings for male escorts. That intrigued me. I wanted a situation I could control, and even though it was illegal I still thought it the safer bet than hooking up with some random person. An escort would not "out" me. An escort would not judge my lack of experience. With an escort, I could feel in control.

I looked at the ads for the Dallas/Fort Worth area. One drew my eye. I was nervous, but I called the number anyway. An older man answered the phone and said he would be sending "Vincent." I tried to talk myself out of it, but I didn't. In less than an hour, a sexy young Latino-looking man named Vincent arrived at my door. He was beautiful, but seemed as nervous as I was. He called his "manager" to tell him he got in okay.

CHAPTER 23

COMING OUT...KIND OF

Vincent told me he was from Puerto Rico, nineteen years old, and this was his first night as an escort. Fortunately for me, there was a genuine attraction. I didn't know that escorts typically don't kiss, but that was the first thing we did. He stayed the night and the following day he left without taking the money. Vincent gave me a number where I could reach him, so we met again the next weekend. He told me that night he quit being an escort and that he had fallen in love with me the first night we were together. I was his first and last client. I think Vincent believed what he was saying, but I thought he was joking. He had a hero-worship attitude toward me, from almost the very beginning. I loved it!

We had what I thought was an understanding. So I started having him over to my apartment, and he often stayed the whole weekend. We would hang out, watch television, and have sex. On our second weekend, we watched football. "I hate football. I know nothing about it, but I would go to a game with you," he said with obvious anticipation.

I answered, "I much prefer to watch it here." Several weekends later, Vincent gave me a big hug and whispered, "Can we please go dancing?"

I hugged him back, but replied as always, "No, Vincent. You know I'm not ready to be out." But Vincent was young and vibrant, so he naturally wanted more.

"Why can't we go dancing? Who's going to know you in a gay club in Dallas? We could have so much fun and you could meet some of my friends."

It wasn't unreasonable to want to go to the bars with me to dance and be seen. But I was building a law practice and wasn't going to jeopardize everything for someone I considered to be a secret boyfriend. I hate to think of myself this way, but I didn't take Vincent seriously. He was a hot sex buddy and someone to spend time with in my apartment. I was so wrapped up in myself that I don't think I saw him as a whole person. It was all about me.

Eventually, Vincent wanted to stay during the week. When I said no, he began making threats that he would out me. He threatened to call people I knew to tell them about us. I knew he just wanted more attention, so I made empty promises. This started an incessant on-again, off-again relationship which always led to more sex.

Vincent was becoming difficult to control. When his demands would start again, I'd try to cut him off for good, but then he'd call me every day. Each time the call ended in a screaming match. Finally, I put my foot down and ended it. I told him never to call me again.

Late one Friday afternoon, I heard the phone ring. The caller ID showed it was Vincent. I picked up. "Hello," I said.

Vincent spoke quickly: "Tate, please do not hang up, I just want to talk. I am not trying to stay together. I just need to talk. That is all."

"Okay, talk," I said.

"No. In-person," Vincent said. I heard the tears and sniffling coming. He whispered, "I promise I will go away after we talk. I promise. If we are going to end it, let us do it in person."

I felt a wave of empathy and thought, "He's right." In our last conversation, I told him I never wanted to see him again. That was it. He was in love, and I was not. The least I could do was give him one last in-person talk. I said gently, "Okay, but this is the last time. No more starting over or staying."

Vincent said, "I know, I know. I get it. Can I come over tonight?"

A feeling of distrust went through me, but I said, "Yes."

After the call, I went to a bar and began to drink. I needed to be home before 8. After several beers, I picked up a 12-pack and headed to the apartment. I was unquestionably horny. Buzzed as I was, I knew having Vincent over was a mistake. How many times had I broken it off, leading him to incessantly call, cry, and beg? Then we'd have sex and it would all start all over.

I went home and showered and tried to relax. I was anxious, very anxious, and tired of wrestling with him. A little after 8 p.m., I heard a light knock on the door. I knew it was Vincent, and I opened the door with a rush that I had hoped I wouldn't be feeling. Here he was again, beyond cute and sexy. He had purposely dressed to get under my skin with a tight white body shirt and black jeans. And oh, his smile, his cologne, his lips! "Can we at least hug?" he said. I was weak at the knees.

"Of course," I said. I gave him a small kiss on his cheek, which brought a smile. Vincent was 5 feet 5 inches, a little shorter than me, which I liked. I could feel him rise on his toes as he gave me another kiss on the lips.

"It feels so good to be close to you," he said. We hadn't yet stopped hugging. I couldn't resist. Finally, I cradled his head in my hands, lifted his face, and kissed him deeply.

I felt devastated the next morning. I had fallen for his "fuck me, or I will die" routine again. But really, it was my need for sex that was the bigger problem. Had I been more aware, I would have known it was my fault all along.

I let Vincent sleep for another hour or so, and when he got up, I said, "I will take you home. You've got to go. Last night was not supposed to happen. We are not doing this."

Vincent looked at me coyly and said, "Doing what?"

I wanted to throw something. The anger was rising into my chest, I felt it, but I had to admit I had agreed to all of this. I stood up and said, "Vincent, we are over. I am sorry this happened. It should not have happened."

At first, Vincent looked at me with a hurt puppy expression, but it quickly turned into something else entirely. His eyes turned almost black as his pupils dilated with rage. Then he shouted, "I am not going anywhere. I am sick of you using me. You can fuck with my body but not with my heart!" He trembled. "The way you treat me is abuse. You are too ashamed to even go to a restaurant with me. You know I am in love with you, but you mistreat me! No. I'm going nowhere."

I walked toward him and tried to stay calm, but I could feel my voice rising to a scream, "Please get dressed. I admit this is my mistake."

"No! You can use my body, but you cannot use my heart!" he repeated.

I walked over and touched him and said, "Please get dressed."

He glared and said, "No!"

I raised my hand, and he flinched. I could see the fear as he raised his arm to block me. I stopped and yelled, "I am not going to hit you, but you get me so angry, Vince!" It bothered me that he thought I would hit him. I got my cool back.

Vincent looked at me. "I have to make a call."

"Who are you going to call?"

"The police would want to know you are threatening me and would likely like to know how we met. How is that for your law career, Mr. Lawyer?" Vincent glared, walked toward the couch, and picked up the phone. I immediately grabbed his wrist and squeezed with all my might. His face grimaced and he shrieked. He yelled, "That hurts!"

"That did not hurt you," I yelled back at him. Truth be told, I wasn't sure if it had or not. Vincent then slapped me in the face with his left hand, and I slapped him right back as hard as I could. He went down for a minute but then went to slap me again. This time I grabbed his left hand and leaped toward him to pin him to the couch, but we lost balance and fell over the coffee table and crashed to the floor. The noise seemed to reverberate through the entire apartment complex. Vince was crying and I was hurting. I took a deep breath as we lay on the floor, entirely spent. Neither of us said anything.

"What the fuck?" I thought. I rolled over and pulled Vince toward me. I held him with both arms. I just said, "Sorry. I am so sorry," again and again.

Vince stayed with me the rest of the day. We watched two movies on cable. As night drew close, I said, "I am taking you home." It was almost an hour to his house, and we drove in silence. He did not resist. When I pulled in front of his house, I finally said, "I am not doing this anymore. I cannot and will not give you what you want. Please find someone who will." I leaned over and kissed him on the cheek.

◆ ◆ ◆

That was when I finally dared to go to my first therapist. A.J. referred me to Katy Ellis, a psychologist with a no-nonsense reputation. When I first met her, I thought she looked like the kind of bouncy cheerleader I wished I could date if I had only been heterosexual. I made assumptions about her cheerful personality before she immediately went for my jugular. After the pleasantries, she asked me point blank, "Tate, why are you here? Something propelled you to me. What is it?"

"Well, uh, I…am…well…torn up on the inside," I replied, trying to be vague. I already worried she would tell people. I knew lawyers who gossiped about their clients. It was against the rules, but they still did it. And I had been living in secret for so long that I never knew who to trust.

"Okay, what specifically is giving you these feelings? This fear, it seems?"

I said nothing.

"Tate, you okay? You want to tell me, so just go ahead."

She was right. I did want to tell her; I needed to tell her. So I blurted out the whole sorry mess. "I have only had two sexual experiences that gave me any satisfaction. Both were with guys. I think about these experiences all the time. I want the experience again! But I cannot be gay. I just cannot." I was happy to get that off my chest, but I hadn't even told her about Vincent.

"Why can you not be gay?" I saw no judgment in her expression, which made me a little more comfortable.

"I will lose everything! My cases, my friends…everything!"

"Tate, do you think you're gay?"

I immediately replied, "No, I just like sex with guys."

Katy didn't react to my blatant denial. "Okay, so tell me about a day in your life."

We talked for an hour. At the end of the session, Katy said, "It sounds like drinking is your hobby."

"It is one of my favorite things to do," I admitted. I was surprised Katy didn't say anything more about the drinking and let it drop. When we ended that first meeting, she gave me a note with several numbers for gay hotline services. I liked Katy just fine but decided I didn't need to return.

After losing control with Vincent, I kept dwelling on everything that took place with him. How did I let myself lose control? I could not shake my feelings. I felt confused, ashamed, and depressed, but I told no one. Not even Katy in our first visit. Eventually, I returned to Katy and told her all about my fight with Vincent. It felt good to tell someone. She asked me how long I expected I could sustain a relationship like that while in the closet.

I smiled wistfully. "I thought I could keep it as long as I wanted to, but he wanted more."

Katy rolled her eyes, "Of course he did. Isn't that what happens when two people have a sexual relationship over time? He had feelings for you."

I felt kicked in the stomach. I hadn't even told her that Vincent had shown up one more time after our fight at my apartment. It was random and unannounced. When I opened the door, he walked in like he belonged. I wasn't sure if he was drunk. I yelled, "Vincent!" He fell to his knees, unzipped my pants, and I stopped him. "No. No. No. It's over," I yelled and pulled him to his feet and made him leave. I know he felt humiliated, but I didn't see any other way.

The next day I called Vincent's mom. He was still living at home, and I told her, "You've got to get a grip on this kid. He keeps insisting we should be in a relationship, but I don't want it."

She said she understood and would talk to him.

About a month later, I got a call from the guy who first connected me to Vincent, his "manager." In a tone that clearly said *I don't want anything to do with you, I asked why he was calling.*

"Because Vincent's mom is calling me," he said, genuinely concerned. "He's disappeared. I figured he ran to you."

I didn't feel any remorse over that. "I have not seen Vincent."

"He loved you," the man said. "He told me that when he quit working for me."

"I haven't seen him in a long time," I said again, trying to rush off the phone.

After we hung up, the worry I was trying to deny began to fester. I called Vincent's mom.

"Tate," she said into the phone, sounding relieved. I hated to tell her that he was not with me, and I didn't know where he was.

She started to cry. "I do not know where he is. He has struggled at school; he struggles with his stepdad. I just do not know what to do," she said. "Tate, he told me about you from day one. I did not like how he met you, but he bragged about you. I always felt better knowing he was with you instead of running the roads."

I felt sick with guilt. While I was with him, I didn't think of him as having a family who loved him. I was attracted to him, but I never let myself feel more. I was empty inside, drunk most of the time, and only concerned about making money with my law practice. I treated him like just another one of my possessions.

Before I hung up, I said, "I am sorry. I promise that if I hear from him or he comes to me, I will let you know immediately. I promise." Then I walked to the fridge, got another beer, sat down in my chair, and took a long swig.

❖ ❖ ❖

I continued to see Katy mostly to process my fear of "coming out," but I always brought up Vincent, and she always pivoted to the same topic. "Tate, what do you do when you are not working, even when you are working?"

I took a deep breath. "I know, Katy. I drink. But I was not drunk when I fought with Vincent."

Katy snapped back, "You were not drunk. But you tell me, is this fight alcoholic behavior? Is this something your dad would do?"

I didn't like that she brought up my dad. I felt protective of him. I didn't feel that any of this had anything to do with him. I felt like getting up to leave, but I didn't. I just said, "I fucked up."

"You're smothering yourself in booze," she continued. "You will never be at peace with who you are if drinking is your life. Gay or straight, you have got to deal with the drinking first. Find some peace so we can work on the other issues."

CHAPTER 24

ONE MORE TRY

After my relationship with Vincent, I met a receptionist named Leanne at the law office where I was sharing space. I knew I was gay, but I still wouldn't say it out loud to anyone, including my therapist. So when I found out Leanne was interested in me, I decided to ask her out. I was fooling myself, but I felt a glimmer of hope when we started dating because I was able to have sex with her. It was sensual and lovely, and so was she. While we dated, I took Leanne to dinner with my friends and even home to Houston to meet my parents.

The most loathsome thing was, like Vincent, Leanne adored me and saw marriage in our future. The feeling of being adored was like a narcotic, and I lived in its glow for a short time. With Leanne, life was the picture I always desired for myself. Being with her was what people expected of a good ole Texas boy like me, but it was a lie.

My self-hatred grew as my conscience fought against itself. It was Vincent all over again. I could not give Leanne what she wanted. I eventually ended our relationship, though I never told her the truth. I am not proud of the fact that she heard of my coming out through others.

◆ ◆ ◆

Finally, I decided I could no longer live two lives. I was just too tired, so I decided it was time to start coming out. The administrator in A.J.'s office was an openly gay guy named George. I envied and respected him because he was "out and proud." I asked him to meet me privately at his office on a Sunday.

In those days, I was known as A.J.'s hatchet man. When he needed somebody fired or some kind of dirty work done, he usually called me to do the job. As we sat down, George asked, "Am I in trouble?"

I laughed, "George this has nothing to do with A.J." Inhaling deeply, I said, "I want to tell you something no one knows. I am gay and I don't know what to do. I've never been to a gay club. I have no gay friends. I just don't know what to do."

George looked unsurprised. "I thought you were either going to come out to me or fire me today. I'm grateful you're not firing me!"

We both laughed. Reaching over and wrapping his arms around me, he said, "This is a hug thing. I am honored you chose to share this with me. You do have a gay friend—me! I'll help you."

And so I began the process of coming out. The next weekend, George and I went to the *651 Club*, a Country and Western gay bar near downtown Fort Worth. I was a nervous wreck. I had always heard horrible things about gay bars, the terrible things that would happen in the bathrooms. Gay men surrounding you, wanting sex if you tried to take a piss, I literally made George go to the bathroom with me the first time. It was insane and silly, but he humored me. By the way, nothing bad happened.

The scene in the club was amazing! All these men spinning and two-stepping with each other. And they were so relaxed. By the end of the night, I had consumed many beers and a couple of shots with George and his friends. In the following months, I would party often with them. I became more confident and the art of picking up guys came to me quickly. But my comfort was in direct proportion to how much alcohol I consumed. After I came out to George, it was as if a dam broke in me. I started coming out to the people I knew in my Arlington world. First, I told Julie and Margarita my paralegals. I laughed when Margarita said, "Oh Honey, you know I love you. You are too good-looking to be straight anyway!"

A.J.'s immediate reaction was, "I don't care, Bubba. You just be safe, we do not have a grip on HIV/AIDS, so you've got to be careful." There was not one negative reaction, even amongst some of the hardcore North Texas rednecks I had befriended.

The next step was to tell my Houston friends, and it was only right to start with Jodie. One weekend I returned to Houston and invited her to meet me at one of our favorite places, the House of Pies. Since we had been high school friends and dated a few times, I figured she would want to know that our lack of physical affection had nothing to do with her.

"Jodie," I said, "I'm gay." I said it quickly. Jodie inhaled sharply and started to cry.

"Michael Tate, I love you. And I don't care if you're gay. I am so happy you told me the truth. I am sure it was difficult." That gave me a perfect opening to share my theory about repression and alcohol.

"I think one of the reasons that I drank so much was because I have been so conflicted about being gay."

Jodie somberly spoke, "I do hope this helps with the drinking. I've been insanely worried about you for some time now." We hugged, and she congratulated me. We both thought it was logical that confronting my demons of repressed homosexuality would tame my drinking. But, of course, it turned out to be much more complicated than that.

After telling Jodie, I was on an emotional high. Next, I headed to see Liane, my other high school friend, and her boyfriend Robin. As I neared Liane's house, I kept thinking, *Why had I waited so long?*

Jodie had been shocked when I told her. Not because I was gay, but because I kept something so essential about who I am from her. It was almost like betrayal. I felt nervous, but instinctively, I knew it would be easier with Liane and Robin. They were artists and they often spoke of their "gay" friends. I nervously knocked on their old wooden door and heard two voices say, "Come in." When I walked in, Liane was relaxing in a red bean bag on the floor and Robin was standing against the kitchen door frame.

Liane smiled, "Hey, honey."

Robin grinned and yelled, "Tater!" his nickname for me. I wanted to tell Liane alone, but it just didn't feel right to ask Robin to leave the room, so I decided to tell them together.

I sat on the couch and did not hesitate. "I want to talk with you both. It is a big deal, at least for me. First, I want to apologize. I am sorry it has taken me so long to come to this point. I love you both dearly and I know you love me. But frankly, it has taken me a lifetime to wrap my head around it and accept it." Robin and Liane looked concerned, so I quickly said. "I am not dying or anything, but I am gay."

Robin spoke first, "Is that it, Tater? Jesus, you had me worried."

Liane giggled a little and said, "Robin!" But she smiled and said, "Really?

Is that it?"

I said, "Yes. That is enough."

"Michael Tate, you know that is okay, don't you? I hope you know that," Liane assured me.

"I think so," I replied.

She lifted herself off the beanbag and hugged me. "I love you. You have been one of my best friends since I can remember. And…and I have suspected for some time. Just a feeling." Liane seemed proud of herself. I stayed a while longer as they asked me about my "type" and if I was dating anyone. It felt good. Like nothing had changed.

❖ ❖ ❖

Leaving Liane and Robin's, I decided to head to my parents house to tell Mom. As luck would have it, Dad was on the road working. When the moment came, I was nervous. Not afraid, not ashamed, just nervous. Mom sat on the couch in her usual spot, and I sat on the floor in front of her. I gently said, "Mom, there is something I need to tell you about myself. I probably should have told you long ago, but I was ashamed and embarrassed."

"What is it?" she interjected before I could finish.

"I am gay." I watched her face.

She startled me with a loud, almost shriek. "Honey, you are gay? Are you sure?" I wanted to laugh at the last part, but I could see tears in her eyes.

"Yes, I am sure I'm gay. I have known for a long time. I tried to fight it but couldn't make it go away."

Mom began to cry. I lifted myself off the floor and gave her a hug. She hugged back hard as she continued to cry. I sat back down on the floor.

"Mom, how are you feeling?"

Mom reached over to the end table and pulled out some Kleenex. "Michael, Son, Mom is going to have to deal with this in my own way. This is hard for me. I want you to be happy, whatever that is for you. I always thought you would have a wife and kids."

I touched Mom's hand. "I may have kids, Mom; you never know."

She looked at me quizzically.

At that moment, I remembered how sheltered her life had been. "Mom, I know it is a lot, but take your time. I am still the same me."

Mom steadied herself, "I'm sorry you had to struggle with this, son. I love you. I am your mom, and I will always love you. I worry for you. I worry you can't be happy in a world that has so much meanness. And what about all the diseases?"

I got up and hugged Mom. "I am conscientious, Mom. Please don't worry about that."

She sat silently with me for a few minutes. Then I asked, "Do I tell Dad?"

Mom shot me a look of concern, "I don't know, son. Now may not be best. Your dad is in a horrible place in his head right now and is dealing with his own things…selfish things. Your dad and I are in a bad place too." She steadied herself, "Bub, your dad and I talked about this when you were in high school, that you were around gay people. Who was your friend you ran around with early on?"

I smiled, "That was Tony. Yes, he was no doubt about it gay. He was my friend, but we were not lovers."

Mom looked at me, "Your dad did not like him very much. He worried about you being around him. Then you had another friend."

I knew who she meant right off, "Rob? You met him several times. He was my first love, my first boyfriend."

Mom wiped her eyes and said, "The two of you were real close, I remember, for a little while anyway."

It wasn't until many years later that Mom explained that Dad was once again up to his philandering ways at that time, and they were in a rocky place in their marriage. My mom was tolerant and strong but unsure how much she still wanted to tolerate from him. Of course, she stuck it out. She loved Dad and was fiercely loyal. But she was right that it was best not to tell him. I wasn't ready and had no idea how long it would be before I could face the man with my truth.

She stood up and hugged me again, "I love you, son, so much! It has been you and me together through all this shit and struggle. You are my son, my light, and I love you."

Mom and I stood there, hugging tightly for a while longer. I thought about our time in the white house, where we had nothing, the Cadillac man, hiding from the cops as we fled to North Carolina, and I started to laugh. Mom pulled back with a smile and said, "What, honey?"

"I was just thinking about some of the times we've had, Mom."

The following day I called my sister, Brandy, and arranged to meet her at her apartment complex pool in Pasadena where she had recently moved in with her boyfriend Jason. I wasn't nervous about telling Brandy. I stopped and bought a 12 pack of Miller Lite on the way, feeling relaxed and hoping to work on my tan while we talked.

It was a classic summer day in Houston, with highs in the mid-nineties and one hundred percent humidity. Brandy and I found choice spots around the pool and kicked back to drink for a bit. After less than thirty minutes I said, "Brandy there's something Bub needs to tell you. It's been very difficult for me for a long time to keep this secret. I want you to know that I've struggled with it for some time, but I'm not willing to hide it anymore, nor am I ashamed by it; your brother is gay."

Brandy looked at me as a gentle smile crossed her face and she said, "Bub, you know that I love you gay or straight, no matter what and I'm so glad that you finally told me, but you know, we figured you were gay some time ago. So, it's okay. I love you, don't worry."

After a few minutes passed, Brandy looked curious and said, "So what prompted you to come out?"

I answered, "A letter Kairy-Tate sent me after I tried and failed to tell her that I was gay the last time I was in Houston. Apparently, she could see I was struggling with something, so she wrote me this beautiful, three-page note that said, 'Bubba, you can tell me absolutely anything. No matter what, I'm going to love you. There's no reason for you to be haunted by secrets and no reason for you to feel shame. You are a wonderful, caring, loving brother, a smart man and I love you, and I will always love you'. After reading that, I knew it was time for me to begin the process of coming out because it's not just about me."

After hanging out with Brandy, I went to see Kairy-Tate. I thanked her for her letter and confirmed her suspicions that I had been keeping a secret and struggling with the shame of being gay. "But now, I am out and happy to accept my true self," I said.

Confirming what Brandy told me, Kairy-Tate said, "Bubba, we figured it out a long time ago and as I said in my letter, I will always love you."

Finally, later that year, Leighann came to visit Mom and Dad while waiting to join her husband Reggie for his next Air Force assignment. I drove to Houston and stayed in my old room and got to hang out around the house with her two boys, Trey and Trevor, who are awesome kids. One afternoon, Leighann and I sat out in the driveway as was our family habit. I quietly said, "I'm sorry to be whispering, but I want this conversation to be just between us. I've told Brandy and Kairy-Tate and I've also told Mom, but I've not told Dad yet. I want you to know that I love you very much Leighann, but I have been hiding something for a long, long time. I've decided not to struggle with it anymore. I want to be who I am. I am gay."

Leighann smiled and stood up to hug me. Then she said something that I didn't see coming, "Bubba, I don't care that you're gay. None of us are surprised by this. I knew back when you were in high school. You're our brother. You're Bubba, so none of that matters to me. You be who you are, and you be happy."

I was stunned. "How did you know? I wasn't effeminate acting."

She said, "No, but do you remember you had a friend who came over, what was his name? Rob, Robert? And one summer any time Mom and Dad were gone, he would come over and you would go to your room. Kairy-Tate and I both figured that he must be your boyfriend." Leighann continued, "It didn't bother us then and it doesn't bother us now. We just love you."

CHAPTER 25

ROCK BOTTOM

I was afraid that coming out to my friends and most of my family would change everything for the worse, but it didn't. My law practice was still thriving. I met the right people and got referrals from other lawyers who helped me build my practice. Being social and loving to party worked well for me, and I learned to pace myself and finish my drinking at home. I was ambitious and wanted to have enough money so I would never again feel the sting of poverty. Too many times I saw my father humiliated because we had no money.

Despite the drinking, I kept it all together and earned enough money to give my mother the first new car she ever had. I also bought a great house with a jacuzzi in the master bath and a hot tub in the backyard. The problem with having money for the first time was that I was always worried someone would take it from me. I spent it as soon as I had it and especially liked "high-rolling", that is buying everyone rounds of drinks and paying for dinners.

But it all started to catch up with me. I needed to drink to be "out", and I had begun to need the steadiness of a drink to focus on my cases. I was incapable of doing anything without some form of alcoholic buzz. A.J. prescribed me Librium, a mild anti-anxiety med that also treats tremors and alcohol withdrawal, to cut down on my drinking during the day, but I started noticing the shakes and anxiety in the morning anyway. Soon thereafter, one of my best attorney friends told me there was talk around town of my heavy drinking. I was embarrassed but dismissed it as gossip, that is, until that New Years Eve party when I parked my car sideways on my lawn. It scared me enough to enroll in the Charter Hospital treatment facility.

When I left the program at Charter Hospital, I stayed sober for forty-seven days. I tried to steer clear of bars and parties. But I missed my friends, so I started going back to my favorite bars where I would drink Diet Coke, root beer, or club soda, anything so I could have something in my hand. It was amusing and sad.

I tried to convince myself I didn't have a serious problem. Before I left rehab, a few friends cleared my house of all my booze and pills. I wanted to return home to no temptation. The program kept emphasizing *Alcoholics Anonymous*, but at the time I thought that was not for me. AA was for drunks. I just needed to set myself straight. I wanted to prove to myself that I was not an alcoholic. All I needed was willpower and a thoughtful plan. After a while, I could go back to social drinking like other people.

My days at home after rehab became tedious. I could only take so many walks, watch so much TV, and drink so much coffee. I felt unnerved and a little scared. I didn't know where to put myself and I tried to fight generalized feelings of sadness and abject fear. I didn't know where the feelings were coming from because they didn't seem to be related to anything. I stopped drinking and thought that would be it. But the feelings stayed.

I decided to try an AA meeting. I found one nearby, and figured I could slip out of the office unnoticed. Like all AA meetings, they began by asking if there were any newcomers or first-timers. I kept my hand down to avoid the attention of everyone in the meeting. I wanted to be unnoticed and didn't want anyone to try to help me after the meeting. I felt it was enough that I was there listening.

It was a fourth-step meeting, which reads, "Made a searching and fearless inventory of ourselves." Several men shared, but one stood out. He was relatively young with jet black hair and a formidable beard. He wore a weathered work shirt with an HVAC company logo. Clearly upset, he spoke to the group. "I hate this step! It sucks! The rigorous honesty this book requires is too much, too much without something to ease the pain. I haven't had a drink in seven months, but dealing with the me underneath my drinking is kicking my ass. But I have to stay sober. I can't hide anymore."

This man's words staggered me. I didn't want to say I was an alcoholic, let alone be an AA member. I viewed AA as a place for the downtrodden, a rough, working-class crowd, and that was no longer me. The people at the meeting had beards and CPO jackets. They wore dirty jeans and boots with mud on them. These people, mostly men, drove utility trucks, and plumbing vans, and there was even a dump truck. They had beat-up cars, the kind my dad's friends parked all along our driveway when they hung out with him in the garage. But now I felt out of place with them. These people needed AA. I just needed to drink less.

I didn't go back to a meeting after that and tried to ignore the grieving I experienced at the loss of my former self. I was edgy, nervous, and afraid of being with people. I hadn't realized how much my social personality stemmed from being wasted most of the time. I tried everything I could to fight my craving to drink. I wanted to stay sober because, as much as I didn't want to admit it, my life was completely unmanageable. But I was holding on. Although I didn't feel any real love for my law practice, it was how I made money, so I kept it together and continued to do relatively well. I played music every morning that I believed would pump me up to face the day. I did self-talk and made sure to dress well. I constantly worked out to get fit and trim. I tried all the ways alcoholics try to recover without AA. Maybe this works for some people, but forty-seven days after my last drink, nothing had changed inside me.

◆ ◆ ◆

One beautiful spring Saturday. I decided to get in my car and drive around. I stopped at a convenience store near Lake Arlington, thinking I would treat myself to real Coke with sugar. As I approached the checkout counter, I spotted a huge bin of iced-down beer in its usual spot. There were two Miller Lite tall boys soaking in that beautiful, wet ice. They looked so, so good. I reached in, grabbed one and put it on the counter. A rush of guilt and a wave of uneasiness passed through me. *What are you doing?* My mind raced. Returning to the car, I pulled the top and drank. The beer eased down my throat and I felt the same bliss that I felt on that Houston bayou so many years before.

Just like that, I relapsed. No more looking at myself and saying, "I do not want to be a guy that's drunk all the time." I was bored, edgy, and frustrated. The voice of my disease became louder than my desire to stay sober. It reminded me of how much fun I had when drunk and wiped out my memory of the car crashes, the lost friends, and the loss of dignity. After that, I thought to hell with all this sobriety business.

Like the character "Norm" in the show *Cheers*, I loved walking into my local bar and hearing everyone excitedly yell, "Tate!" There was nothing better than sitting down and ordering a Miller Lite and a shot of Jack Daniels. It wasn't the same watching sports with my friends and drinking a Diet Coke. I wanted to be like them. I had no idea if they were alcoholics. For all I knew, they had a few drinks and went home to a full life. This routine was my life, and I made no effort to change it once I picked it up again. I was mostly relieved that it was over, that the abstinence and the suffering was over. But mostly the conflict in my head was gone. I could drink responsibly. I was in control.

It is amazing how quickly an alcoholic can return to old habits. The next day, I bought a six-pack, took it home, and put it in the fridge. After drinking two beers, I decided I needed to leave the house. I knew if people saw me drinking again it would raise eyebrows, so I thought it was best to get it over with and demonstrate my newfound self-control.

I drove to my favorite local bar and sat down. The bartender said, "Diet Coke?"

Looking around the room triumphantly, I said loudly, "No, I'll take a Miller Lite."

"Okay," he said hesitantly. "Are you drinking again?"

"Yes!" I said, "but now I know how to control it."

I don't remember how I got home that night and I woke up the next day with a wicked hangover. Once again alcohol dominated my life like a lost lover.

After Charter Hospital, my brain was occupied with trying not to drink, so I told myself it was better that I was drinking again so I would not be so distracted. I just needed to get back on track. But my drinking escalated yet again, and as word got out, the complaints grew. Friends kept telling me to take it easy.

Several months after the relapse, I tried a case. My client was a condescending white guy, claiming the Defendant, an African American gentleman pulled out in front of him and caused an accident. The Defendant seemed to be a pleasant, genuine guy. I must have signed up my client, the Plaintiff, during a drunk because he was not my typical client. The Tarrant County jury clearly figured out the parties, and I lost the trial. I did, however, get through it without drinking, which was a big win for me. Afterward,

I walked over to Billy Miner's Saloon in downtown Fort Worth. The next thing I remember, a Fort Worth police officer and my opposing counsel were putting me in a cab. Apparently, I had passed out and the bartender called my opposing counsel having seen his phone number on some of the pleadings I had out at the bar.

Yet again, I'd been graced by God. I was not arrested for public intoxication, and my opposing counsel graciously came to Billy Miner's to vouch for me, telling the officer that I'd had a difficult day in court and just had too much to drink. I had dodged another bullet.

The rest of the year was a blur. I was back to my old routine, Bailey's Irish Cream in the mornings with my Valium and three or four Miller Lites on my drive before lunch every day. Returning to the office to pretend I was doing something for thirty or forty minutes, and then departing for lunch where I would have three Absolut vodka sodas with a lemon twist. After lunch, I would come back to the office and try to work, but by 4:00 p.m., it was time for happy hour at my favorite local bar. My biggest stress was Saturday night. Texas did not allow you to buy alcohol before noon on Sunday. It was critical that I had all the beer and booze I needed for Sunday morning, making sure that I did not have a moment where I would run out of alcohol. I only made that mistake once.

Somehow, I managed to make decent but not great money during this time. Margarita and Julie were pushing my claims and cases along, and I would do my bit where I had to. I could rally from time to time, attending hearings and managing to settle several relatively lucrative cases. Margarita became very good at manipulating me so I would rally at just the right moment to make payroll. But I was starting to see my referrals drop and my chiropractors were pushing back since I started asking them for the first time to cut their bills, making it easier for me to settle cases.

Margarita left a year after my relapse, telling me, "Tate, I want to be a part of something exciting and growing. I love you, but I cannot keep you focused and sober." Soon thereafter, I learned one of my chiropractic sources told a lawyer friend, "If you haven't seen Tate recently, you are not missing much. He is nothing but a drunk."

I couldn't pretend anymore. My client base and referral sources dried up, Julie left to work with A.J. full-time, and I was alone with almost no cases. I closed my practice, sold my house, packed up, and moved back home to

Mom and Dad's. While I should have felt embarrassment, I only felt relief. I had no responsibilities, and nothing was weighing me down. I could drink and relax without any interference.

From the first day back at Mom and Dad's, all I did was stand in the garage leaning against the washer and dryer, thinking about how I needed to stop drinking, which made me drink more. After a while, I became oblivious and stopped thinking about even slowing down. I didn't notice that I had once again gained weight because I drank all day and ate huge amounts late at night. My father taught me one of his ridiculous drinking rules: "Don't waste $100 drunk on a $10 meal." But now I ignored even that rule. I just couldn't get enough of anything that I thought would make me feel better. Everything I did had to be to excess. I stopped looking in mirrors or reaching out to friends.

I tried to get work through an attorney placement service as a project lawyer reviewing documents and landed gigs here and there. But I couldn't get through a day without making an excuse to get out and drink. I was going through a case of beer a day, easy, and often called in sick. During one of those gigs, I called in sick and I went on a two-week drinking binge deluding myself into thinking I could return to the office as if nothing happened. But of course, they had fired me, so later that day when my mom got home from work, she found me passed out on our couch. Dad was traveling and Mom was never one to say much, but she asked me to shower and made me supper. It was the first of many such episodes.

My drinking escalated during the fall of 1998. Then, the day before Thanksgiving, before the rest of the family arrived, my dad and I drank nonstop into the night. I only wish this was my rock bottom because I cringe when I think of it. But instead, I woke up on Thanksgiving morning covered in my own urine. I felt like a five-year-old as I pulled the evidence off the bed and peeled off my soiled clothing. I ran the shower over my bloated body and cried.

When I came into the kitchen for some coffee, my mother looked me up and down.

"What's wrong, Bubba," she asked. It was as if she felt my pain.

"I really messed up, Mom," I confessed. We walked together to my room, and without saying a word, she got out the bleach, and we both sponged off the stains. Mom took care of it all, like always. After that, we never spoke of it again.

My sister Kairy-Tate invited me to a New Year's Eve party, but I felt too fat and awful to go. She insisted, so I started drinking early on the day of the party. My parents had gone out of town, so I had the garage to myself. I found a bottle of Dad's Johnnie Walker Black and poured some into my coffee. I was no longer getting the buzz I needed from beer. I heard my voice say, "This is hopeless; you can't stop." I burst into tears. Daily living at the most basic level required so much alcohol. The next thing I knew, I had blacked out.

I woke up on the garage floor sticky from urine and my own feces. I have no clue how long I had been out, but it was clear much time passed. My whole body ached; my head was killing me. I felt like I had fallen into a void. As I laid there I thought, *I can't go on.* I knew I had a bottle of at least twenty Valium pills my doctor had prescribed for the shakes, with the explicit instruction, "Not to be taken with alcohol." With the bottle of Johnnie Walker tucked under my arm I went to the bathroom where I kept the pills.

I hadn't prayed or asked for help in a long time. I was ready to give up. But before I poured the Valium in my hand, a flash went through my head. I remembered a friend telling me about a treatment facility called Hazelden in Minnesota. I thought it would be easier just to slip away into a haze of Valium and Johnnie Walker Black. But for reasons I still cannot quite explain, I called Hazelden instead. The call lasted over an hour; long enough for me to regain some lucidity and hope.

The only way I could afford Hazelden was with money I had stashed away with my friend, Greg Barta. In a fit of drunken paranoia, I sent Greg money to hold it for me in case of emergency. This situation was absolutely an emergency. I called Greg and he took care of the rest.

I would love to say I had an epiphany and went to Hazelden with a few days of sobriety already under my belt, but that was not the case. Instead, I did everything I could to get shit-faced drunk before getting on the plane. I found an open bar at the airport and managed to get through four Miller Lites, four Jacks, and a couple shots of Peppermint Schnapps for good measure before heading to the gate. I was fighting back tears the entire time, telling the bartender some bullshit about going to a relative's funeral.

I drank continuously during the flight and drifted off to sleep. When I woke up, the pilot was announcing we were about to land, and I panicked. How the hell did I fall asleep? I practically begged the flight attendant for one more beer, but she refused, and I barely controlled my upset. My only thought was "I might never drink again."

PART III

Men

CHAPTER 26

HAZELDEN

I had no idea how sick I was. Checking into Hazelden was humiliating. They searched my stuff for contraband like I was some addict from the streets. I still didn't think I was like *them*. I had yet to acknowledge that, had I not had a family to run home to, the streets would have been my next destination.

The medical exam was debasing. I remember feeling victimized by all the probing and prodding. I was embarrassed by my naked, fat, and bloated body. My 5 foot 7 inch frame was hauling around 225 pounds which caused me to waddle rather than walk. Looking back, I am amazed at how out of touch with reality I was. The doctor said my blood pressure was dangerously high and I was in a state of medical emergency. It didn't sink in that they kept me in a special infirmary for several days under observation because I wasn't medically well enough for rehab. They needed to bring down my blood pressure to avoid a stroke. I am convinced that my moment of urine-soaked clarity in the garage may have truly saved my life. I wouldn't have admitted it then, but that was the first of many miracles where God helped me realize I was worth saving.

As much as I thought I was in control of my life during my drinking years, underneath I was still that insecure chubby boy struggling with self-hatred. I was addicted to alcohol on a physical level, but I would learn that I was committing a slow suicide. Despite all my bravado, I liked the feeling of oblivion, because it was the only time I felt okay with myself. When I entered Hazelden I was totally numb from the heart up and my brain was ready to explode from within.

When I was finally released from the infirmary, a young man came into my room. Smiling, he said, "Mr. Barkley, I've come to take you to the Cronin Unit. It is an all-men's unit." We gathered my luggage, without any perceived contraband. They took away my Nyquil, my Halls cough drops and my Listerine due to their alcohol content. Then the young man led me to a very large room that had two beds and a set of bunk beds. Everything seemed to be in order, the beds were neatly made but there were personal items throughout the room. I was shocked! I was being forced to share a room! As a wave of anxiety rolled through me, I thought, *who are these people I am going to live with? How humiliating. I'm a lawyer for god's sakes.* It was like I'd been beamed back to the seventh grade at South Houston Intermediate School, where for the first time I was required to take a shower with everyone else. The young man pointed. "This is your bed. Here's a schedule. Once you're settled, Jim will come see you."

"Who's Jim?"

"He's your unit supervisor and your counselor," the young man said. Then he left the room.

I sat on the bed and took a deep breath. I could have cried, but I didn't want to humiliate myself any further. My mind raced through possibilities to get back to the airport, out of there. I found no rational solution. Twenty minutes later, Jim Atkins, a solid guy with unruly black hair and a full beard, walked into the room and introduced himself. He spoke quietly. "I will be your unit supervisor and counselor, coordinating your care and recovery. If you're settled, come on down to my office and we'll chat."

"I am not settled. I am not built for roommates," I said defiantly. Jim just laughed and said, "I know you're special, but this is how we do it at Hazelden. We are a community. Follow me please." I followed Jim through an open area that looked like a large living room into his office.

I was in a fog as he explained how Hazelden worked. "Everyone here, including staff and the other patients, are committed to your recovery. You can come talk to me any time if you have any problems or challenges. Hazelden is a 28-day chemical dependency recovery program. Our protocol here is the standard for the world. Are you aware of AA and the Twelve steps?"

I nodded "Yes," thinking to myself yet again, *AA is not for me.*

"Our goal is to get you through at least the first three steps. You will meet with doctors, pastors, psychologists, and all manner of counselors. We go to three AA meetings a day led by staff, patients, visitors and people from the community. And when you are ready we will also take you to an AA meeting outside of these walls." Jim hit me hard with AA right out of the gate.

He then added, "It concerns me that you smoke. At some point, you will need a tobacco cessation program, but for now, you just worry about alcohol. You can smoke, but only in between required events and outside." It was January in Minnesota, so this rule made smoking painful, whether by coincidence or design.

Jim was straightforward and friendly and I couldn't help but like him. Still feeling anxious about my roommates, I followed him back to my room. There I met John, a huge man around fifty years old, who was a carpenter from a little town near International Falls. His Minnesotan accent was immediately noticeable to me which made me feel even further from home.

Next was Matthew, a good-looking, nicely-dressed fellow who made my gaydar go off like crazy. Finally, there was Mark, a skinny black-haired guy about 5 feet 10 inches. He was pleasant but quiet. They all seemed nice enough. In an attempt to break the ice, I joked, "My name is 'Luke.'" No one laughed. "You know, Matthew, Mark, John, and Luke from the Bible?" I got blank looks, so I re-introduced myself as "Tate."

After Jim left, Matthew and John took me to eat lunch. As we ate, Matthew explained our daily schedule, "There's a unit meeting for meditation and daily readings every morning. Then three AA meetings a day, mostly speaker meetings where other alcoholics tell their stories. And then, we go to meetings about the first three Steps." Matthew grimaced and said, "They beat AA into you. Have you ever been to AA?"

"Not really."

"Okay. For the benefit of the uninitiated, the first three steps that we focus on are as follows:

Step One: We admitted we were powerless over alcohol - our lives had become unmanageable.

Step Two: Came to believe that a power greater than ourselves could restore us to sanity.

Step Three: Made a decision to turn our will and our lives over to the care of God as we understood him.

These three steps will be pounded into you daily. There are study sessions on all Twelve Steps." With a sympathetic look, Matthew paused and said, "I know that is a lot, but it will make sense soon."

In the following days, despite my resistance, I found myself enjoying the small group discussions and especially the speaker's meetings. They sincerely poured their hearts and souls into their talks. The level of sharing and deep, unbridled honesty took me aback at first, but I found myself relating to every speaker as they recounted how they each reached a point of desperation. I could feel my defenses wearing thin because, unlike my prior assumptions, these were people from all walks of life, and their experiences with alcohol were much like my own. I couldn't deny it. They were like me and I was beginning to believe I belonged here.

I had never been shy about speaking in front of people, but for some reason I struggled in my early meetings at Hazelden. I sat silently for my first few meetings but finally felt comfortable enough to speak, straining to keep the emotion from bursting through my words.

"Hi, I'm Tate and I am an alcoholic."

The room responded with "Hi, Tate. Welcome."

I continued, "I cannot seem to control my drinking. I lost my house, my law practice, most of my friends, and my self-respect. I have no trust in myself."

I saw the other men nodding as if they really understood. None of them were judging me. In fact, I could feel an acceptance that I had never experienced before. I said it all out loud, and when I did, it didn't seem horrifying. For the first time, I felt there was hope for me to live a different life than the one before.

In these meetings, I learned that alcoholics develop a craving. After the first drink they crave another, then another, then another and simply cannot stop. They have a compulsion to drink even though they know it is certain to cause them grief or harm. I was the perfect budding alcoholic when I tasted my first beer on the bayou so many years before.

Somehow, the term disease made me feel better about things. I had spent so many years trying to exert my will over my drinking and it always failed me. Addiction is complicated. Even if you stop drinking on your own, there are always the inner cravings telling you one drink will be okay. The disease is a liar. It is "baffling, cunning, and powerful," as *The Big Book* says.

On day three, I was taken off medical supervision and the Librium prescribed by the Hazelden doctor was taken away. Now I really had to face the world clean and sober. I was already anxious, but without the Librium my sense of nervous foreboding started to take control. I felt like I was on a roller coaster. One minute I would feel okay and maybe even a little bit happy. Then I would swing into anger, agitation, and hostility. Finally, I fell into a deep, unyielding sadness. Everyone around me could sense it. Somehow, I understood that this wasn't a mood. It was what was underneath all the masking and avoidance. I was sad, and for the first time, I had to sit with the pain. It was consuming me.

During the second week at a small group meeting, we were discussing our progress and feelings. Sue, the staff member that led the group called me out, "Tate! What is wrong with you? You've been moping around here like you lost your best friend. What's up?" I froze. Usually sharing was on a volunteer basis, but apparently not that day.

My mind raced, scrambling to come up with something wise and insightful to say that wasn't about me. I had nothing. I gave up and just decided to tell the truth.

"I'm sad." I blurted out. "Usually, I can't figure out why, but now I think I do know why. I can't drink. I'm aching like I lost my best friend because I have. It's easy not to drink here, but what am I going to do out there?"

I caught my breath and continued. "I paid a lot of money for this! I understand that alcohol was on the verge of killing me. I don't need all your well-thought out, well-intentioned reasons as to why I should quit. I get it! I'm the one that has lived in the path of my own goddamn self-destruction. Still, I'm sad, and I'm afraid because I drink to help me get through the days. How will I get through the days if I can't drink?"

I paused and Sue smiled broadly. "Thank you, Tate. We needed that honesty. No offense, but it is the first time you've been real with us since you've been here."

I thought I had already been real with them. Admitting that I was an alcoholic was huge for me. But I hadn't admitted how much I missed the person I was when drinking. And I had not admitted my fears. My fear of being poor; my fear of being gay; and my fear of not being enough.

◆ ◆ ◆

When I arrived at Hazelden, I made the commitment not to hide my sexuality, and I was completely accepted by the staff and my fellow patients. It was an awesome feeling. At the end of the second week, a new member joined the Cronin Unit. David was a doctor in his late thirties. He was gay and worked as an AIDS researcher at UCLA. With so much vulnerability and raw emotion in rehab, closeness happens fast. David, Matthew, and I immediately hit it off. I had never experienced a friendship where I felt so comfortable sharing my most personal feelings. It was liberating. I didn't fully understand at the time how important this was to my ultimate recovery. The term "rigorous honesty" hadn't entered my vernacular, but this honesty with myself and others would soon be my salvation.

At the end of the third week, at my debrief with Jim Atkins, I complained, "I'm three weeks into this program, and no power greater than me has restored me to sanity. I am frustrated. I feel this constant thump in my head and body. I need some kind of liberation or satisfaction, but everything leads to more work, more meetings, more self-examination. I am angry at the relentlessness of the expectations here."

Jim nodded gently. "Spiritual awakening comes after working all Twelve steps, the order is intentional. One follows the other. Do you believe you're an alcoholic whose life has become unmanageable?"

"Without any doubt," I said.

"So has your higher power restored you to sanity?"

"No!"

"Have you had a drink in three weeks?"

I was caught off guard, "No."

Jim smiled. "That sounds sane to me. Remember, one day at a time."

Wow, I thought. I had never taken anything one day at a time. I heard everyone talking about it, but for the first time it made sense to me. I was anxiously thinking way into the future wondering how I could live without drinking, but for one day only I could do anything.

Jim asked me to come back later so we could talk more.

When I arrived he asked, "Would you mind sharing your drinking history with me?"

"Sure, but it's a long story."

Jim grinned and nodded, encouraging me to start at the beginning. "I'm in no hurry." He was a very attentive listener and made full eye contact. I could tell he was truly interested.

I went all the way back to that night on the banks of the Houston bayou where I felt a feeling like no other, total bliss. "I have been chasing after that same perfect buzz ever since. The only time I have ever felt real comfort and honest acceptance is when I was drinking with my friends."

"That is not unique," Jim said. "For many of us, we felt our best selves when we were drinking. It was the only time we felt like enough." I had forgotten that Jim was also in recovery.

I nodded. "It was the only time I felt relief. I was anguished about being gay, being poor, and not being as smart as those I hung out with. That feeling of fear, being less than, never left me. The booze helped."

For over an hour I shared every excruciating detail with Jim. All the humiliations and pain that I experienced in my time drinking. When I finished, I was teary-eyed but still holding back. With a look of compassion, he asked, "So what do you think?"

"Jim, I'm sad and exhausted. I feel sad for myself and yet surprised. I can't explain why I'm not dead or how I managed not to kill someone. I don't know why I've never been arrested. I don't understand why I haven't contracted an STD or had a stroke."

Then it came over me, a moment of deep understanding. The Second Step says, 'came to believe that a power greater than ourselves could restore us to sanity.' I realized that only a power greater than me could explain all those things. The next day began my last week at Hazelden.

For 28 days, with each passing AA meeting, counselor session, group discussion, and collective morning prayer, I stayed sober and clean, one day at a time. It was a humbling and frustrating yet empowering experience.

The program worked because I finally worked the program, and I have been sober since 1999. It hasn't been without ups and downs, and the craving still rears its ugly head, because I am, and will always be, an alcoholic.

CHAPTER 27

GROWING UP IN PUBLIC

My last week at Hazelden was likely the most critical. I had excelled at being institutionalized. The hyper structured daily schedule and constant drumbeat of recovery had done me good. I had no spouse, no kids, no job, and no business to worry about. I was extremely lucky to have entered Hazelden with nothing to lose. But after 28 days of sobriety, my identity was changing. My recovery was paramount and now I had something too important to lose. The thought of going back to my old ways terrified me. The staff at Hazelden made a real effort to help me with my greatest worries about leaving, including giving me the name of a recovery contact in Houston.

When I arrived back home, any thought I had to continue my routine would have been impossible. Aside from Dad being drunk when he picked me up at the airport, as soon as we got home he berated Mom and Kairy Tate for going to an Al-Anon meeting. I decided I couldn't stay there even one night if I was to protect my newly found sobriety.

I tried to be open-minded. At first, Dad was just insulting. That I was used to. But he quickly became mean-spirited. There were so many times during the years that I bit my tongue because Mom wanted to keep the peace. But now, I could not protect her from his anger, and I knew it would drag me down. Jim warned me that Dad may be threatened by my newfound sobriety. "It's typical for former drinking buddies, even those who are related to us, to think your stopping puts pressure on them to stop. They will also miss the companionship and feel judged." He was right. The chaotic presence of an active alcoholic was not a recipe for success so early in my recovery. I resigned myself to a sudden change of plans.

Thankfully, my sister Kairy-Tate was there when I arrived at Mom and Dad's. As Dad spewed vitriol at Mom, Kairy-Tate touched my hand, "Bubba, you need to come live with me." I put my suitcase in my black Dodge Intrepid and drove to Kairy-Tate's. She understood that I needed to do whatever I could to stay sober.

Kairy-Tate and my brother-in-law, Brian had been married a short three months when I moved in with them. With any other brother-in-law, none of this may have been possible. Brian now had his unemployed brother-in-law, recently retrieved from chemical dependency lockdown, moving in with him. You have to be a good man to accept that arrangement. At minimum, I knew for sure how much he loved my sister and how much she loved me. I stayed with them for seven months as I got on my feet.

The challenge of trying to stay sober hit me right in the face. I was still not a big fan of Alcoholics Anonymous. Despite endless meetings at Hazelden, I was uncomfortable going to AA meetings by myself. In fact, I was afraid to go anywhere by myself. Everything made me nervous. I was afraid to even see a beer, afraid I would just walk over and grab it, and "poof," all the Hazelden work and sacrifice would be for nothing.

From day one at Kairy-Tate's house, I felt more relaxed and safe. I knew instinctively that I needed to continue the work on my own and tried to build the daily structure that they talked about in recovery. I'd not prayed regularly since I left Grandma Kirkman's house in 1972, but I vowed to get on my knees and pray every morning. Then with a cup of coffee in hand, I would read my meditation books and a chapter in *The Big Book of AA*. Afterward, I would go to the park and exercise. I had no excuse since I was unemployed and had nowhere to be. I was eventually able to jog and then work up to a run. I immediately began to feel better about myself. My tattered self-esteem would not rebuild itself until I lost weight and got in shape. I was scared to death that if I remained too down on myself my depression would lead me to a cold Miller Lite.

I eventually gathered the courage to meet my recovery contact, Hank, in the lobby of Houston Methodist Hospital where Hazelden counselors had directed me to attend the after-care therapy program. Hank was a former marine and trial lawyer in his mid-fifties who had been sober for three years. He was tall with a deep voice and was a little intimidating.

"Tate, good to meet you. You want coffee? We have time before the meeting." Hank gestured and I followed him into a coffee shop. He got right to it. "How can I help?"

At this point I wasn't sure I liked him or his intensity, but I said, "I'm just not confident I can go without drinking."

Hank smiled and assured me, "I am willing to help. You can call me anytime. Anytime."

The group meeting was in a room with about twenty chairs in a circle. Hank and I walked in together and he immediately introduced me to Scott, a good-looking guy with cool Clark Kent glasses and brunette hair. But before we could really talk, the room filled with about eight others. This was not just an AA meeting, though everyone was checking in about their recovery and drug use. When it was my turn to share, I felt a surge of anxiety. But I could hear Jim of Hazelden say, "Just be honest."

I took a deep breath. "I am Tate, and I am an alcoholic. I have only been home for a week or so after 28 days in Hazelden. I am not currently working. I am too afraid to, really. My dad was drunk when he picked me up at the airport. I am now living with my newlywed sister and her husband. Frankly, I am afraid that I will not be able to drive by a liquor store without stopping for a beer. Coming here today has been my biggest event yet. I have a big ego, and I hate saying these things to you." It all blurted out before I could stop myself.

Suddenly, I felt small, filled with regret. Hank gently patted me on the back with his big hand and said in his authoritative, Marine-trained, trial lawyer voice, "Tate, I hope like hell that one day I will have your courage to be that honest."

After the meeting was over, I walked down to the lobby with Hank and Scott. Hank said, "You boys exchange numbers. You have a lot in common and it never hurts to have lots of people to call." As we followed his instructions, he continued. "Who is calling who tomorrow? Tate, why don't you call Scott? Scott, when is a good time for you?" We arranged a time to talk and made a plan to meet for lunch or coffee.

AA strongly encourages having a sponsor with whom you work the Steps, so when Hank and I met two days later, despite being intimidated by him, I asked him to be my sponsor. I decided to be honest first, "Hank, I'm gay. How do you feel about that?"

He looked at me very seriously and said, "I think homosexuality is a sin.

But it's no greater sin or lesser sin than any of the others and I happen to be a world champion sinner, so I think you and I will be just fine." I was dumbfounded. He burst out laughing and said, "Tate, you have nothing to worry about, we'll be fine. It is my honor to be your sponsor."

Things got a little better as I worked the Steps with Hank. The stories in *The Big Book* began to sink in. I related more and more to the feeling of helplessness shared by the alcoholics in the book. Hank did not demand that I attend AA meetings, but the drumbeat of Hazelden was still in my head—*you need to attend meetings to stay sober.* I finally decided to attend a meeting at Palmer House Episcopal Church, which was somewhat famous in the recovery community as the location where Palmer Drug Abuse Program started many years earlier.

As is the custom, the leader asked if there were any newcomers to the meeting or to AA. I begrudgingly raised my hand along with two others. When it was my turn to introduce myself, I said, "I am Tate, and I am an alcoholic."

The group of about eighty people said in unison, "Welcome, Tate." As the meeting continued, a topic was introduced, and people were asked to share. About halfway through, the leader said, "Let us hear from Tate, our newcomer." I had never shared in a meeting with this many people. My first thought was *don't be ridiculous, you are a public speaker and a trial lawyer*, but this was different. Honesty with these people was the key to my survival. So I began, "My name is Tate, and I am an alcoholic. I just got sober on January 12, 1999. I went to Hazelden in Minnesota in the depths of winter, so for a southern boy like me, I knew I wanted to get sober." The room laughed. I continued, "I feel like I'm fourteen and about to go to high school. I am afraid of everything. It took me three weeks to muster up the guts to come here. Leaving the safety of my house, passing a bar or a convenience store is still too much for me. I don't trust myself, but I made it today. Thanks for letting me share."

After the meeting, the leader approached me, "Tate, sharing at the gut honest level like you did takes courage. Getting sober is like starting over. It's our belief that our maturation, our growth, stops when we become alcoholics, so getting sober is like learning life all over again, as if we are kids or adolescents and know nothing." He put his arm around me and said, "We recovering drunks call it growing up in public. He gave me a card and said, "The phone weighs eight hundred pounds in early recovery. But the more calls you make to fellow alcoholics, the lighter the phone becomes. I need you to help me stay sober. Would you please call me tomorrow?"

I hugged him and said, "Yessir, what time is best?" That first call was instrumental in teaching me that other alcoholics will take the time to talk with you because the human connection is essential to recovery, especially in the early days.

◆ ◆ ◆

Part of my public growing-up process eventually included getting a job. I needed to find something that paid decent money but was not stressful, a job that likely didn't exist. As luck would have it, a recruiter offered me a document review job with a downtown firm.

"Tate with your background this is easy breezy, and the money is good. You can work as much as you like."

With little hesitation, I told her, "I'm in." How hard could a document review job be? I had very little time to get my mind right before I started the next morning. As it turned out, the firm was in the same building as Hank's office where we did Step work together every week. So, after 106 days of sobriety, I had a source of income and the security of my sponsor just upstairs.

After a few lunches and coffees, Scott and I also became good friends. I learned that he was also gay and living a gay life. Together, we would go to other AA meetings around Houston, including several predominantly attended by gay men. This was the first time I was around a lot of gays without drinking. It was like the early days at the gay bar, so I stuck close to Scott. This began my introduction to sober, gay life in Houston.

That summer, I began spending time with Jodie and her new husband, Loren. They owned a two-story duplex in Montrose, known as the "Gayberhood." It was a fixer upper in every sense of the word. Jodie and Loren lived upstairs, but the downstairs remained a mess and their plans to fix it up kept getting postponed. After six months living with Kairy-Tate and Brian, it was time for me to be back on my own. So I approached Jodie with an idea, "You know honey, if you got the downstairs of your duplex done, I could rent it from you, giving you an income stream. I would have my own place, but my support community would literally be on top of me, and you would get rent money."

Without hesitation, she agreed. Completing the downstairs became a community project for me and my friends. I moved in a few months later and it was just what I needed. I was standing on my own two feet, with Jodie right beside me.

The following month, I took a second job at another law firm. My life suddenly became very busy, very organized, and disciplined. It seemed to me that the best elixir was to work, work, work, and not allow myself access or opportunity to drink.

I was still not going to Mom and Dad's very much. When I visited, I would mostly speak with Mom. She lamented, "I don't see you much, son." Though I knew it would be painful, I was honest with her. "Mom, Dad is just toxic for me. I need to focus on my recovery. I'm not tough enough yet to handle him and stay sober."

CHAPTER 28

LAMBDA

There were a lot of advantages to living near Jodie. She loved me and constantly checked on me. And when she became pregnant, I was happy to help her in return. My friends, Liane, Fairan, and Jodie were fully engaged in my recovery. My social life was tame compared to years past. I hung out with Scott and Hank, Jodie and her family, had dinner with Fairan most Fridays, and Saturday was for Liane, Robin, and their little girl, Emily. Their support helped immeasurably.

Jodie's house was three blocks from the Lambda Center, a recovery center for the gay, lesbian, bisexual and transgender communities. When my document review job ended, I had a lot of time to think about myself, not particularly helpful for an alcoholic. I was proud of my sobriety, but I had not really worked the Steps as thoroughly as I wanted. I had no valid excuse not to go to an AA meeting at Lambda.

You would've thought that I was jumping out of an airplane the first time I walked into the Lambda Center. I was scared to death for reasons I no longer understand. I had resisted AA, and the thought of it with a room full of gays was just too much, but I went anyway.

As I sat down before the meeting, everyone was way too friendly. Several people wanted to hug me right away, which I declined. Looking around the room I saw two small, odd-looking guys and a huge guy wearing leather from head to toe sitting between them. I later learned that this was a "throuple" and this big guy was their submissive sex slave. They took him everywhere with them. I also met a crack and meth addict who was a male prostitute. Then there was the quirky, chubby guy who wore his hair like Princess Leia of Star

Wars. Jesus Christ! What had I gotten myself into?

As the meeting began, the leader read a chapter from the *Alcoholics Anonymous 12 by 12*. Then the group spent time writing and working the Steps. Unlike other AA meetings, which are short, part of the appeal of the Step Study is that it lasts one and a half hours. After the first few meetings, two attendees, Ron and Jesse, invited me to go to lunch with them. I declined each time they asked. I knew that I needed this Step Study, but I did not need any new friends.

But I grew a little more comfortable. The vulnerability, honesty, and kindness these "queers" exhibited grew on me, and garnered my respect. I found the Step Study meeting thoughtful and brutally honest. It became the one thing that I looked forward to all week. More importantly, I was managing to stay sober. I finally agreed to go to lunch with Ron and Jesse just so they stopped asking. That first lunch lasted over two hours and the tainted lens through which I viewed these two gentlemen fell away. I realized that I was often prejudiced and judgmental of other gays, not by intention, but rather by indoctrination.

Ron and Jesse's story was my story, just with a few different facts. They were two men, struggling with addiction, like me. So we began a tradition of going to lunch every Sunday after Step Study. Over time, our lunch group grew to twenty or more. My self-acceptance and pride in being an "out" gay man was growing with each day of sobriety.

It occurred to me that in a way I had come full circle. My happiest memories of love and acceptance had been Sunday dinners at Grandma Kirkman's. Now I had a familial group of people to share my spiritual work with a great meal to follow. It helped me feel at home.

CHAPTER 29

DÉTENTE

D ad and Mom were still having their Sunday dinners and Dad insisted that all the kids be at the house. My sisters and their spouses complied, but I boycotted. Finally, one Sunday, after I celebrated my second AA birthday, I decided to go. Dad and I were out in the garage like old times. He was drinking a Miller Lite and I was drinking water. He stood beside me and put his arm on my shoulder. "Bub, I wish I saw you more. I miss you!" I said nothing. Dad continued, "I don't care. I don't care that you no longer want to drink. I know you are a teetotaler now. You do not have to stay away. You're not working as much now. You could come over during the week, say every Wednesday; we could go to the gun range. You need to learn to shoot your guns, particularly your handguns. I will show you."

I stood quietly for a moment and said, "We will see." I left shortly after. I was not ready for gun ranges and weekday excursions. Sunday lunch was the best I could do. But as time passed and I became more comfortable in my sobriety, I spent more time with Mom and Dad.

◆ ◆ ◆

The whole family was relieved when Dad was home from the hospital, but there remained a sense of foreboding. We all knew this would be the first of many trips to the emergency room. Dad was not one to change. Surprisingly, this heart attack did convince him to finally stop smoking, but, true to form, he just started dipping Copenhagen snuff instead.

Mom was never a fan of his smoking, so she resigned herself to Copenhagen and the heightened caretaking required to slow Dad's inevitable demise. Cancer, diabetes, and heart and lung disease ran rampant throughout both families. All my uncles smoked, as did most of my aunts on both sides of the family. A few of my uncles made it into their seventies, but none reached their eighties. They all had some form of emphysema. Neither Dad nor I quit smoking soon enough. Dad was diagnosed with emphysema in 2003, and I was diagnosed in 2010. History, genetics, and hard living made it almost inevitable.

I understand why Dad reacted the way he did when I got sober. He was an incredibly intuitive man, particularly when it came to his kids. He knew that I had harbored intense resentment toward him because of his treatment of my mom over the years, not to mention when he abandoned us in Florida. He was incapable of saying, "I'm sorry," but somehow I still expected the heartfelt apology that never came. When I started drinking, we managed to loosely patch this up, but when I got sober, our relationship was torn again. Dad not only mourned the loss of his favorite drinking buddy, but he realized that all the old wounds would resurface. He was right.

To our credit, we both tried, once again, to build back our relationship. The effort was real but not necessarily the healthiest approach. We just left so much unsaid. It was easier that way.

◆ ◆ ◆

On December 8, 2004, I bought my first home in sobriety. My house on Briar Bend was aging and a little beat up but otherwise solid, stable, just like me. Still, it was a statement, a symbol of my recovery. I had finally overcome so much of what I had lost in my drinking days. I was honestly prouder of myself now than when I bought my first luxury home at the age of 28. The minute I stepped into the house, I knew I wanted to buy it.

As I settled into Briar Bend, I was teaching Communications Law and Ethics as an Adjunct Professor at the University of Houston. I was often asked by my students and others to speak about ethics in the community, so I began writing *Successful Ethical Decision Making: Get What You Want Without Getting in Trouble* in 2006. I had never written a book before, and I certainly didn't realize what a challenge it could be. Finally, with the help of my friend John, it was completed and published in 2007. The next thing I knew, I was booked on national radio shows. It was an absolute blast! I was plugging the book, teaching, and I even garnered the occasional paid speaking gig.

One day, just after returning from an ethics keynote address in Austin, my mom called. "Your dad is not feeling well. He wants you to come over immediately!" I would not have been overly concerned, but I heard the urgency in her voice. I had gotten so used to high alert with him that my fight-or-flight response was dulled.

Since his first heart attack, the trips to the hospital were becoming more frequent. By this time, Dad had been diagnosed with COPD/emphysema, coronary artery disease, and an assortment of other issues. He was also terribly overweight. He had no qualms about outright lying to a doctor, and my mom would not correct him with the doctor or nurse present. If she did, she knew he would lash out at her later.

As a result, I had begun attending my dad's doctor visits. His automatic response was always, "I drink about two beers a day," when in fact it was two *cases* a day. He also loved to tell them, "I stopped smoking," but he never divulged that he dipped a can of Copenhagen every day too. I was the only person who could redirect and force the truth out of him without him getting angry.

When I arrived at Mom and Dad's he was clearly struggling to breathe. He seemed frightened, an expression I had not seen before. I knew we didn't have time to waste so I said as calmly as I could, but with urgency, "Dad, we have to go now." I helped him up and slowly we made our way to my truck. We drove to the closest hospital less than half a mile from their house. After we checked in, Dad said, "All I need is breathing treatment and a B12 shot," his remedy for everything, but I knew that wasn't going to help this time. There was no waiting. The ER doctor saw that his vitals were out of control and administered an EKG. He said, "I saw your history, so I paged the on-call cardiologist."

The cardiologist handed Dad some nitroglycerin and told him to put it under his tongue. Dad again lobbied for a B12 shot and breathing treatment. The cardiologist agreed to the breathing treatment, I think, just to placate him.

"I need an echocardiogram and ultrasound, stat," the doctor said, addressing the nurse. The machine arrived quickly, and I watched the doctor's brow furrow. "We have got to get you out of here!"

There was an enormous collection of liquid around Dad's heart and this hospital wasn't equipped to handle such an emergency. The doctor went to a nearby room to make some calls. We could still see him through the window. He spoke frantically, pacing back and forth, which didn't help my anxiety. There was no time to waste, and I had to prepare myself for anything. There wasn't even time to call my siblings. This was the day I was dreading.

Despite struggling to breathe, Dad actually chuckled watching the doctor from behind the glass. Looking at me with a grin he said, "Bub, it looks like we are way too much for the good doctor to handle. He doesn't want to have anything to do with us!"

The doctor returned, walking like a man on a mission. He touched my dad's left shoulder and said, "Mr. Barkley, please understand I must transport you immediately to another hospital. I see a life-threatening condition. You have collected enormous amounts of fluid around your heart. This can cause death. I believe you need a thoracic surgeon, and we do not have one. An ambulance is already on the way."

Mom rode with Dad in the ambulance, and I followed behind. When he arrived at Memorial Hermann Southwest Heart and Vascular Institute, he underwent a series of tests. Within the hour, I was called back to be with him. His breathing was horrifically labored, even though they had him on oxygen. Standing next to my dad was the thoracic surgeon who touched my right elbow and led me to an adjacent room with a computer, and after a couple of clicks on the keyboard, he said, "You're looking at footage of the area around your dad's heart."

I didn't need any medical explanations to see the prognosis was bleak. There was a massive amount of fluid around Dad's heart. The doctor continued, "This is an exigent, life-threatening circumstance getting worse by the second. I have a team ready to operate." I felt tension rising in me and asked him, "Specifically, what do we need to do? And why is that approach the right one?" He looked puzzled, almost offended, then he patiently said, "The surgery will open a pericardial window on the fibrous sac called the pericardium surrounding the heart. This sac has two thin layers with a small amount of fluid between them which helps with friction. When too much fluid builds between these layers it is called a pericardial effusion. If we do not operate immediately, your dad's heart will implode."

"I need a minute," I told him, and I left the room to be with Dad.

I moved a chair and sat directly in front of him. He smiled as broadly as he could and said, "Goddamn, Bub, I just wanted a breathing treatment and a B12 shot." I busted out laughing and Dad joined me.

Then I got serious. "Dad, you saw the pictures. We both saw them. They need to operate."

Dad sighed, "I know, son, but I could die on the table."

"You could. But if we do nothing, you'll die today for sure."

An air of sadness descended on his face. "I know, Bub. There's no choice. Go get the doctors."

I stepped out and found them huddled in the hallway. I said, "Let's proceed ASAP."

I went downstairs and walked outside. I needed a smoke break. I knew that Dad's surgery would take a good long time so there was no rush.

Lighting a Marlboro Light, I thought, "Here I am again." I let my father go into surgery with so much left unsaid. The mixed feelings were bubbling up again and for a minute I wished I could drink.

I had to admit to myself I loved the man so much and yet I loathed him. Only my dad could fill me with such dissonance.

Here I was, 42 years old, a recovering alcoholic and addict, finally reconciled as a proud gay man, but I had never told him I was gay. In fairness, acceptance of my alcoholism and true acceptance of being gay came together as one for me. It was part of the process of my being whole.

And early on, Dad had rigorously shamed my recovery, so I was for damn sure not going to tell him then that I was gay. I rationalized that he did not deserve to know the truth. I said all this to myself in a sanctimonious tone. And there it was, I could feel it, shame. It washed over me like I was a teenager all over again. I realized at that moment that I was still living without addressing that last stubborn bastion of shame, which sat there obstinately between my father and me. I thought, *I can't have the gay talk now. Dad is just too sick for it. Why am I even thinking about this?*

After his surgery, another ten days passed before Dad was released. Relieved as we were, by that time he had ceased to be our primary concern. The stress and lack of sleep had taken their toll on Mom. She needed to be back home just as much as Dad. Her dedication and loyalty to him were unwavering, but none of us ever really understood why. If we ever brought up how he treated her sometimes, she'd reiterate what she had said many times: "I love him." After sitting vigil with her and thinking about losing him, I started to understand how she felt. He was a fixture in our lives, and as much as I hated him sometimes, he was hard not to love. When we got this chance for more time with him, I made it a point to try to build a better relationship with him. After all, acceptance and forgiveness were part of my recovery.

Over the next six years, there were constant issues with Dad's heart, lungs, circulation, liver, and kidneys. All his organs seemed to be in rebellion at one point or another. Within eight months of his surgery, we discovered his right carotid artery was almost completely blocked, and he was back at Memorial Hermann. Three months after the carotid artery surgery, Dad had fourteen days in the hospital with pneumonia. But thankfully, after this bout of pneumonia, he had a good, healthy patch of time. I needed to take advantage of it.

CHAPTER 30

PENSACOLA

Ever since Dad's major heart surgeries I knew my time with him was limited. If I was ever going to work through my feelings and heal the relationship it would need to happen before another health crisis, and I would need to initiate it.

He and I had always had our best times and talks while on the road together. With no recent hospitalizations and clear improvement in his mobility, it seemed like Dad was doing better. So I decided it was time for one more road trip. I had high hopes that I could find the courage to tell him the truth during our time together.

For years, Dad talked about us going to the Naval Aviation Museum in Pensacola, Florida. So we finally planned a road trip. We left at the crack of dawn, driving my 2005 champagne-colored Dodge Dakota pickup. Dad and I usually split the driving, but not this time. I just wanted him to enjoy the ride. I enjoyed watching him out of the corner of my eye. He seemed truly relaxed. We both always liked to get to where we were going no matter the toll on ourselves, so I drove in a straight shot all the way there. The weather was perfect, traffic was manageable, and Dad was relaxed but very reflective.

He always told me stories while on the road, and I loved hearing them. This time it was different. I sensed an urgency—like he wanted to make sure I heard all his stories before he could no longer share. I felt sad and more aware than ever that I had stories I needed to tell him. *He needs to know,* I thought. But we were having such a good time. I didn't want to be a downer. For years I had pictured his reaction, so I decided since Dad was having a good day, physically and emotionally, I would leave it alone.

After checking into our hotel, we spent the entire next day at the National Aviation Museum. Both Dad and I were wide-eyed at all the exhibits. I remembered the books he gave me when I was a child and here were all of those planes on display. We barely spoke, walking around in a joyful daze.

As luck would have it, we ran into a WWII Pilot of the F4-U Corsair, Dad's favorite aircraft. The pilot was a marine, land-based pilot in the Pacific theater. We invited him to have coffee with us and I observed my father in all his glory as the two men spoke about the plane and the pilot's experiences during the war. I loved to see Dad so animated. He was truly in his element. I couldn't have planned the day any better than it turned out.

The following day, we toured the beaches of the Florida Panhandle and talked about how hurricanes Frances and Jeanne had come through spreading destruction in their wake. We saw all the new construction everywhere and it reminded me of the story of the phoenix rising from the ashes. Dad and I had both risen up from ashes of our own design. But we were having the time of our lives together with nothing but fun. There were no complications or uneasiness and even the beaches were serene. We drove up and down the coast and since it was off season, there were very few people and only light traffic. It was perfect; so perfect that I decided I didn't want to ruin it by talking about being gay. It may have been an excuse, but in my mind, it was a very good one. Why ruin the best time I had with my dad in ages—maybe ever? It just wasn't the right time.

Sadly, and as I expected, Pensacola would be our last father-son trip. When we were drinking buddies, Dad and I traveled the country together, partying and sightseeing all along the way. But when I got sober, all of that ended. Our return drive to Houston was more sedate. As we approached downtown Houston, Dad said, "Bub, do you remember how excited you were when you first saw all those buildings?"

"Yes," I said, trying to keep my voice from shaking. "I remember."

He touched my right arm. and said, "It changed our lives, Bub, coming here to Texas. We needed the change, the whole family needed out of North Carolina. We needed to leave our past behind."

I quietly said, "I know, Dad, I know."

CHAPTER 31

THE PROMISES

By pure happenstance, or maybe because the fates thought I was ready, on December 22, 2011, I met a guy named Anson. He was the cutest thing I'd ever seen. He stood 5 feet 4 inches tall, and was lean and fit with a beautiful, bright smile and perfect brown skin. Anson's parents had emigrated from India, but he was born and raised in Houston. His mom was a critical care nurse, and his dad was a respiratory therapist. Anson went to medical school in Europe after he graduated high school and returned to the States for his residency in New Jersey. That December, he was visiting his parents in Houston for Christmas. At the time, Anson had a fellowship for Developmental and Behavioral Pediatrics at Children's Hospital Philadelphia. We met through a mutual friend at a Christmas party. I was smitten from the very beginning. Anson and I went out three times during Christmas break. When he returned to Philadelphia at the end of December, we talked almost every day. I really wanted to see him again, but my schedule was full, with no chance to see him before April.

While I was waiting on a flight back to Houston after an eight-hour deposition in Dallas, Anson texted me asking if I thought there would be any time before April for me to come to Philadelphia. I scrolled through my calendar. I was totally booked and I was set for trial in Dallas the following Monday.

Fucking unbelievable! I finally met someone I would fly halfway across the country to see, and I had no time! I took a deep breath. I wanted to see Anson more than anything; this guy really got to me. Deep down, I felt he was different. I stopped texting. I closed my eyes and said the Serenity Prayer,

"God grant me the serenity to accept the things I cannot change, the courage to change the things I can, and the wisdom to know the difference." Then I texted Anson back, "I am coming this weekend." I didn't care about the trial settings and deadlines; I just wanted to see him.

As if God himself intervened, the case set for trial the next week settled the night before my flight to Philadelphia. When I saw the signed deal come across my email, it was like the weight of the world had been lifted off my shoulders. Now I could go to Philadelphia and be with Anson without the worry of a trial on Monday. We could just be together. I arrived in Philadelphia that Friday and enjoyed a weekend that changed my life.

CHAPTER 32

THIS IS MY SON

I knew with certainty when I flew home from Philadelphia that I had met the love of my life. By late March, Anson and I had traveled back and forth every other weekend to see each other. Never in my adult life had I fallen in love with anyone before Anson. I had accepted the fact that I was just not cut out for a long-term relationship, but Anson turned that notion on its head.

The last weekend in March 2012, I was in Philadelphia with Anson when Mom called me saying she had to drive Dad to the ER at Southwest Memorial. He had been feeling especially bad the week before. He hardly felt like eating, and was losing weight, and getting noticeably weaker. I told her I would come to the hospital as soon as I got home. I was having an awesome time in Philadelphia with Anson. I told him, "Welcome to the family, my dad is in the hospital, again."

◆ ◆ ◆

After the last surgery and for a good while, Dad seemed fine. I would get worried every time Mom called with another problem, but I never felt the fear as I did back when it was an emergency. I was happy and relaxed and took the Sunday noon flight out of Philadelphia as usual, assuming all would be well in time, as it typically was with Dad.

I arrived back in Houston late Sunday, and Monday morning I was in Dad's room at Memorial Hermann Southwest. The doctor told me that they were bringing in liver and blood specialists on his case. There was serious leakage around his aortic valve. Dad's lungs were now filling up with fluid, and his blood was super thin, so they took him off the blood thinners. His blood was so thin they did not believe that he could sustain a surgery—they feared he could literally "bleed out on the table."

It turned out that it wasn't internal bleeding that was the problem. The doctors eventually discovered Dad was suffering from chronic liver disease. Of all the great ironies, heavy drinking had finally caught up with him. The cardiologist said, "The extent of the diseased heart tissue may be too great to repair, but I cannot be certain until your dad is opened up." Things were not feeling good at all. I felt a twinge of guilt for feeling so relaxed when Mom said Dad was back in the hospital.

I walked outside. I had stopped smoking by this point, but I did take a big dip of Copenhagen. I needed to be alone. I said out loud, "I wish I had a $5 bill every time I walked outside of the hospital to think about my dad's health."

Over the next three weeks, little changed. Fluid had to be removed from his lungs twice. The doctors were trying everything they could think of to improve his platelet count, but nothing seemed to work. He was not getting better. The Sunday morning of his third week in the hospital, I woke up harried and stressed. I put on the coffee, sat in my chair, and tried to read the paper. Too many things were running through my head, so I decided to take a good long walk. Usually by April, Houston is hot and humid, but not that day. I took a brisk walk around my neighborhood, and I returned home.

Mom had been holding vigil at Dad's bedside the entire time he was in the hospital, and she was starting to look as tired as he was. At our insistence, she agreed to let Brandy take her home. Kairy-Tate was with Dad that day, but she was pregnant and not feeling that well herself. She called me that morning before I left for the grocery store asking if I could come stay with him. I told her that I would be there after I bought groceries, so she could go ahead and head home.

When I returned to the car after grocery shopping, Anson called and we chatted for a good twenty minutes. It felt good to talk with him. When we ended the call, this intense, liberating wave of gratitude coursed through my body, the kind of feeling that comes from being in love. I took my groceries home and headed to the hospital. Before getting out of the car, I put my head on the steering wheel, breathing deeply. *This is the day he needs to know, because I want him to meet Anson. I want Dad to be in our life.* I did not cry, nor did I feel shame. I just felt ready.

Dad had a private room, of course, but I knocked on the open door and said, "Dad, it's Bub." I walked in and found him up and dressed, sitting on his bed. The Sunday news programs were blaring on the TV; he turned it down. Dad looked at me and smiled broadly. He could give the best smiles. He always seemed to be glad to see me. He was wearing his trademark khaki cargo shorts and what looked like a freshly ironed black pullover shirt. I looked down and he was barefoot. If my dad was not working a job, he was barefoot no matter what the weather. It was his natural state.

I had been there a good twenty minutes and he said, "Bub, you're fidgeting, what do you have on your mind?"

I smiled. "Dad, do you want a cup of coffee? I know I could use one."

"Sure."

The fourth floor had a fancy coffee machine that I liked. I got a couple of Columbia Supremes and thought to myself, *Do not chicken out!* I returned to the room, handed Dad his coffee, and sat back down. He wouldn't stop looking at me. I remember thinking to myself, *Why is he giving me a sympathetic look? He's dying, not me.*

I was taken aback by my own train of thought. I let it shower over me. "He's dying." I thought about AA. I knew that I owed my dad an amend, an apology, no matter how he took the news. He deserved an apology for my waiting this long to have such an important conversation about something so essential to my life.

"Dad, there's something I want to talk with you about."

He looked at me with his full attention.

Looking him in the eye, I firmly stated, "Dad, I'm gay. This is something I have struggled with for a long time. Frankly, I did not begin to truly accept that I was a gay man until I got sober. I did not really feel the need to say anything because there hasn't been a need for you to know. I was also afraid of how you might view me. The reason I'm finally telling you is that I've met someone special. We met over Christmas. I feel like I'm falling in love. I realize that I cannot be a whole man for whatever reason until I tell you."

Dad looked at me, partly puzzled, clearly concerned. He tilted his head slightly and said, "Bub, Dad knows you're gay. In fact, your Mom and I talked about it when you were in high school. We knew then that you were likely gay and we worried about your safety and happiness in this world. So, Bub, I know."

He looked at me now with even more concern and said, "I assumed you never came to me because you were afraid that I would be disappointed in you or ashamed of you. But Bub, I'm not disappointed, nor am I ashamed. You have never, ever disappointed me as a son. You are the light of my life. You are without doubt my best work, my finest achievement. You are my son, yes, but you are also courageous, kind, loyal, funny, and the finest man I've ever known. I know you're gay and I love you with all that I am."

He fell silent. I could feel the tears welling up inside of me, but I was more stunned than relieved. I didn't know what to do, so I stared at him glassy-eyed and in silence. Finally, I got up and I sat by him. I was in shock, I think. I sat by Dad on the bed and laid my head on his shoulder. He rested his head on mine while gently holding my right hand. In a life with many special moments, this was the most special moment of my life. We stayed there in silence. There was nothing I could think to say. I could not fully digest what had just happened. He had known all this time. He had been waiting for me. Eventually, there was a loud knock on the door, "Mr. Barkley, it's time for your breathing treatment." An older South Asian gentleman with a delightful smile walked in and said, "Mr. Barkley, it's that time again. And who is this?"

Dad said, "This is my son."

EPILOGUE

MAY THE CIRCLE BE UNBROKEN

The world had been lifted from my shoulders. When I left the hospital later that day, I called Anson from the hospital parking lot. Then when I got home, I called my three younger sisters and told them I had finally talked to Dad. They were thrilled. Then I called Fairan and Jodie. I was on Cloud Nine. After holding it in for all those years, despite all the anguish, the fear, the repression, and the angst, my dad had known. He had been waiting all this time for me to come out.

Once the euphoria subsided, I took a moment to sit in my study and reflect on what had happened in that hospital room that day. He had said it with such power: "I would never ever feel ashamed of you." For a moment, I couldn't breathe. How could I have anguished in this shame and worry for so long? Why did I not do this sooner? I thought, *I cannot emotionally handle any more analysis or deal with the obvious truth.* I could not yet accept that I had carried my shame so long. Dad was so wonderfully human. He wore his defects and dignity like badges of honor. It was not Dad who was ashamed of me; I had been ashamed of me. I took a deep breath and whispered to myself, *Enjoy that it is done. You can hyper-analyze it all later.* I closed my eyes and drifted off to sleep.

Dad spent 48 days in the hospital during his final illness. He was released to hospice care on April 25, less than two weeks after our talk. None of his providers believed he was capable of surviving the risky surgery to repair or replace his valve. His blood was too thin, his lungs too broken. He relied on full-time oxygen because of his emphysema and bronchitis, and that was never going to change.

When the decision was reached to send him to hospice care, my dear friend Fairan was there every step of the way. We loaded Mom and Dad into her car with his huge oxygen tank.

Once we arrived at home, the hospice organization, arranged by the hospital, sent a representative to the house. Dad, still lucid, basically said, "We're private people and we don't need you." He smiled politely but very firmly. "We'll be fine with just family." Then he took a big dip of Copenhagen.

I helped him up and out of his recliner, where he had spent so many of his final years, and we walked out to the patio behind the house to look at his plants. Dad had an assortment of flowers and shrubs on the back porch. He coddled his tomato plants and doted on his collection of begonias, purple cone flowers, and periwinkles.

That night, Dad seriously deteriorated. He woke up and walked all over the house speaking gibberish. At one point, I clearly understood him saying something about planting strawberry bushes behind the barn. His voice sounded just like Ma Barkley's. I was up all night with him. It was truly eerie, the things that were coming out of his mouth. He fell three times, and each time I struggled to get him back up.

By 7:00 a.m., I had a private ambulance in my parents' driveway and we headed to St. Luke's in the Houston Medical Center. If a miracle was to be had, I figured they could deliver.

When we arrived, Dad was in respiratory distress. It wasn't long before they put him on a bi-pap. Not long after that, he was intubated. With many doctors strolling in and out, conferencing amongst themselves in the hallway and in Dad's room, and finally conferencing with me, the decision was made that nothing could be done to save his life. We were turned over to the palliative care team and we knew the end was near.

Dad died on April 27, 2012. When he was born in 1939 on that farm in North Carolina, all of his brothers and sisters and their husbands and wives surrounded him as he came into the world. He was the youngest of seven children. All of Dad's siblings were significantly older, so he was the center of the entire family's attention. He insisted on the same with his own family. Dad left this world the same way he came into it, surrounded by his family, and commanding the attention of all.

When he died, he knew that I had met Anson, though he never met him, and he was pleased for me. As luck allowed, Anson found a job in Houston.

We bought a house together and we married in February 2017. Anson swears my dad's spirit permeates every room of the house. It is likely so.

NOTE TO READERS

While this book is a memoir containing true stories of my life and relationship with my father and our family, it includes many people with whom I have not had direct contact in many years. All of the places mentioned are real, however in an effort to fully tell these stories I have changed some names to protect the privacy of the real people who were involved.

ACKNOWLEDGEMENTS

There are so many special people who have contributed their love, spirit and intellect to the creation of this book. My husband, Anson, who is my true love and the joy of my life. My mom, Linda, to whom this book is dedicated and my Dad, Tate G. who is at the core of who I am and the journey I have taken. My sisters, Vickie, Leighann, Kairy-Tate and Brandy-K who have been the center of my life, all of my life. These beautiful women have provided me with the greatest role of my life: Uncle Bubba. I am so grateful to my nephews Devin, Trey, Trevor and Liam and my nieces and grand nieces, Kristian, Drew, Reese, Kate, Mia and Devin Grace. A special acknowledgement to Trevor who typed, edited, cut and pasted seemingly endless versions of this book, all in an effort to help "Uncle Bubba."

I also want to thank all the staff of Bain & Barkley all of whom were tasked or trusted with some request to "help with the book," A special thanks to my dear friend, Steve Bain, and his wife, Annette. Steve has been my steadfast friend, coach and confidante for over two decades and so much of my success I owe to him.

Everyone has angels in their life and I have been blessed with many angels throughout mine. But, the brightest and best of them all is my friend and soulmate, Fairan Jones. Fairan has known me in every phase of my life, drunk and sober, broke and affluent, broken and emboldened, thin and overweight, lost and leading. No matter what she has been there for me. I love you, Fairan!

A special thank you to Lisa Phillips whose contributions to this book and to me cannot be measured. She has walked the path of writing, editing and organizing this book with me every step of the way. Lisa has made this book her own and for that I am forever grateful. I want to acknowledge Sam Russek, my copy editor whose edits and insights were thoughtful and on target.

Finally, I want to thank Janet Switzer for her guidance in turning my feelings into a vision for a book. But most of all, I thank Janet for referring me to Jeff and Deborah Herman. In our first call, Jeff said, "You need my wife," and boy was he right. I cannot well express my gratitude to Deb Herman who served as my developmental editor, co-writer, creator, awesome friend, intuitive and my publisher. *Sunday Dinners, Moonshine and Men* is a labor of love for us both. Thank you, Deb, for all your help and friendship.

— Michael "Tate" Barkley